English in Practice

ALSO AVAILABLE FROM BLOOMSBURY

How to Read Texts: A Student Guide to Critical Approaches and Skills, 2nd edition, by Neil McCaw

Studying Literature: The Essential Companion, 2nd Edition by Paul Goring, Jeremy Hawthorn and Domhnall Mitchell

Studying Poetry, 2nd Edition, by Stephen Matterson and Darryl Jones

Studying the Novel, 6th Edition by Jeremy Hawthorn

ENGLISH IN PRACTICE
In Pursuit of English Studies

2nd Edition

PETER BARRY

B L O O M S B U R Y

LONDON • NEW DELHI • NEW YORK • SYDNEY

Bloomsbury Academic

An imprint of Bloomsbury Publishing Plc

50 Bedford Square	1385 Broadway
London	New York
WC1B 3DP	NY 10018
UK	USA

www.bloomsbury.com

Bloomsbury is a registered trade mark of Bloomsbury Publishing Plc

First published 2014

British Library Cataloguing-in-Publication Data
A catalogue record for this book is available from the British Library.

ISBN: PB: 978-1-7809-3033-6
ePub: 978-1-7809-3107-4
ePDF: 978-1-7809-3105-0

Library of Congress Cataloging-in-Publication Data
A catalog record for this book is available from the Library of Congress.

Typeset by Fakenham Prepress Solutions, Fakenham, Norfolk NR21 8NN
Printed and bound in Great Britain

Contents

Acknowledgements ix
List of illustrations x

PART ONE Studying English 1

1 Introduction 3

Your starter for ten 9

2 Reading Poetry 23

The end is nigh: reading short poems 23
Spenser's 'second hand' 31

3 Reading Fiction 37

The facts of fiction 37
The narratee 39
The narrator 40
'Site' or 'domain' 41
The narrator's fear of the narratee 44

4 Reading and Interpretation 49

Context and intertext 49
'He could not escape those very words' 51
Intertextuality and authorship 57
Dove Cottage, gender and intertextuality 59
Total textuality: 'The Lady of Shalott' 63
Current trends in interpretation 69
Four kinds of interpretation 71
'Synoptic' interpretation 74

5 English and Creative Writing 79

Teaching elephants: creative writing in America 79
Creative writing in UK higher education 81
Creative writing and English departments 84

6 English Now and Then 91

Early English in America 92
Early English in the UK 94
Early English in practice 96
Two revolutions and a 'turn' 98
Coda: English here and there 101

7 Online and Digital English 105

A backward glance 105
Databases and topic sites 106
Being choosy online and referencing 108
Going through the gate 112
Four sites with foresight 118

PART TWO Progressing in English 125

8 Literary Criticism and Literary Theory 127

A brief history of criticism 127
British and American criticism – key differences 128
'Intrinsic' and 'extrinsic' criticism 130
'Theory has landed' 132
Sonnet 73: reading with theory 134
History 135
Language 137
Gender 138
Psychoanalysis 139
Doing it deconstructively – 'HD' and Adrienne Rich 140
Contradictions 143

Linguistic quirks and aporia 143
Shifts 144
Absences and omissions 145

9 English as Language 147

Stylistics 148
'Shifters' and deixis 149
Taking a ghost for a walk 150
Sociolinguistics 153
Reading the papers 154
Language and gender 154
Jargon 156
Brave new words 157
Historical linguistics 160
Clandestine relationships 162
Meanings on the move 164
Borrowed words 167

10 English and History 171

How much context is there in text? 171
Is Keats's 'To Autumn' about Peterloo? 181
Is History the new English? 186

11 The Essay: Crossing the Four Frontiers 191

Description 191
Commentary 192
Discussion 193
Analysis 195

12 The Undergraduate Dissertation 199

Shaping the dissertation 200
Preliminary reading 206

13 The Text as Text 209

On avoiding textual embarrassment 209
'In two minds' – Blake and Keats 212
Searching for the one true text 219
Editorial primitivism 221
Last intentionalism 222
Syncretism 224
Populism 225

14 English at MA Level 227

Varieties of MA in English in the UK 227
Variations of teaching format 232
Scholarliness vs readability 235
Your voice and 'their' voices 237
Book chapter vs journal articles 239

Postscript 243
What Next? Annotated Bibliography 245
Index 255

Acknowledgements

The author and publisher would like to thank copyright holders for permission to quote the following: 'I Know a Man' from *Selected Poems of Robert Creeley*. Copyright © 1991 by the Regents of the University of California, reprinted with the permission of the University of California Press. 'Brief thoughts on Maps', by Miroslav Holub, translated by Jarmila and Ian Miller (in *Notes of a Clay Pigeon*, Secker & Warburg, 1985), reprinted with permission of the Random House Group Ltd; 'Oread' by HD (Hilda Doolittle), from *Collected Poems, 1912–1944* © 1982 by the Estate of Hilda Doolittle, used by permission of the New Directions Publishing Corporation; 'Transit' by Adrienne Rich © 2013, used by permission of W.W. Norton & Company, Inc. and the Adrienne Rich Literary Trust.

Millais's *The Boyhood of Raleigh*, © Tate, London 2013, is reproduced with permission. The diagram 'The Indo-European language family tree' is by Jack Lynch of Rutgers University and is reproduced with his permission. The source of the image 'Julia Jackson, possibly by Julia Margaret Cameron' is currently unidentified; the copyright holder is invited to get in touch with the publisher.

List of Illustrations

Figure 3.1 Millais, 'The Boyhood of Raleigh' 38

Figure 5.1 Julia Jackson 88

Figure 9.1 The Indo-European language family tree 161

PART ONE

Studying English

1

Introduction

The aim of this book is to provide an overview of English Studies, covering basic aspects of the subject in Part 1, and in Part 2 moving on to discuss issues and concerns likely to arise in the later years of an undergraduate course. In addition, the last chapter looks at the transition to MA level, for the benefit of those who may be interested in continuing their studies and doing postgraduate work. An overview is a kind of map, and the notion of mapping brings to mind a poem about a map which I used for several years at the start of university courses in English. It is by the modern Czech poet Miroslav Holub (1923–98), whose work became popular in English translation through the medium of the *Penguin Modern Poets* series. Maps are strange things. None of us has ever seen an accurate map, for the only accurate map of a place is the place itself. Think, for instance, of a road map: if the map were a strictly accurate, true-scale representation of the country concerned, then the roads depicted on the map would be miles wide. On the other hand, if the roads were shown in accurate scale, you wouldn't be able to see them on a map that you could hold comfortably in your hands: this couldn't function as a 'road map' at all. The purpose of a map, then, is to be helpful, showing you what you need to see in order to achieve your purposes at a given moment. The same is true of the map of English Studies provided in this book: it offers a way of looking at the terrain, one which I hope will be helpful to you now. Later on, you will notice lots of complexities not included in this map, but found, perhaps, in others that strive to meet different needs. We don't have to anticipate all those needs now, and a book like this could never be written if we did. If the map is to work at all, it will do so not because

1

of my input, but because of yours, which is more or less what the poem – which is about a particular map, one that saves lives, and which is entitled 'Brief Thoughts on Maps' – says.

> Albert Szent-Gyorgi, who knew a lot about maps,
> according to which life is on its way somewhere or other,
> told us this story from the war
> due to which history is on its way somewhere or other:
>
> The young lieutenant of a small Hungarian detachment in the Alps
> sent a reconnaissance unit out into the icy wasteland.
> It began to snow
> immediately, snowed for two days and the unit
> did not return. The lieutenant suffered: he had despatched
> his own people to death.
>
> But on the third day the unit came back.
> Where had they been? How had they made their way?
> Yes, they said, we considered ourselves
> lost and waited for the end. And then one of us
> found a map in his pocket. That calmed us down.
> We pitched camp, lasted out the snowstorm, and with the map
> we discovered our bearings.
> And here we are.
>
> The lieutenant borrowed this remarkable map,
> and had a good look at it. It was not a map of the Alps
> but of the Pyrenees.
> Goodbye now.[1]

This book provides you with a map to keep with you as you set off into the Alps of English Studies. As the blizzards of set texts, literary theories and essay deadlines set in, it is easy to panic. But perhaps when all that starts happening, you will remember the map, calm

---

[1] 'Brief Thoughts on Maps', *The Times Literary Supplement*, 4 February 1977, p. 118, and reprinted in Holub's collection *Notes of a Clay Pigeon*, trans. Jarmila and Ian Milner, London, 1985.

down and pitch camp till the blizzard clears. Much later, when the crisis has passed and you take out the map again in a moment of idle curiosity, you may well find that it isn't really a complete map of English Studies at all, just as the map which saved the soldiers in the Alps was actually a map of the Pyrenees. But the important thing is that, when it was needed, it gave you a feeling of security, a sense of direction and the confidence of knowing what you have to do not just to survive as an English student, but also to enjoy your studies and eventually move beyond them.

*

I should say something now about the name and scope of the discipline of English Studies. The word 'English' in 'English Studies' is often felt to be unsatisfactory and misleading. For one thing, on English degrees we don't just study the literature of England, but usually a sample, at least, from that of Ireland (James Joyce, Eavan Boland, Seamus Heaney, for instance), of Scotland (Robert Louis Stevenson, Edwin Morgan, Kathleen Jamie) and of Wales (David Jones, R. S. Thomas, Gwyneth Lewis). So, even when we are thinking only of the British Isles, doing English involves the literature of the group of islands sometimes known as the 'British Archipelago'. But, of course, on English degrees we also study world literature *in* English, that is, writing from the United States (Herman Melville, Edith Wharton, Toni Morrison), from the Caribbean (Derek Walcott, V. S. Naipaul, Jamaica Kincaid), from Canada (Margaret Atwood, Alice Munro, Fred Wah), from the Indian sub-continent (Rabindranath Tagore, R. K. Narayan, Anita Desai), from Australia (Patrick White, Peter Carey, Les Murray), from South Africa (Athol Fugard, Nadine Gordimer, Ezekiel Mphahlele), and so on.

But even these wide-ranging national divisions of literature in English are hardly satisfactory or sufficient. In the United States, for instance, the various ethnic communities all have their own bodies of literature, and many of these have grown dramatically in recent years both in scope and variety and in terms of national and international prestige. A selective listing would need to include African American writers (Ishamel Reed, Gloria Naylor, Toni Morrison), Asian American writers (Carlos Bulosan, Amy Tan, Maxine Hong Kingston), Native

American writers (N. Scott Momoday, Louise Erdrich, Sherman
Alexie) and Chicano/a writers (Rolando Hinojosa, Rudolfo Anaya,
Sandra Cisneros).[2] Furthermore, all four of these 'trans-national'
groupings are themselves a yoking together of writers from many
different regions, and to approach a true picture of the range of
contemporary literary activity in English they would all need to
be further sub-divided. For instance, the broad category of Asian
American writing includes (but is not confined to) Chinese American,
Japanese American, Korean American, Filipino American and South
Asian American literatures, and in each of these fields there is a
wide range of available literature, mainly prose fiction, often vividly
representing the multicultural history and experience of each of
these groups.[3]

But even if we were to extend our listing along these lines, so
that a wide range of national and trans-national groupings of writers
in English were represented, we would still be offering a very
conservative map of 'English Literature' (in the sense of Literature
in English), when viewed from a different angle. For instance, if
our viewpoint were 'generic' (which is to say concerned with the
various forms and genres of writing in English), then it would have
to be admitted that most of the writers just listed are novelists. So
while the list just given is progressive in one way, it is conservative
in another, for it doesn't even cover the privileged generic trio of
fiction, drama and poetry, making no attempt to include those forms
in which the boundary between literature and other kinds of writing
is blurred (such as travel writing, biography and narrative history).

For instance, we might argue that accounts of extreme experiences, like prison or captivity narratives, constitute an important
kind of writing which deserves close study. This might lead us to
a collection like *Women's Indian Captivity Narratives* (ed. Kathryn
Derounian-Stodola, Penguin Classics, 1998), representing a form of
narrative which is, the editor suggests, 'arguably the first American
literary form dominated by the experience of women' (the ten

---

[2]The work of all 12 writers mentioned in this sentence is discussed in detail in
Beginning Ethnic American Literatures, ed. Helena Grice et al., Manchester, 2001.
[3]For suggested reading in each of these areas see Grice eds, et al, *Beginning Ethnic
American Literatures*, pp. 185–7.

examples in the collection cover the period 1682–1892 and show considerable diversity). Likewise, we might wish to study the narratives not just of a *period* of captivity, but of *lives* of captivity, as represented in a volume like *The Classic American Slave Narratives* (ed. Henry Louis Gates, Jr, Signet Classic/New American Library, 2002). Equally, it might be the increasingly popular and significant genre of travel writing, as found, for instance, in *Colonial American Travel Narratives* (ed. Wendy Martin, Penguin Classics, 1994) about which we wish to learn, or, on the other hand, voyage accounts (a very different genre, since the main thing to be discovered on a long sea voyage is yourself). And we could go on to include conversion narratives (that is, life narratives which pivot around the moment of religious conversion or transformation) or, more recently, 'coming-out' stories (life accounts in which the focal moments are those of recognising, acting upon and making known one's true sexual orientation).

But even a list supplemented with all these would remain a fairly conservative sketch of the generic coverage which studying English might, or should, involve – where is the cyberpunk prose, the steampunk novels, the graphic novels, the 'sudden fiction' (also known as 'short-short-fiction'), the performance poetry and the improvised drama?, you might be asking. All these different kinds of writing have valid claims for inclusion on English courses, and one of the great transformations of the past twenty years has been that many of these claims have been met, so that the kind of material cited in the last few paragraphs is increasingly indicative of the exciting scope and scale of English degrees in the twenty-first century.

*

I have kept the structure of the book as simple as possible, so the two parts each contain seven chapters. Following this introduction, the next three chapters (2, 3 and 4) are about the 'core' activity of English, which is reading: we learn to read the lines, and then between the lines, and then beyond the lines. I illustrate the first with poetry, the second with prose fiction, and the third with poetry again. The preponderance of poetry examples is not meant to imply that poetry should take precedence over prose, or that it should form the culmination of our studies: it's simply that I hate working with extracts and like to use whole-texts for illustrative purposes whenever possible. However, the example used in the second half of chapter four is Tennyson's 'The Lady of Shalott', which is a substantial narrative piece rather than a short lyric, and it can be seen as an example of 'poetic fiction' (a form much liked by the Victorians) rather than just poetry. The brief Chapter 5 registers the rapid rise in the popularity of creative writing as an element in English degree courses, a trend which is having profound effects on the culture of English departments. Chapter 6 concerns the history and development of English Studies, a topic which can help us to be aware that the 'scope of the possible' in the discipline may extend beyond currently approved or prescribed modes. Chapter 7, 'Online and Digital English', is about the huge body of texts and study resources available on the internet. Chapter 8, the first chapter in Part 2, is about literary theory, and does two things: firstly, it gives an overview of the arrival and impact of literary theory in English Studies since the 1970s; secondly it gives two detailed examples of how theory can operate in actual reading practice. It does not give a detailed exposition of the various kinds of literary theory because I have done that in another book (to which I – naturally – refer you in the bibliography). Chapter 9 is the longest, because it looks at a cross-section of the different kinds of language study that can be included on English degrees. This too can be a contentious area, and the friction between literary study and language study has a long history. To some extent, the friction is inevitable – it's like that always felt between adjacent cities, and I try to show that the closeness can be beneficial, provided that outside forces don't try to make the two cities amalgamate into a new disciplinary megalopolis. Chapter 10, on English and History, is about the contentious issue of context in literary studies. Chapter 11 gives advice on essay writing, and Chapter 12 considers the 'dissertation' (that is, the extended essay on a topic of your own choice), which is the culmination of many English courses. Chapter 13 looks at how the literary text we study in class and write essays about comes into being as a printed artefact: in other words, it's about the shadowy world of textual editors, those literary midwives who move in their mysterious ways to bring literary texts into the world, often labouring for decades over the (re-)birth of a single work. I have included the chapter because I believe that some basic awareness of 'the text as text' should be part of degree-level study, and it is a topic that will loom larger if you decide to continue your studies to a higher level. Chapter fourteen, finally, looks briefly at some of the characteristics of English Studies at master's level.

The bibliography at the end of the book is conceived on very simple principles: it is annotated, and it lists five books relevant to the topic of each of the chapters.

Your starter for ten

At its most basic, English is about reading the text, but then, you could say, so is history or philosophy. What distinguishes English from other textual subjects is the intensity of the reading: English is super-charged reading, and it can produce its own characteristic mental atmosphere in which the words seem to have an aura of high verbal energy. Sometimes we scan them rapidly, perhaps driven by an accelerating current of dawning comprehension, and sometimes, when becalmed, we scrutinize them minutely, almost one by one, turning them this way and that, in the light of an idea which is still only half formed in the mind. Either way, it's the words themselves with which we are engaged, and everything worthwhile that happens in English has to begin happening there. The interpretation and evaluation of literature can be learned by guided experience, and that is what an English course should provide. It is unusual to attempt to break down such gradually acquired expertise into a list of identifiable sub-skills, but it can be useful to make the attempt – here is mine, from one to ten.

(1) *In reading a work of literature, look first for some overall structural pattern – that is, something which provides a structural frame or backbone for the whole.*
These over-arching frames are particularly important in large-scale works like novels and plays, and we can call them 'macro-patterns' (to distinguish them from the smaller-scale patterning referred to

later in point 8). For example, two characters or two couples in a novel may be paired and contrasted throughout, like the two sisters in Jane Austen's *Sense and Sensibility*. Elinor (representing 'sense') is thoughtful and naturally prudent, while Marianne (representing 'sensibility', which today we might call 'sensitivity') is impulsive and passionate. The novel asks which set of characteristics offers the best foundation for a lifetime, whether it is possible to attain a balance between the two extremes, and whether experience will help both personality types to temper their excessive leanings towards one pole or the other. The contrast between the two types may be supported by image-patterns linked to each, such as a contrast between indoor and outdoor locations for their respective key scenes, or preferred types of reading (such as a preference for romantic novels on the one hand or philosophical essays on the other) and contrasting styles of dress or speech. Although the basic thematic contrast may seem simple, the devil, as always in literary studies, is in the detail. But so is the angel, meaning that the potential for readerly enjoyment and the scope for a student or scholar to make original points based on non-clichéd evidence, lie at the level of taking in details. So the working out of this strongly thematized plot is not simple or predictable, and there is much critical debate about which side 'wins' and whether the outcome is really a satisfactory resolution of the issues.

'Issues' can be raised in a novel in many different ways, and usually a combination of methods will be used, some implicit and some explicit: for example, the author/narrator may raise them directly, or the characters may talk about them, or be shown as thinking about them. Raising an issue implicitly might involve, for example, embodying it in action or incident, as in another Jane Austen novel, *Persuasion*, when Louisa Musgrove's impetuous leap into Frederick Wentworth's arms on the Cobb at Lyme Regis results in her injury and ultimately has a transformative effect on her character. While everyone else panics, Anne Elliott, who had rejected a proposal from Wentworth eight years previously (persuaded by her family that he was beneath her), calmly tends the injured Louisa until medical help arrives. Until that moment he had been determined to marry someone else, partly to slight this woman who had once rejected him, but now he begins to see her in a more kindly light. Clearly the incident again raises the issue of the relative merits of caution and impetuosity in matters of conduct and asks what amount of self-protective foresight it is sensible to exercise at a given moment. For Austen is well aware that unless we accept some element of risk, we will never enter into any relationship, or undertake any worthwhile enterprise at all. So the issue is implicit in the overall plot-structure and design of the novel and embodied in contrasts or parallels between different characters.

(2) *In reading a work of literature, look for similarity beneath apparent dissimilarity, or vice-versa.*
Victorian novels commonly feature two central, paired characters whose marriage is the culmination of the action. There may also be a rival love interest for one or both, and a series of plot strands which connect the two in various ways to the wider society in which they live. The 'minor' characters in the subordinate plot-strands will be 'thematized' in some way in relation to the main pair. A frequent motif in the main plot of the nineteenth-century novel is the 'double proposal', as seen, for instance, in *Jane Eyre* and *Pride and Prejudice*. In this kind of plot, the initial proposal is unworthy of acceptance (for instance, because it is made for motives of ambition, complacency, lust, pride, etc.), and so is rejected. Thus, Jane Eyre rejects Rochester after the existence of his insane and estranged wife is revealed to her: his immoral concealment of his true marital circumstances render him unworthy, and this is compounded when he begs her to elope with him to France and live with him as his wife, even though they cannot be legally married. She separates herself from Thornfield Hall and moral temptation, and is in due course rescued from desperate circumstances by the ardently religious St. John Rivers, eventually agreeing to marry him and go to India with him as a missionary. He seems the opposite of Rochester, in his moral uprightness and selflessness, but she perceives that beneath that dissimilarity there is a similar willingness to use her for his own purposes, 'higher' though they might seem (to himself) to be. Thus, St. John Rivers is exposed as an exponent of another kind of immorality, as he tries to persuade Jane to enter into a loveless marriage for exalted reasons. So the reader's interpretive trajectory

involves realising that two opposites are only opposites on the
surface.

(3) *In reading a work of literature, we often need to distinguish
between overt and covert content – that is, between apparent
content and real content.*
For example, the American modernist poet, novelist and essayist
e. e. Cummings (1894–1963) has a poem about driving a car, usually
called 'She being brand' after its first line, though this makes little
sense as a title, and it would be more sensible to call it 'She being
brand-new', taking the first *two* lines as the title. On the surface, that
is 'overtly', the poem describes taking a new car for a test-run, but
beneath the surface, that is 'covertly', it is immediately obvious that
the poem is actually about making love.[4] By today's standards, this is
a hopelessly sexist piece of writing, with an active male participant
and a passive female who succumbs to his attentions. I said just now
that the poem 'is actually about making love', but a poem cannot
entirely disown its overt content, so it must in some way be about
both its 'overt' and the 'covert' meanings – the poem celebrates the
exhilaration of both driving *and* making love, deriving its effect from
juxtaposing the two. Hence, it is more accurate to say that the overt
content describes driving a car, while the covert content is about the
alleged parallels between driving and love-making.

The overt/covert content distinction is also relevant in the case of
a poem by Vicki Feaver called 'Ironing'. It describes three different
attitudes to ironing which the speaker passes through at different
points in her life: in the first stage she irons everything, in the second
she irons nothing, and in the third she returns to ironing, but with a
difference, so that it becomes a savoured and elective activity which
gives the self room to breathe, rather than being driven and frantic,
as it was in the first phase. All this is the overt or open content of
the poem; at the covert level, the reader realizes that the speaker's
changing attitude to ironing is indicative of the broader issue of
seeking a balance in life, an issue not unlike those mentioned in
relation to the Jane Austen novels. But again, it is not a matter of

---

[4] 'She being Brand//-new', pp. 15–16 in *E. E. Cummings: Selected Poems 1923–1958*,
London, 1960.

perceiving the covert meaning and then discarding the overt subject matter, for the former is really a fragment of the latter, so that the meaning beneath the surface includes the surface meaning as part of itself.

(4) In reading a work of literature, it is often useful to distinguish between its meaning and its significance.
'Meaning' is like something *inside* the work, whereas 'significance' is something we *perceive* in the work, something which is necessarily shifting.[5] If a literary work is regarded as being like the sea, then 'meaning' is like the salt – it is one of the 'ingredients' of the water, whereas significance is like its colour, which is an attribute that changes with the prevailing light conditions. When we look down from a height, the shallow water nearer the shore is a lighter blue than the deeper water further out, but if you were to fill one bottle with water from in-shore and another with water from further out, no difference in colour would be detectable. The significance of a work of literature likewise shifts according to our angle of view, the concerns, assumptions and anxieties that we bring to it, and the nature of our times: thus, Conrad's novella *Heart of Darkness* will have a particular urgency, intensity or significance for a reader from a recently de-colonized nation. Significance, then, is always shifting, and it is difficult to put a limit on it. Here is my favourite illustration of that difficulty: in his book *Literary Theory: An Introduction*, Terry Eagleton says that we can probably be sure that *King Lear* is not about Manchester United Football Club. He should have said that Manchester United is not part of the *meaning* of King Lear, for it may well be part of the *significance*. *King Lear* is about somebody who retires, but can't entirely let go of the reins of command. He still wants a hand in team selection: he wants to be able to name his squad of a hundred knights and keep on having a say in running the club (or the kingdom). In other words, the parallel between *King Lear* and the one-time Manchester United manager Sir Matt Busby is actually pretty close. It is a play about the paradox of a king who stages a public display of devolving power and dividing his kingdom between his daughters, and yet tries to hold on to power. The great Russian

---

[5]The distinction is put forward in E. D. Hirsch, *Validity in Interpretation*, Yale, 1967.

novelist Leo Tolstoy went so far as to say that all old men are King
Lear, all reluctant to admit that others can step into their shoes, or, at
best, admitting it in theory, but in practice finding it difficult actually
to let it happen. And after all, the play does mention football, when
Edmund says to Kent 'Out of my way, you base football player', as if
it had anticipated the reading that Eagleton maintains is impossible.[6]

*(5) In reading literature, we think in terms of genre or literary type –
that is, we ask how the literary genre affects the content of the work.*
For instance, in a Renaissance stage tragedy, an evil character
may openly declare his evil intentions, as when Richard, Duke
of Gloucester, in the opening soliloquy 'Now is the winter of our
discontent' in Shakespeare's play *Richard III* describes himself as
'subtle, false, and treacherous' and makes the announcement that
he will plot his way to the throne, for 'I am determined to prove a
villain'. We could conclude that Richard is a person of unusual self-
knowledge and honesty, but it would be wrong to do this, because
this kind of announcement is one of the conventions of the genre;
Richard's long opening speech is partly a way of supplying the
historical back-story, allowing the author to address the audience by
proxy through the character, so that the action can begin strongly
with a scene of immediate dramatic impact. In this sense, the speech
anticipates the kind of direct authorial comment on characters and
their situation which would develop in later centuries with the rise of
the novel. The soliloquy (which is usually quite a lengthy speech) and
the 'aside' (which is usually much briefer) are ways of representing
thought on the stage by turning it into spoken words. Thoughts
are not always verbally formulated as full-scale sentences, and an
inner decision to act in a certain way, or adopt a certain goal, will
not usually be conducted within like a formal spoken debate. So the
apparent crystal clarity of Richard's self-address and the beauty of its
poetry are not so much part of his character as part of the dramatic
medium in which he is being represented.

---

[6]This response to Eagleton on *Lear* is Professor Ken Newton's. It originally appeared
in an article entitled 'Interest, Authority and Ideology in Literary Interpretation' in the
British Journal of Aesthetics, 22 (1982), pp.103–14 and in expanded form in his book *In
Defence of Literary Interpretation: Theory and Practice*, Macmillan, 1986.

A second relevant 'generic' point is that Richard is an example of a stock character, for he represents a distinct literary type in early modern drama, a type which is now usually called the malcontent: the malcontent is a male figure of great intelligence and ability who is at odds with the society in which he finds himself: he is cynical and contemptuous of the aims and motives of others and derives satisfaction from thwarting their aims, spreading mischief, humbling those he sees as more favoured than himself. The brooding, self-despising form of bitter introspection with which Richard opens the play immediately signals to the audience that Richard is one of these and sets up the expectation of a plot full of multi-layered scheming leading to bloodshed, cruel acts of revenge and a period of general chaos. Other examples of this character type are Iago in Shakespeare's *Othello*, Bosola in John Webster's *The Duchess of Malfi* and Malevole in John Marston's *The Malcontent*. Being aware of the conventions of a particular literary form and of the existence of stock character-types or situations are examples of what is meant by 'thinking in terms of genre or literary type'.

(6) *In reading literature, we frequently read the literal as metaphorical, especially in the case of reading poems.*
For example, a contemporary poem mentions a person who has a 'bullet lodged inside before we knew it was growing'.[7] At first this seems to suggest an assassination by some outside figure. But literal bullets can't grow, and this is the clue which shows that it is actually a metaphorical bullet, and it soon becomes clear that it is a metaphor for a fatal illness from which the person mentioned is found to be suffering. This kind of interpretive move (apparently literal objects being read metaphorically) is very common in the reading of poetry. You will probably have realized that this is quite closely related to point 3, above, but the difference is that if we map the overt/covert distinction on to it, with the bullet being the overt sense and the fatal disease the covert or underlying sense, then it is clear that here we have to discard the bullet and replace it with the disease, for there isn't actually any bullet there, even though a bullet is mentioned. By contrast, in the case of the ironing in Feaver's

---

[7]See 'The Forked Tree' in Marion Lomax, *The Peepshow Girl*, Northumberland, 1989.

poem, 'Ironing' is literally what it says and remains present along with the wider sense we attributed to it and cannot be discarded when we recognize that it is also emblematic of a wider category of attitudes or activities. Of course, the metaphor linking the bullet and the disease works because of the similar effects the two have – they both strike suddenly, have fatal consequences, and so on. But as with all metaphor, the link depends upon a perceived difference as well as a perceived similarity, the difference in this case being the ability of the metaphorical 'bullet' to grow, which in effect deletes the literal bullet.

(7) In spite of this, we read the surface of the work accurately – in other words, we recognize the importance of the precise literal words of the text and do not take liberties with them.
For example, a poem discussed in Chapter 8 contains the lines 'When sisters separate they haunt each other / as she, who I might once have been, haunts me'. It is important for the reader to realize that these lines do not say that the two persons mentioned are sisters – they merely say that they haunt each other as separated sisters do. A reader who failed to notice the presence of the word 'as' would misread the line and regard the two figures as sisters. So interpretation often works at the level of minute textual detail and often seems to turn upon apparently insignificant linking words.

For a prose example, consider the moment in Conrad's *Heart of Darkness* when Kurtz's African mistress curses the departing steamboat from the shore. In writing about this episode student essays have sometimes suggested that the African woman is stereo-typically portrayed and depicted as unable to articulate or control her actions and reactions. But read closely, it is evident that, on the contrary, she puts on a carefully orchestrated theatrical display in which every move is calculated to produce maximum impact on her audience, as if choreographed move by move in advance. For instance, notice in this trimmed extract the effect of the italicized words:

> She walked with *measured* steps ... there was something ominous and stately in her *deliberate* progress ... She ... stood still, and faced us ... A whole minute passed, and then she made a step

forward … and she stopped *as if* her heart had failed her … She looked at us all *as if* her life had depended upon the unswerving steadiness of her glance. Suddenly she opened her bared arms and threw them up rigid above her head, *as though* in an uncontrollable desire to touch the sky … A formidable silence hung over the scene.

The words 'measured' and 'deliberate' show that every movement is calculated, the timing rigidly adhered to, every action slowed down till the movements are mesmerising, and when an action is performed which suggests a loss of control of her actions and emotions it is preceded by 'as if' (twice) or 'as though'. A careless reader will miss all this calculated art and theatricality and, spotting the phrase 'uncontrollable desire', will write that this woman is shown as being unable to control herself, failing to take into account the crucial phrase 'as though'. These are some of the elements, then, of understanding the vital importance of the 'precise literal words of the text'.

(8) As readers we look for patterns in literary works. Not over-arching structural patterns this time, but 'micro-patterns', such as a series of words with the same tone, or register, or flavour.
Often the significant point is where the perceived pattern is broken, for the pattern-breaking item must have been chosen either *in spite of* breaking the pattern, or *because* it breaks the pattern. Either way, it is thereby 'foregrounded' in the reader's attention. In the same way, if you see a hundred rows of flowers in a wallpapered room, the only ones which will catch your attention are the ones which are not properly aligned – all DIY people know this. In this poem, for instance, by the American 'Black Mountain' poet Robert Creeley (1926–2005), every element of the style is 'talky', colloquial and informal, except for one phrase:

I know a man

As I sd to my
friend, because I am
always talking, – John, I

sd, which was not his
name, the darkness sur-
rounds us, what
can we do against
it, or else, shall we &
why not, buy a goddamn
big car,
drive, he sd, for
christ's sake, look
out where yr going.

The air of spontaneous, slice-of-life informality is re-enforced by
abbreviations mostly used only in casual jottings made for private
use, such as 'sd' for 'said', '&' for 'and', 'yr' for 'you're', and by
typographical features like the omission of quotation marks and the
use of a lower-case initial letter in 'christ's': The poem also features
the kind of self-interrupting asides which seem to typify spontaneous speech, as seen in 'because I am / always talking', 'which
was not his / name', and '& / why not'. But right in the middle is the
stark, philosophical pronouncement 'the darkness sur- / rounds us,
what / can we do against / it?' Presumably, the car is surrounded by
darkness during an epic road trip, but that is not the kind of darkness
the speaker seems to be worried about, and he craves distraction
from ultimate questions by meaningless materialistic consumerism
('shall we & / why not, buy a goddamn / big car'). So the positing of
the ultimate philosophical question gains force from the way it breaks
the jokey, blokey colloquial tone that otherwise makes a consistent
pattern throughout the whole poem. Here, then, the perception of
something consistent in a text, plus a single inconsistent element,
and the interactive 'spark' between them is crucial to an appreciation
of the text and both its humour and its seriousness.

*(9) As readers we identify stages and phases within a literary
work, and doing so is often itself a useful stage in the process of
interpretation.*
Some of these stages are formally marked by the divisions of
a work into Acts, or Books, or Chapters, or Verses. These are
formally marked breaks in the text, and often they will be formally

numbered (Act 1, Chapter 1, Book the Second, and so on). Further, in the nineteenth century each chapter in a novel would often be provided with its own 'epigraph', usually a couple of quoted lines from a well-known poet or dramatist, which would give a thematic clue or pointer to the content or outcome of the chapter. The larger formally marked divisions would probably also have individual titles (such as 'Book 1, Miss Brooke', 'Book 2, Old and Young' in George Eliot's *Middlemarch*). These formal divisions lead us to expect that the designated segment of the whole (the chapter or 'Book' in question) will form a distinct, quasi-free-standing link in the chain of circumstances and events which make up the whole novel. In the twentieth century a good many of these formal indicators were removed. For example, in Virginia Woolf's novels there might not be formally numbered chapters at all, just a section break in the page to indicate a switch of time or place, possibly with a centred asterisk inserted, but this kind of 'low-profile' break is still a residual form of 'chapterization' (to coin a term I hope will not catch on).

But in literature, transitions are just as important as breaks. Thus, an Elizabethan sonnet sequence may contain a hundred or more sonnets, and they would usually be numbered (with formal Roman numerals in the original editions and with the more familiar Arabic numerals in modern ones). But across the sequence there are also phases which are not formally marked. For instance, in a courtship sequence, there may be a gradual transition from rejection and disappointment to eventual acceptance and gratification, with possibly a cluster of three or four 'hinge' sonnets in which the shift seems to be instigated. Picking up on-going shifts in the emotional 'weather' and tone of the sequence is an important aspect of the reading experience. Gradually, the frostiness of the 'exposition-phase' begins to thaw, sliding into the more inconsistent weather of the 'development-phase', and then another phase will begin, putting everything in place for the dénouement. The reader needs to be aware of the moment when the introduction of setting, circumstances and characters pivots into the first significant moment of choice, or denial, or tentative drift towards intimacy. This kind of 'staging' can even be important within the narrow confines of a single sonnet. For example, in Shakespeare's Sonnet 73, which is commented on in Chapter 8, it is important to decide whether the three images of aging are meant to represent some kind of progression and development, or just three static examples of the same thing.

(10) Finally, as competent readers, we read in linguistic period, aware (among other things) of semantic change, that is, changes in the meanings of words.
Even in quite recent literature, words and phrases have different meanings from those they have today, so their very familiarity can be a snare. For instance, in the Victorian novel, the word 'lover' does not mean what it means today – in the title of Elizabeth Gaskell's novel *Sylvia's Lovers*, for instance, 'lovers' means 'suitors', and when Jane Austen tells us in *Pride and Prejudice* that the Bennets were seeing less of Mr Collins than hitherto because 'the business of love-making relieved them from a great deal of his company', she means simply that he was preoccupied with his courtship of Miss Lucas. 'Love-making' to the Victorians meant making flattering comments, whispering sweet nothings and the like. In earlier texts, it is often more immediately obvious that a familiar word can't mean what it means now, as in Shakespeare's *Henry V* when Falstaff talks about his womb ('My womb undoes me', he says). Do we conclude that he is unmanning himself, or claiming some kind of double-gendered universality? Well, it is tempting to some critics to make this claim, but the explanation is simple. In Elizabethan times the word 'womb' still had its older meaning of 'stomach' and was used of both men and women. Falstaff is simply saying that his large stomach prevents him from being a brave and agile soldier. (For more about such changes of meaning see the section 'Meanings on the move' in chapter nine). In general, then, 'reading in period' is an important element in appreciating earlier literature, and these instances of possible confusion arising from individual words and phrases are less significant than cases where a whole 'mind-set', as we would call it, separates us from the situation, experience, expectations and assumptions embodied in the work we are reading.

These, then, are some of the main ways in which readers and critics engage with literary texts and begin to put forward accounts of what they mean. We will always need these ten elements of interpretation, for literary criticism can never outgrow them, and they can never be superseded. In other words, it is impossible to do English without them. But, as we will argue in later chapters, though we can never grow out of them, we will need, as we progress through degree-level study, to supplement them with techniques and attitudes ultimately derived from literary theory.

2

Reading Poetry

This chapter concentrates on poetry and the next one on prose, but poetry and prose do not occupy, of course, separate universes. Poems tell stories as well as fiction (often in both senses of 'as well') – they just do it differently. The contemporary poet Ian Duhig once defined poems as 'novels without the waffle', and he was, I think, only half joking.[1] Likewise, we may admire Coleridge's famous definition of poetry as 'the best possible words in the best possible order', but this should not lead us to imagine that novelists are by nature content with something inferior (more-or-less adequate words in an on-the-whole acceptable order, for instance). But many poems are very short, and that does allow and demand an especially close scrutiny of a disciplined and thorough kind. So this chapter begins with a suggested method.

The end is nigh: reading short poems[2]

'Reading should be a predatory activity'
(Thomas Kinsella, contemporary Irish poet)

The practice of 'unseen close reading', still taught at school and university as the main way to read short poems, can seem to invite

---

[1] Duhig is the author (most recently) of *The Speed of Dark* (2007) and *Pandorama* (2012), both from Picador. He made the remark in an edition of the British TV arts programme *The South Bank Show* broadcast in 1997 to celebrate the 'New Generation' poets.
[2] This method was jointly devised by Peter Barry and Marianne Taylor of the Department of Information Studies at Aberystwyth University.

a *reverence* for poetry, building a mystique of invulnerability about the poet, and inviting us merely to *contemplate* poems, a process which can seem intimidating and disempowering for readers. We seem to be asked to enter the poem as if entering a church, taking off the cycle-clips of day-to-day thinking and standing in awkward reverence, like the speaker in Philip Larkin's poem 'Church Going'. But what we need to do to make ourselves feel comfortable within the space of the poem is to *intervene* in it in some way. The white space around the poem on the page seems almost sacramental, like the space between priest and people at a church service: it seems a kind of barrier between word and world, as if the poet were a priestly being and the poem a service going on in the distance at the 'holy end' of literature, which we readers are called upon to witness passively. The method recommended here, by contrast, involves taking back the surrounding white space and talking back to the poem. It involves writing on the poem, changing some of its words, in order to see how this changes the poem as a whole, and dividing the poem up into sub-sections – *doing* things with it, in fact. In this way, we try to make connections between ourselves and the poem – to read ourselves back into it, so that it can become a part of ourselves. All this will perhaps help us to re-appropriate poetry, refusing it the status of a revered and unapproachable 'verbal icon' in the inner temple of literature. So the method described here is a way of 'negotiating' with a poem, and it should provide you with plenty to say in circumstances where you are expected to write analysis or commentary as part of an essay or exam. To begin with, read through the poem two or three times. Then ask yourself the basic questions: Who is 'speaking' or 'thinking' in this poem? Who is being spoken to or thought about? To what end or purpose, and in what setting or circumstances, is this activity taking place? For instance, what has just happened or is about to happen? What seems the most likely outcome? What is the overall mood or atmosphere of the whole poem? Having jotted down a few notes on these preliminary matters, move on to the four main stages of this poetry-reading method, which are as follows:

Focus on the flow of the poem as a whole

Poems (no matter how short) have 'phases': there is a part which is introductory, then a development or transition which adds some new element, or twists or re-shapes the material of the first phase in some way (probably, but not invariably, this phase will be the longest section); then there may be another development phase, in which a further shift or re-alignment of attitude or viewpoint is evident; finally there will be will be a concluding part (which may double back, or break off from the logic of the development, or transpose what had been merely literal and one-dimensional into something more complex). Mark the phases in some way on the printed poem itself (for example, with dotted lines across the page). This 'phasing' activity helps you to look for an overall containing structure, enabling you to see the poem as meanings cumulatively unfolding, moving forwards, or sometimes looping back and repeating, or rephrasing what has gone before. Identifying 'stages and phases' can give us a strong sense of familiarity with the poem, of 'ownership', even, as we begin to get a sense of how it works, how it moves and where it might be bound.

Focus on a point in the poem

Few poems are easy all the way through. Nearly all have a section which is more difficult than the rest, and because of this, we may tend to shy away from its greater complexity, preferring to direct our attention elsewhere, to parts of the poem which seem more straightforward. So at this second stage, we make ourselves stop and home in, grasping the nettle of difficulty, and remembering that difficulty may take many different forms. For instance, it is by no means always a matter of unusual or unfamiliar words, or complicated grammar – on the contrary, sometimes the words in a puzzling passage can be bafflingly simple, making their precise significance or effect hard to pin down. Sometimes the meaning seems to hover right in front of us, but somehow just out of reach. At other times the passage has what the poet J. H. Prynne calls an 'ardent obliquity', meaning, more or less, a passionate or intense

ENGLISH IN PRACTICE

indirectness. Whatever type of difficulty the intimidating section of your poem seems to have, pencil a box around it on the page and spend some time with it: write about it in the margin; talk back to it; 'brain-storm' it; free-associate round it. Difficulty in poetry often indicates the presence of thematic significance: facing up to this part of a poem can be a cure for poetry phobia – in other words, for that panicky feeling readers get when the words on the page don't quite make sense, even on second, third or fourth reading. But word puzzles can be engrossing to grapple with and suddenly realising how to unravel them can give great satisfaction. Keep in mind, too, the other side of this coin, which is that no poem in the whole world is difficult all the way through.

Focus on the flow of the poem again

All poems have patterns. Identify some in the poem and, again, find a way of marking them on the printed page. Having identified a pattern, look for a point where the pattern is broken. Breaks in a pattern are always significant. Patterns can be made out of almost any aspect of a poem. An obvious example is line-length – in most poems, most of the lines are of roughly the same length, even when there is no rhyme pattern, and no fixed metre to determine the number of syllables per line. Hence, a line which is longer or shorter than most of the others usually has a special reason for being so, and exactly the same point could be made about stanza length. Patterns of rhyme and rhythm are a familiar feature of poetry, and again, the moment when a regular rhyme scheme is broken with a half-rhyme, a rhythmic break or 'hiccup' may be significant. Patterns may also be formed by the type of vocabulary a poet uses – for example, a succession of words which are romantic and tender in tone, perhaps interrupted with one which is strikingly different, containing overtones or violence or the uncanny, for instance, or a string of phrases of a technical, erudite or scientific kind, among which is a phrase that seems much more homely or familiar.

Focus on a point *in the poem again*

Circle the word or phrase which is for you the strangest or most surprising in the poem. This word or phrase can become a focal point of your view of the poem. Look across the poem for others that seem related to it; circle them too and link them to your focal word. Try the experiment of changing the focal word to one which you would initially consider less surprising. Then ask yourself how the overall effect of the poem is now changed. Later you can ask what it is that makes your focal word stand out: it may seem to have unexpected connotations or tone; or it may be connected in a surprising way with other words that feature in the poem; or it may be part of a phrase in which the words are unusually ordered, or seem in some way counter-intuitive.

These four activities are ways of becoming actively involved with the poem so that we engage purposefully with it, looking both at the whole poem in the first and third stages of the method, and more closely at particular parts of it in stages two and four, going close up to a particular section in stage two, and then ultra-close-up, so to speak, at stage four. Writing on the page and making various marks on it in the course of this engagement enhances the feeling of active involvement with the poem, and should help to dispel that feeling of semi-religious awe and reverence which many approaches to poetry-reading seem to induce. The shorter the poem, the more it seems to have that intimidating 'gem-like' quality which can make close readerly and academic engagement with it very difficult. As a reader, you may find the stark simplicity of an ultra-short lyric like Robert Frost's 'Stopping by Woods on a Snowy Evening' to be mesmerising and dazzling. But merely saying so doesn't make any critical point, or contribute to any possible analysis, so it is of very little use for study purposes. To write about a poem we have to get beyond our sense of awe and set up some kind of dialogue between ourselves and the poem. The four stages of 'dialogue' just described try to help in doing this.

Let's see how this approach could work with a suitable short poem: the piece below is by contemporary poet Johnston Kirkpatrick and originally appeared in the *Times Literary Supplement*.[3] Kirkpatrick says that his main subject matter has mostly been his 'growing up in working-class Belfast', and this poem is about a blind friend he remembers from his childhood:

Aposiopesis

Wet days, Sammy Hill's sitting room,
Sammy on holiday from the 'Blind School',
his spectacles thick as bottle bottoms,
reading buff-paged riddled books of Braille,
nervous fingers divining the words.

I held the page to the window.
My dumb touch read nothing in spite
of seeing the bullet-proof page,
groped over the stopped rivets,
the darkness of dot dot dot dot.

On the matter of the 'stages and phases' of the piece, clearly the first stanza of the poem is mainly about Sammy and the second mainly about the speaker himself. The first shows Sammy reading; the second shows the speaker trying to read what Sammy reads. Sammy may be awkward and nervous, but he is succeeding, and in this sense he penetrates the darkness which surrounds him. The speaker, by contrast, fails – his touch is 'dumb' and he can merely grope in the darkness. Structurally, then, the second stanza is a kind of mirrored reversal of the first.

On the second stage (concerning the most difficult-seeming section of the poem); for me this occurs in the last two lines of the first stanza: 'buff-paged' simply describes the nature of the paper – it doesn't look or feel like the pages of an ordinary book because it has to be thick enough to hold the perforations which form the

---

[3] *Times Literary Supplement*, 1980: Kirkpatrick's work has also appeared in *Trio Poetry 3*, Belfast, 1982 (as one of three poets in the collection); in *English*, 1991, 40 (167), pp. 135 and 162; and in the anthology edited by Frank Ormsby, *A Rage for Order: Poetry of the Northern Ireland Troubles* Belfast, 1992, rpt 1994.

text. So the page is 'riddled' in two senses, firstly in the sense that it is full of holes (as in the expression 'riddled with bullets'), and secondly it is 'riddled' in the sense that it poses a 'riddle' or problem for the sighted reader because it is written in code (like the Morse Code suggested by the 'dot dot dot dot' at the end). The remaining difficulty, though, is the word 'divined', which oddly suggests that there is something supernatural or uncanny in the decoding Sammy is learning at the 'Blind School'. Of course, it *looks* that way to the person who has not learned the code, but there is something here of our own tendency to invest this disability (blindness) with an aura of the supernatural, as if we want to romanticize it by believing that in return for the physical disability, some kind of spiritual '*in*sight' is given to blind people – hence the recurrent figure in literature and legend of the blind seer ('seer' meaning 'prophet'), such as the Tiresias who features in Sophocles' play *Oedipus Rex* and in T. S. Eliot's poem *The Waste Land*. Another example is Gloucester in Shakespeare's *King Lear* who, after he has been blinded, tells us 'I stumbled while I saw', meaning 'I was morally blind until I lost my sight'. Does the poem collude with this sublimating spiritualization of a physical disability or does it expose it, saying that blind people differ from everybody else only in not being able to see?

On the third stage, concerning patterns within the poem; the major one is a pattern of reversals between the two stanzas: Sammy's fingers may be nervous, but they *are* reading, but the speaker's touch is 'dumb' and can read nothing. He holds the page to the window, but he can see nothing. The indicators of disability are shifted from Sammy to himself as the poem progresses, so that the speaker becomes dumb and gropes in darkness. Looking at Sammy in the first stanza, he sees an awkward, ill-at-ease character (the thick glasses, the heavy pages of the book, the nervous fingers), but in the second, as the awkwardness is transferred to himself, he gropes in a darkness which his sight cannot help him to penetrate and seems to achieve a degree of empathy with Sammy, an achievement to which either seeing or not seeing is irrelevant.

Concluding, then, with stage four, which involves homing in on the single word which seems to be the focal point of the poem; I suspect that the title word itself might well be the one which took much of your initial attention, for its air of technical precision is strikingly at odds with the ordinary and simple language of the poem itself. It isn't a word in common usage, and most readers would need to look it up. The dictionary informs us that it is the term for a printed indication that something is missing from a text. Some common examples are such devices as: (1) the apostrophe, as in a word such as *can't*, which indicates that in this contracted version of the word 'cannot', the 'o' of 'not' has been omitted; (2) the dash which indicates an item of held-back information (as in a Jane Austen novel, when we might be told of a character that he is 'a Colonel in the ——shire Regiment'); and (3) the full stops (...) which indicate omitted material within a quotation. The last example is the most relevant to the poem. Aposiopesis, notice, is not the act of leaving something out, but the graphic means of *indicating* that something has been left out. The root meaning of the word is to pass over something in silence (from the Greek *apo* + *siopesis*, together meaning 'in silence'). The pages of Braille writing held up to the light by the speaker look like an endless aposiopesis – dot, dot, dot – as indeed they are, in the sense that for him the *entire* sense of the words is omitted by the Braille, since he understands nothing of it at all. The 'dot dot dot dot' at the end of the poem tells the speaker that there is something he doesn't understand, and indicates the existence of a gulf between himself and his friend.

'Aposiopesis', in my view, is an excellent poem which is artful in its apparently artless simplicity. Paradoxically, its not being complex on the surface makes the poem easy to enjoy, and yet at the same time difficult to write about. I hope that the four-stage method just described and exemplified suggests some ways of working out worthwhile things to say about poems, and in doing so gaining some insight (pun intended) into the way poetic excellence is built up throughout a poem. But 'excellence' is a loaded term. If some pieces of writing are indeed 'excellent', then others must be less than excellent, and yet others must be mediocre, or even downright poor. These are evaluative terms which express judgements about degrees of quality. On what kind of criteria can literary judgements of this kind be based? That is the topic of the next section.

Spenser's 'second hand'

Writing about literature is not exclusively concerned with making judgments about literary quality but attempting to make such judge-ments is a significant part of it. Evaluation is not the same thing as interpretation (which is what we have talked about so far in this chapter), though in practice the two often work in combination.

Literature, then, is inescapably a world in which some works are more equal than others, and identifying the strengths and weaknesses of literary works is one of the skills you might reasonably expect to develop over the course of an English degree. But it is as well to be realistic about the amount of agreement likely to be achieved. When a dozen competent mathematicians take up a calcu-lation they will, I suppose, all come up with the same answer, but if you ask a dozen critics to evaluate a poem or a story, the likelihood is that you will end up with a dozen different opinions (perhaps more, as literary critics will even argue with themselves). The problems arise because evaluation is usually highly contested and often very personal. But let's see to what extent it might be possible to agree on some general evaluative principles, even though we realize that the application of these criteria to specific instances will probably not produce universal agreement.

Let's start by emphasising that poetic excellence means different things in different literary periods. My admiration of Kirkpatrick's poem is heightened by the fact that it dispenses with many of the conventional external features of poetry (such as rhyme and a fixed metre) and appears 'naked' before the reader. But such 'unadorned' poetic excellence is not of a kind which was available to, say, a Renaissance poet, for the English poetry of earlier centuries kept to laid-down rules of poetic form and diction and poets had to find a way of being original within the restraints of that kind of framework. In the same way, a chess player has to be daring and original *within the rules of chess*. Placing a pawn on an opponent's head, though original, and probably quite daring, can never be a brilliant move in a chess game. So in making a judgement about the quality of a piece of writing, the piece has to be considered within the context of the rules to which the writer has subscribed, by the mere fact of writing, say, a sonnet. It would therefore be difficult to devise criteria of excellence that would apply equally to Kirkpatrick, writing in the late twentieth century, and Edmund Spenser writing in the 1590s. But let's see how far we can get in formulating some general criteria for poetic excellence. Let's suggest, firstly, that every word in a text should earn its keep and have a specific job to do and a definite *semantic* role to play (that is, one concerned with establishing the meaning) – words in poems shouldn't just be decorative. Much of the 'practical criticism' and 'New Criticism' which was prevalent from the 1920s to the 1970s (see Chapter 8) seemed to subscribe to this criterion, but it should soon become apparent that we can't really accept it in these absolute terms, for it is actually very *genre-specific*. An epic poem, for instance, could be much more effectively evaluated by thinking about the impact of complete episodes rather than that of single lines or phrases. So, let's refine our original formulation to take this into account: this gives us the final form for our evaluative criterion in the area of language – *the briefer the verbal structure, the more important it is that every word should have a precise semantic function*. This is a *contingent* criterion rather than an 'absolutist' one, for it is genre-sensitive in a fairly precise way.

In practice, I suspect, the above criterion will turn out to be still not flexible enough, partly because it doesn't make any distinction between the poetic tastes and practices of different historical periods. However, for the moment, let's see how useful it is in evaluating the following sonnet, from Edmund Spenser's *Amoretti* sequence:

75

One day I wrote her name upon the strand,
But came the waves and washed it away:
Again I wrote it with a second hand,
But came the tide, and made my pains his prey.
Vain man, said she, that doest in vein assay,
A mortal thing so to immortalize.
For I myself shall like to this decay,
And eek my name be wiped out likewise.
Not so, (quod I) let baser things devize,

To die in dust, but you shall live by fame:
My verse your virtues rare shall eternize,
And in the heavens write your glorious name.
Where whenas death shall all the world subdue,
Our love shall live, and later life renew.

The sequence was written the year before Spenser's marriage (at
the age of 40) to Elizabeth Boyle, who may be taken as the 'she'
addressed in the poems. What the criterion we are testing does,
in essence, is to condemn mere decorative padding, insisting that
every word and phrase in a short poem should be 'load bearing',
that is, should be necessary in some way to conveying *the sense* so
that 'verbal redundancy' should not occur. Now, this is a test which
Spenser's sonnet might have some difficulty in passing, for there
seems to be a clear example of verbal redundancy in line three. The
speaker opens the poem by telling us how he once wrote the name
of his beloved in the sand of the seashore; it was washed away by
the tide, so he wrote it again – 'Again I wrote it with a second hand',
he says. But isn't the entire sense of this line conveyed by its first
phrase, 'again I wrote it'? The second phrase, 'with a second hand',
adds nothing to the sense. So it fails the 'verbal redundancy' test. Is
that the end of the matter, though? Is the poet really guilty here of
faulty technique?

Well, let me argue against myself, as I said critics are prone to do.
In drafting this argument, the phrase 'adds nothing to the sense' was
originally written as 'adds nothing at all to the sense'. Why did I add
'at all', since 'nothing' cannot become more nothing by intensifying
it to 'nothing at all'? That, of course, is true in terms of strict verbal
logic, but adding the words 'at all' after 'nothing' is, in real life, a more
emphatic way of making the point – people say things like 'nothing
whatever' or 'absolutely nothing' when feelings are running high, and
it would be fussily pedantic to point out that the 'whatever' and the
'absolutely' are in fact semantically and logically redundant. So if we
apply a strictly utilitarian test to the words in the sonnet, it may be
that we would rule out of court many of the effects which sonnets
are most geared to creating. In other words, we need to redefine
the notion of *utility* with specific reference to the sonnet, taking into
account the fact that in a sonnet, the concept of 'utility' (what works

and what doesn't, what has a job to do and what doesn't, and so on) is more various than mere semantic precision and logical economy. The sonnet's primary requirements are for verbal and conceptual ingenuity within the framework of a tight and inflexible set of rules for rhyme and rhythm. So its principle of utility would be anything that is conducive towards these ends. One aspect of the verbal ingenuity found in sonnets is the use of (to take a phrase which post-dates Spenser) 'elegant variation', which can involve, for instance, repeating what has already been said, but using a different form of words. For example, lines two and four of Spenser's sonnet describe exactly the same thing (the incoming sea washing away what is written in the sand), but they use different verbal formulae ('waves' becomes 'tides' and 'washed it away' becomes 'made my pains its prey'), so that the principle of variation is maintained. In this light, the phrase 'with a second hand' may be said to conform to the sonnet's generic requirement for 'repetition-with-variation', so that it doesn't actually fail the redundancy test at all.

This approach involves seeing the sonnet as a form of compressed verbal entertainment akin (let's say) to tweeting. Tweeting too has its own verbal conventions which are imposed by the genre, and within which those who employ the medium strive to be witty, incisive and inventive. It wouldn't make sense to accuse the tweeter of not using the proper grammar and spelling of standard English or to condemn the medium as an inadequate vehicle for conducting a conversation about the meaning of the universe. Not even Milton would have tried to justify the ways of God to man in a sonnet (much less a tweet) – he realized it would take an epic, at least, to do that (hence *Paradise Lost*). Nor would it be sensible to try to use tweeting to teach (say) open-heart surgery. This amounts to saying, again, that it doesn't make sense to set up open-ended criteria (like the absolute condemnation of verbal redundancy) which don't take into account the *totality* of the aims, customs and capabilities of a medium of communication (whether we are talking of sonneteering or tweeting). Every medium or genre, then, has its own norms of appropriateness or 'decorum' which determine what can be said, and how, within it. Thus, you might text a friend to let her know what time you will all meet this evening, but not (surely) to tell her that her grandmother has died. If you had to do that, you would go round to see her if you could, or phone her if you couldn't. And it wouldn't make sense to judge your way of breaking the news by the criterion of verbal redundancy – on the contrary, the more verbal redundancy you employ, the kinder your manner is likely to seem and the more genuine your sympathetic concern. If we consider the sonnet, then, as verbal entertainment, or even just as effective communication, we might conclude that the strict verbal redundancy criterion is not really an appropriate one to apply – indeed, it may well be one which is at odds with the 'decorum' of the sonnet medium.

So, have we convinced ourselves that Spenser's 'second hand' is OK after all? Well, in my case, not entirely. The phrase about the second hand does seem to be a moment when the current goes slack and simply marks time for a few beats.[4] It seems to puncture the flow of the sonnet, because it is such an inert repetition, too obviously just needlessly saying the same thing a second time. It will be clear (and this may well have been in your mind while reading the last couple of pages) that in evaluating the poem in terms of strict linguistic concision, we have inevitably strayed into wider territory, and this will often be the case in literary discussion. Indeed, the defence just mounted essentially involved switching our attention strategically to broader aesthetic issues and arguing that the pleasure afforded by sonnets often has to do with patterns of repetition combined with variation. In the same way, if we were trying to judge the aesthetic quality of (say) a Georgian town house, it wouldn't be a valid criticism to say that a given window was merely the same as the ones on either side of it and therefore added nothing (at all) to the overall design, since the whole concept of Georgian buildings involves elements which are repeated and have an effect *collectively*, that is, as a *row* of windows.

---

[4]The ideal poem (if we accept an aesthetic principle of concision) is above all an economical *arrangement* of words, and the result should be as clean and spare as a piece of Shaker furniture. Johnston Kirkpatrick, writing about his own working methods, describes something very similar: 'As soon as I begin telling, I am aware of complications. That's when the work begins, the toil of packing the right words in the right place, the desire for form, the ear listening for the click of the snib [i.e. the lock].' Author statement in the poetry magazine *Windows* (10), Janet Ashley, Peter Barry, Robin Haylett and Marianne Taylor (eds), East Sussex College of Higher Education, 1982.

My point in raising all this is partly to show how 'close reading' can sometimes be *too* close, ignoring aspects of the movement and dynamic of the poem as a whole and fixing somewhat artificially on just one item within it. The distinctive feature of this poem is that it relates an incident which might actually have happened (the speaker's writing his lover's name in the sand) and that we hear the affectionate banter between the two of them. Most of the other sonnets in the sequence, by contrast, develop an elaborate and traditional metaphor which expresses the speaker's love within the 'courtly love' tradition of the period. Perhaps the reader of Spenser who enjoys this more informal glimpse of day-to-day reality in the poetry of the 1590s is reading 'out of period', for such moments are more likely to be found in (for example) Romantic poems of the 1790s. Likewise, a reader who wants to pass every word through a fine sieve may have arrived at this early modern poem with expectations more appropriate to the reading of a minimalist poem from the 1970s. Our conclusion must be, to reiterate, that the reading practices we develop should be appropriate in terms of period and genre, and that is just another way of saying that we need to approach the literary text with realistic and informed expectations. That is the only way to gain access to the enjoyment which the writing of all periods has to offer.

In this chapter we have considered in a practical way the two basic literary-critical activities of interpretation and evaluation, taking poetry as our focus. We have emphasized reading close, and this seems entirely appropriate for smaller-scale poetry, but towards the end we began to think about larger works, and here it makes less sense to focus exclusively on individual lines. In reading prose, even more so, we will need to begin to shift our attention away from the impact of the localized phrase and the individual line, and on to the cumulative movement and unfolding of the whole work. In the next chapter we move from poetry to prose, in which the practice popularly known as 'reading between the lines' is often important. In fact, saying that we have to read between the lines is perhaps a way of reminding ourselves again that sometimes close reading can be *too* close.

3

Reading Fiction

The facts of fiction

'Every picture tells a story.' So goes the familiar cliché. But what can a picture tell us which shows someone telling a story? The one I have in mind is a famous painting called 'The Boyhood of Raleigh' completed in 1870 by the Victorian artist John Everett Millais. It shows the young Walter Raleigh, later explorer and naval hero, listening (along with a companion) to a veteran sailor who is telling them stirring tales of adventure at sea, and, we must suppose, inspiring Raleigh to take up his future career. It's a picture which has greatly interested literary academics: Kate Flint discusses it in her book *The Victorians and the Visual Imagination* (Cambridge University Press, 2000, pp. 285–8), and Jeremy Hawthorn uses it as an emblem of the story-telling process in his edited collection *Narrative: from Malory to Motion Pictures* (Edward Arnold, 1985). This is what Hawthorn says about the picture at the start of his preface:

> In Millais's famous painting *The Boyhood of Raleigh* two young boys stare with rapt attention at the figure of a sailor who is telling them a story. The sailor points out to sea with one arm, but his other arm forms itself into a familiar interpersonal gesture directed towards his auditors. His gaze does not follow the direction of his pointing arm but is fixed upon the two boys who, in return, stare not out to sea but at the person who is addressing them: the narrator. (p. vii)

©Tate, London 2013

Figure 3.1 Millais, 'The Boyhood of Raleigh'

I am grateful to Hawthorn for the idea of using the picture to discuss the narrative process, but it has to be said that this is not quite an accurate description of the painting, as I think you can see by looking at the illustration (the original is in the Tate Gallery in London). Is it really true that the two young boys 'stare with rapt attention at the figure of a sailor'? Surely Flint's description is closer to what we see; she says that

> The eyes of one of the small boys are fixed intently on him; those of the other, Raleigh himself, are directed more downwards, suggesting an inward, imaginative visualisation of the sailor's words. (p. 285)

This is more accurate, but still not completely so, for even the second boy does not seem to me to have his eyes 'fixed intently' on the sailor. He too, though with less intensity, seems to be looking at something which is suspended, so to speak, between the mind's eye and what is physically before the eye. And what do *we* look at as we look at the picture? Our viewpoint is low down, as if we too are auditors of the tale, sitting or reclining like the two boys, and constructed by this perspective as fellow childish listeners to the stirring tale. And though the sailor's finger points out beyond the horizon, our gaze, like that of the children in the picture, doesn't follow it, but fixes, surely, on the pale, inward-seeing face of the young Raleigh.

The narratee

Already we have touched upon a number of the salient points of the narrative process, but let's try to use the picture in a more systematic way to bring out some of the major elements of story telling. Firstly, though the story points out beyond the frame of the narrative to the 'real' world, as the sailor is doing, the tale actually happens within the 'narratee', which is to say the hearer, auditor or reader. It is the narratee (who may indeed mentally 'sub-vocalize' the narrating voice) who produces the tale by a process of sustained, imaginative intro-spection, which is triggered, of course, by what the teller points to, and yet is not limited by that. This imaginative collusion will vary in intensity from reader to reader (as it evidently does for the two boys), but it will always involve the vicarious (that is, 'proxy') living out of the depicted events, as if they were happening to ourselves, as if we were Elizabeth Bennet in Jane Austen's *Pride and Prejudice*, or Dickens' David Copperfield, or Toni Morrison's Seth in *Beloved*. This vicarious identification does not depend upon our being a woman, or working class, or black – on the contrary, a reading of *Pride and Prejudice* in which the male reader's vicarious identification is with Mr Darcy rather than Elizabeth is necessarily a misreading. In other words, we put ourselves imaginatively into the frame of the book, just as the young Raleigh is 'living' the sailor's tale as it is told, reacting mentally as if it were happening to him. The reading of fiction, then, requires this kind of collusion, this coming out of yourself, so that you allow the thoughts of another person to 'think' within yourself.

Yet, at the same time, we are not asked as we read to *lose* ourselves in the story, or to believe that we are actually somebody else and that the narrated events are really happening. Rather, what is required is what the poet Samuel Taylor Coleridge finely called a 'willing suspension of *dis*belief' (my italics). In other words, we have to stop *not* believing in the truth of what is said, without quite going so far as to believe that what is happening is real. Hence, a fearsome ghoul on the cinema screen may make you cringe in your seat as if terrified, but it probably won't make you run from the cinema screaming in fright, for you are taking the events on the screen as both real and not real at the same time, suspending, as Coleridge said, your rational disbelief in the reality of what happens on stage, or on screen, or in the inner-projected theatre of the mind which operates as we read a novel. So, Raleigh's eyes in the picture are not closed. Even though they are focused on an image projected from within, he is still in touch in some way with an external reality. He doesn't look in the direction of the sailor's pointing finger because he doesn't need to, since the story isn't taking place out there beyond the horizon, but within his own mind.

The narrator

The narrator, however, strives for a kind of invisibility; we only look directly at the teller when we are sceptical about what is being said, when the spell is broken. If we were to look directly at the pointing finger we would become conscious of the narrative process, and aware of how we are being manipulated, and when this happens the implicit trust between teller and auditor would have broken down, and the narrative would falter. Of course, many twentieth-century writers were profoundly interested in the narrating process itself, and deliberately cultivated a technique whereby the teller of the tale is recalled from anonymity and rendered visible again, perhaps even receiving the main spotlight of attention, so that as we read we constantly speculate about whether the narrator is 'reliable' or not; authors felt anxious about the rapt, inward gaze of the auditor, and about the comparative vulnerability of this state. They found something disturbing or morally distasteful in the kind of authorial hypnotism which placed readers in this state, and in any case, the spell of realism no longer seemed an artistic challenge – on the contrary, working this spell seemed all too easy, so that a whole body of early twentieth-century writers (Joseph Conrad, James Joyce, Virginia Woolf and many others) began to experiment with ways of re-directing the reader's 'gaze' away from that projected inner theatre of imagined events, away from the things the teller pointed *at*, and on to the teller, and the act of telling itself. Hence, they would deliberately draw attention to the voice and actions of the teller (that left hand of the sailor, for instance, which seems to manipulate or orchestrate the boys' reactions as a puppeteer determines the actions of the puppet – what is it doing, exactly, and how is this trick achieved?). Indeed, the sailor's is the only gaze in the picture which is unambiguously directed – his attention is unswervingly on the reactions of his auditors as he produces his finely calculated effects. Significantly, he does not follow the direction of his own pointing finger. As developing readers of literature, we need to look both at what is pointed at, and at the pointing itself (to use a distinction made by Hawthorn), asking such questions as Why now? Why at this? Why not at that as well?

'Site' or 'domain'

In the painting, it is perhaps obvious that we should 'read' and interpret the two boys and the sailor, since they are clearly the collective focus of the picture. But there are plenty of other things in the picture which also need to be read, for we must read the 'site' or 'domain' of the action as well as the action itself. Flint, for instance, reads some of the objects in the 'site' as follows:

> On the left of the picture, a toy sailing ship, placed on the same diagonal as the sailor's outstretched arm, suggests how childhood enthusiasms, mediated through the narratives and inspiration of the sailor, will transform into adult exploration and adventure. The red ensign on this ship signals its Englishness; the strange feathered cap, and the exotic plumage of a dead bird behind the

sailor, represent the cultural and natural trophies awaiting the voyager across the ocean. (p. 285)

Flint reads these objects plausibly in emblematic or symbolic terms, but it is clear that there is a degree of subjectivity here; this cannot be avoided, but we ought to be conscious of it, as we slide from *delineation* (noting that the object in the left foreground is a toy sailing ship, for instance) to *interpretation* (suggesting that its meaning is that 'childhood enthusiasms ... will transform into adult exploration'). Obviously, such details would lend themselves to different interpretations, for instance, that the ship in the left foreground is a 'proleptic' (that is, anticipatory) emblem of the eventual outcome of Raleigh's brilliant career (that is, his disgrace and beheading), for it is positioned so as to look like a ship wrecked on a rocky shore. In the right foreground are objects representing a different possible outcome – we can see the fluke of an anchor, the anchor (associated with landfall and homecoming) being a traditional symbol of hope and fulfilment, with the parrot suggesting a return from distant parts of the globe. Nobody in the picture is pointing towards these objects, so it takes an effort to pick them out and figure them out, but being aware of this kind of peripheral significant detail is an essential way of adding depth and nuance to our reading. Yet, with the interpretation of such details it is notoriously difficult to know when to stop – once we become readers we sometimes become obsessives who are determined to leave nothing at all unread. So we might see the enclosing wall of the rampart as the protective horizon of childhood, behind which the boys are still sheltered, pending the time when they will face the open horizon beyond, its dangers perhaps suggested by the cliff just visible on the left. Furthermore, we might speculate about the ship's timbers, upon which the sailor is seated: are these the detritus of a shipwreck, rotten timbers in which weeds have taken root, or is it wood still being seasoned from which the ships of the future will be built, just as the boys will supply the 'hearts of oak' from which the future navy will be fashioned? Here we have moved away from what seems to be the central focus of the picture and have started to construct a kind of alternative narrative.

This other narrative is implied by the objects in the picture, which we read as emblems or symbols that construct a series of 'silent statements' constituting (to use a musical metaphor) a kind of *counterpoint* to the main narrative, which is to say, another tune which is interwoven or contrasted with the first one, making the overall musical experience more complex. A slightly different way of putting this (though still keeping to the musical analogy) is to say that the 'silent statements' made by the emblematic devices are a kind of accompaniment which harmonizes with the 'tune' being played by the main narrative line, giving it added depth and subtlety, in the way that the 'chordage' played by the pianist's left hand sets off the basic melody played by the right. But the emblematic dimension of a narrative is easily misread or over-interpreted, and unless we can reintegrate this narrative 'shadow line' with the basic patterns set up by the central narrative elements (these being plot, character, direct authorial commentary, and so on), then we ought perhaps to be cautious, and should at least pause to ask ourselves whether we have gone too far.

So far, then, what have we said about narrative? We have commented on the role of the listeners or readers and the way they bring the story to life by their inward gaze, which becomes unconscious of the narrating voice, and on the role of the objective world beyond in which the events take place. We have also commented on the narrator and on how the manipulation of the reader's response is his or her exclusive concern – 'Have eyes only for your reader', novelist Ford Madox Ford (1873–1939) said to writers, a phrase which perhaps reminds us of the sailor's intense gaze at the two boys who are 'taking in' his story. Narrators may point outwards to events in the real world, but their real concern is with what happens within. Finally, we commented on a more loosely defined aspect of the story which lies beyond the main events of the plot and the protagonists. This is the realm of significant details of setting, emblem, or symbolism, which adds nuance and depth to the overall effect. We have called this aspect of the text the 'site' or 'domain' of the story, and defined it as those parts of the narrative which are present, but not explicitly pointed to during the process of narration.

The narrator's fear of the narratee

A while ago, we said that early modernist writers engaged in a sceptical foregrounding of the narrating role, employing a device often known as the 'unreliable narrator'. Many of these features of narrative come to our attention only when the story-line 'pauses' in some way, which authors sometimes deliberately make it do. A famous example occurs in Joseph Conrad's 1899 novella *Heart of Darkness*, when the narrating persona, whose name is Marlow, interrupts his own story with anxious introspection about the inevitable limits of knowing and telling. For Marlow is struck in mid-tale by the sheer impossibility of ever conveying to others the unique flavour of an occurrence, or the precise nature of another human being; it's as if an acrobat, crossing a cataract on a high wire, were to look down suddenly and become aware of the immense vulnerability of his own position. Marlow is trying to convey to his hearers, through his tale, the precise lure of the corrupt Mr Kurtz, but he breaks off with 'Do you see him? Do you see the story? Do you see anything?'[1] Here, as it were, that other old sailor, the one in Millais's painting, breaks off and asks those two boys, who are not looking at him as he tells his tale, what exactly (if anything) they see in their minds' eyes. And then, of course, the spell is broken, not just because the tale which the boys are projecting within themselves is interrupted, but also because the story teller has lost faith in a fundamental way in the narrative process itself, and is suddenly floundering. This is Marlow:

> He was silent for a while.
> '... No, it is impossible; it is impossible to convey the life-sensation of any given epoch of one's existence, – that which makes its truth, its meaning – its subtle and penetrating essence. It is impossible. We live, as we dream – alone ...'
> He paused again as if reflecting, then added –
> 'Of course in this you fellows see more than I could then. You see me, whom you know ...'

---

[1] Robert Hampson ed., London, 2000, p. 50.

What we see here is the narrator's fear of the gaze of the narratee (the 'recipient' of the tale). The former's desire is that the auditors should look anywhere but at him, for if they look at him they will inevitably see more than he himself can, because they will also see his 'bias', which is to say the point of view which determines the limits of his vision. In other words, the telling of a story is always an act of self-exposure, for in the process we inevitably reveal our obsessions and our weak spots, making it embarrassingly obvious precisely what 'makes us tick'. So what makes Marlow able to continue? Crudely, it is the cover of darkness, which restores narratorial invisibility. As they sit on deck, listening to Marlow's tale and waiting for the tide to turn, darkness has descended, so that Marlow loses his solid individuality as a real person – the person his old friends know only too well – and becomes a kind of disembodied voice, an impersonal narrating function, the voice not of the teller, but of the tale:

> It had become so pitch dark that we listeners could hardly see one another. For a long time already he, sitting apart, had been no more to us than a voice. There was not a word from anybody. The others might have been asleep, but I was awake. I listened, I listened on the watch for the sentence, for the word, that would give me the clue to the faint uneasiness inspired by this narrative that seemed to shape itself without human lips in the heavy night-air of the river.

This powerful passage again seems in accord with the story-telling in the Millais picture. In Conrad's tale, the listeners are isolated from each other, each one projecting a different realization of the tale in his mind, just as the two boys in the picture are both isolated in a private world of vicariously lived experience (not, for instance, looking at each other and sharing open-mouthed wonder, as a cruder representation of the narratee might have had it). The unnamed 'principle narratee' in the Conrad story will later (presumably) write down the tale Marlow told, so that it can be relayed eventually to us, but for the moment the energising thread is not mere suspense (the desire simply to know what happened next), but the desire to identify the source of the vague feeling of unease which Marlow's tale induces in his listeners. This isn't a desire for mere narrative closure, then, which is to say that it is not a desire to *know* but a desire to *understand* which is the deep-down narrative drive, rather than the surface motor. Yet, too, the remarks of Marlow already quoted show an awareness of the fact that this is a desire which can never be fully satisfied, so that, in a real sense, *every* story is a never-ending story, or (to say this differently) a story which ends differently every time we read it. In the lines from the tale just quoted, this sense of endemic uncertainty is built into Conrad's very grammar – is it the narrative which 'seemed to shape itself without human lips' or the 'faint uneasiness' which that narrative inspires? In Millais, it is the narrator himself who is least likely to know the ending of the tale he tells (it continues in Raleigh's life, and ends with Raleigh's execution): in Conrad, Marlow supplies a false ending to his tale of Kurtz's life when he confronts the dead man's fiancée and deceives her into believing that 'The last word he pronounced was – your name.' Since we know for certain that Marlow deceived *her* on that point, how can we ever be sure that he isn't also deceiving *us* on others?[2]

The account of stories given in this section has, as you will have noticed, focused mainly on story-*telling*. Its primary emphasis has been not on content but on the act of representation, that is, on how narrators present matters and how readers respond. Its end-point has been to recommend a certain scepticism about what the story-teller says, and this scepticism will necessarily prize the reader away a little from the 'spell' of the story, and set up a space in which readers, in effect, can enter into a kind of dialogue with it. However, this is not to plump for a wholesale dethronement of authors, since if reading is to be seen (as I believe it usefully can be) as a form of conversation between reader and writer, then it still remains the case that the conversation is initiated, and largely directed, by the author. Likewise, it isn't to assume that readers know better than authors what authors mean, and hence are always able to expose authorial ideologies and purposes to which authors themselves are naively

---

[2] A good answer to this question would be to say 'because he himself reveals to us his deception of the Intended – it isn't something he tries to hide'. All the same, it remains true (even though he himself is the one who says it) that as readers we can always see more than he (or any tale-teller) sees, because we see the tale-teller too.

blind (an illusion common in literary critics). After all, the scepticism about narrative omniscience which came to a head in the high modernist period of the early twentieth century was not instigated by a readers' revolt in which they refused any longer to believe in authorial omniscience – rather, the writers (James, Conrad, Joyce, Woolf, and many others) were themselves the instigators of that kind of scepticism. Thus, one of the linking factors between the way we discussed poetry in chapter two and the discussion of fiction in this chapter has been precisely this emphasis on the reader 'writing back', or talking back, to the text. We could even say that this kind of 'writing back' (and talking back) is supremely what doing an English degree is all about.

The next chapter takes matters a stage further, going 'beyond the lines', so to speak, in the sense that it begins to take into account some of the external factors which impinge upon the text, starting with those texts which have a prior relationship with the text under discussion – that is, with its sphere of *inter*textuality. It then opens up the question of how it relates to the world beyond, that is, its *con*textuality. Both the examples used in the next chapter are poems, but they are also narratives, thus bringing together some of the concerns of chapters two and three.

4

Reading and Interpretation

Context and intertext

No literary text exists in a vacuum. Every text is intimately related to a great web of circumstances outside itself (that is, it has *contex*tuality) and every text has relations with other texts, some literary, some not (that is, it has *inter*textuality). I suspect that as literary scholars we have in recent years exaggerated the amount of literary understanding which can be derived from the study of context. So we need (sometimes at least) to entertain the counterview that there is a sense in which we can only understand and appreciate the literature of the past by *detaching* it from its web of contextual strands and filiations. This is to advocate a *combination* of historicism (see chapter ten) and formalism (see chapter eight), rather than the current disciplinary fashion, which often requires the rejection of the latter and the embrace of the former.

The study of *inter*textuality is generally less problematic than that of context, because the area of relevance is usually much more limited and specific and less the selective construction of the individual critic. Many literary works, for instance, have close relationships with other printed texts, from which they derive, or to which they respond in some way. For instance, the Victorian poet Gerard Manley Hopkins wrote his epic-scale poem 'The Wreck of the *Deutschland*' in response to an account of this tragic shipwreck in *The Times* newspaper of 11 December 1875. It is possible to compare the two, and by doing so gain an insight into the poet's thinking and methods of composition. Beyond this (as we might call it) *primary* level of intertextuality, there are in the case of this poem other levels of more generalized intertextuality, such as the poem's relationship with the Victorian sub-genre of shipwreck poems and ballads, with its expectation of set-pieces which provide 'vivid and repeated descriptions of the storm, heroic drama, prayer, a powerless crew ... and horrific detail', so that 'Hopkins was drawing on literary convention for subject, details, emotion, and vocabulary'.[1] Hence it was natural then, as it would not be now, that when Hopkins discussed the newspaper account of the event with his religious superior, the latter should make the comment that somebody ought to write a poem about it. And there are further layers of intertextuality which come into play when we go on to consider the form of the poem: Hopkins used as his verse form an adaptation of the Pindaric ode (the form used by the Classical Greek poet Pindar) and he incorporated into this his own version of the sound patternings found in Welsh verse, especially *'cynghanedd'*, which makes intertwining patterns of sound in ways very much to Hopkins' taste. (At the time he wrote the poem he was at a Jesuit college in Wales and was studying Welsh poetry and experimenting with its forms.) Clearly, gaining a full-scale understanding of the intertextual affiliations of this one poem would be a challenging undertaking, and only a limited amount of the knowledge so gained would be transferable to other aspects of our literary studies. And this is a consequence of the fact that the study of *inter*textuality has an inherent specificity which is often lacking in approaches which are primarily *con*textual. Of course, the corollary is that a good deal of contextual study *is* transferable to the study of other literary works – the Victorian social and political context which you might unearth in connection with work on a Dickens novel will probably be equally relevant when you are studying the novels of other Victorian writers.

---

[1] For the Hopkins data see Norman White, *Hopkins: A Literary Biography*, Oxford, 1992, ch. 21, pp. 250–60, 'The Wreck of the *Deutschland*'.

'He could not escape those very words'

However, one advantage of studying a text from the viewpoint of intertextuality is that it can indirectly bring in those big concerns with such matters as gender, identity and ethics, which make the contextual approach so attractive to literary scholars. At the same time, this approach can give us profound insights into the nature of writing, and the sources of writers' ideas as well as, sometimes, a strong sense of a writer's limitations. The material which follows is a kind of case-study in intertextuality which asks you to consider the extent of William Wordsworth's debt to his sister Dorothy Wordsworth by making a comparative analysis of one of his poems and one of the entries from her diary, which he used as a source. In 1800, when her diary was started, William (born in 1770) and Dorothy (born in 1771) had just moved to Dove Cottage at Grasmere in the English Lake District. Orphaned as children, they had been brought up separately by relatives, and when re-united in early adult life they had determined to set up home together, which they did in the year 1795. The unmarried Dorothy remained part of the household after her brother's marriage, and both lived into old age. Dorothy began to suffer from premature senility after a breakdown in 1829. William died in 1850 and Dorothy in 1855.

The opening entry in Dorothy's diary explains that she first decided to keep a journal in May 1800 when her two brothers were away. But over that three-week period, the journal-writing habit was established, and so continued. She says that her motive was to give her brother pleasure by keeping the diary, and I think she meant by this that she would record for him the details of weather, nature and scenery which he would have observed himself on their daily walks had he been present. In the interval, he would be enabled, by means of the diary, to 'see' by proxy – she would view their environment in the meantime on his behalf. This 'proxy-witness' function is an important element to keep in mind in what follows. The journal contains an amazing number of accounts of beggars, pedlars, discharged veterans, odd-jobbers and the like who were constantly tramping the countryside in this politically troubled period, giving readers today a vivid impression of the amount of social destitution which existed in this era. Thus, a typical passage in the diary begins, 'As I was going out in the morning I met a half crazy old man. He shewed me a pincushion and begged a pin, afterwards a half-penny.' Wordsworth was fascinated by these sombre outcasts and many of his best poems tell of encounters with them. Not surprisingly, then, these are the passages from Dorothy's journal which he often uses as sources for his poetry. It is easy to see why they are so attractive to him, for they have a vivid, eye-witness quality which could never be faked ('He ... begged a pin and afterwards a half-penny') and they provide him with ready-made 'incidents from common life' of the kind he is explicitly committed to using as the basis for a new kind of poetry. Furthermore, the diary language is plain and prosaic (as is fitting for that kind of writing) and so seems to leave something for the poet to do, in terms of transforming the accounts imaginatively into something heightened and significant.

There is often a delay of a couple of years between Dorothy's diary entry and William's related poem. For example, on 3 October 1800 William and Dorothy together encountered an old man gathering leaches: during the period May to July 1802 William wrote a poem called 'The Leach Gatherer' (later renamed 'Resolution and Independence'). In the poem the meeting is presented as a solitary encounter between the male speaker and the old man, with Dorothy written out – 'I was a traveller then upon the moor', the voice in the poem tells us. Another example, and probably the best known, concerns a scene witnessed by brother and sister together on 15 April 1802 when they walked by the lake known as Eusemere and came across a long belt of daffodils, which (as Dorothy describes them) 'tossed and realed and danced' in the breeze. Two years later, William wrote his famous poem 'Daffodils', using Dorothy's journal account as a source, but again writing her out of the scene – 'I wandered *lonely* as a cloud', the poem begins [my italics]. Why does William omit Dorothy from these poems? (It is worth bearing in mind that there may be a different reason each time it happens.)

We will consider a final example in more detail. On 27 May 1800 Dorothy opened the door of their cottage to 'a very tall woman, tall much beyond the measure of tall women', and described the ensuing encounter in her journal. There is, in fact, no indication that this person was seen at all by William, but on 13 March 1802 she read her account of the meeting to him, and (she says) 'an unlucky thing it was, *for he could not escape from those very words, and so he could not write the poem*' [my italics again]. In fact, the poem *was* finished, the following day, and William's inability to escape from Dorothy's words may partly be due to the fact that he had not actually seen the woman himself. Yet once again, in the resulting poem, Dorothy is written out of the incident and the encounter becomes a solitary one, transferred from the cottage door to the open countryside. The question for us to ponder, put bluntly, is 'Whose poem is it?' Here is the journal entry in full, followed by the poem.

A very tall woman, tall much beyond the measure of tall women, called at the door. She had on a very long brown cloak and a very white cap, without bonnet. Her face was excessively brown, but it had plainly once been fair. She led a little bare-footed child about two years old by the hand, and said her husband, who was a tinker, was gone before with the other children. I gave her a piece of bread.

Afterwards, on my way to Ambleside, beside the bridge at Rydale, I saw her husband sitting by the roadside, his two asses feeding beside him, and the two young children at play upon the grass. The man did not beg. I passed on and about a quarter of a mile further I saw two boys before me, one about 10, the other about 8 years old, at play chasing a butterfly. They were wild figures, not very ragged, but without shoes and stockings. The hat of the elder was wreathed round with yellow flowers, the younger, whose hat was only a rimless crown, had stuck it round with laurel leaves. They continued at play till I drew very near, and then they addressed me with the begging cant and the whining voice of sorrow. I said 'I served your mother this morning.' (The boys were so like the woman who had called at the door that I could not be mistaken.) 'O!' says the elder, 'you could not serve my mother for she's dead, and my father's on at the next town – he's a potter.' I persisted in my assertion, and that I would give them nothing. Says the elder 'Let's away.' And away they flew like lightning.

They had however sauntered so long in their road that they did not reach Ambleside before me, and I saw them go up to Matthew Harrison's house with their wallet upon the elder's shoulder, and creeping with a beggar's complaining foot. On my return through Ambleside I met in the street the mother driving her asses, in the two panniers of one of which were the two little children, whom she was chiding and threatening with a wand which she used to drive on her asses, while the little things hung in wantonness over the pannier's edge. The woman had told me in the morning that she was of Scotland, which her accent fully proved, but that she had lived, I think, at Wigton, that they could not keep a house and so they travelled.

'Beggars'

1.
She had a tall man's height or more;
Her face from summer noontide heat
No bonnet shaded, but she wore
A mantle, to her very feet
Descending with a graceful flow,
And on her head a cap as white as new-
                                        fallen snow.

2.
Her skin was of Egyptian broan:
Haughty, as if her eye had seen
Its own light to a distance thrown,
She towered, fit person for a Queen
To lead those ancient Amazonian files;
Or ruling Bandit's wife among the Grecian isles.

3.
Advancing, forth she stretched her hand
And begged an alms with doleful plea
That ceased not; on our English land
Such woes, I knew, could never be;
And yet a boon I gave her, for the creature
Was beautiful to see – a weed of glorious feature.

4.

I left her, and pursued my way;
And soon before me did espy
A pair of little boys at play,
Chasing a crimson butterfly;
the taller followed with his hat in hand,
Wreathed round with yellow flowers the
        gayest in the land.

5.

The other wore a rimless crown
With leaves of laurel stuck about;
And while both followed up and down,
Each whooping with a merry shout,
In their fraternal features I could trace
Unquestionable lines of that wild supplicant's face.

6.

Yet *they* so blythe of heart, seemed fit
For finest tasks of earth or air;
Wings let them have, and they might flit
Precursors to Aurora's car,
Scattering fresh flowers; though happier far, I ween,
To hunt their fluttering game o'er rock
        and level green.

7.

They dart across my path – but lo,
Each ready with a plaintive whine!
Said I, 'not half an hour ago
Your mother has had alms of mine.'
'That cannot be,' one answered – 'she is dead' –
I looked reproof – they saw – but neither
        hung his head.

8.

'She has been dead, Sir, many a day' –
'Hush, boys! You're telling me a lie;

It was your Mother, as I say!'
And in the twinkling of an eye,
'Come! Come!' cried one, and without more ado
Off to some other play the joyous Vagrants flew!

How far, then, does the poet succeed in 'escaping those very words'? And just as importantly, how far is he more generally dependent on Dorothy's treatment of the subject? To answer these questions we need to consider actual verbal similarities between the two texts as well as more general similarities (e.g. viewpoint, emphasis, progression, tone) and also significant *dis*similarities between the two (e.g. William's omissions, additions, re-orderings and alterations).

Firstly, some key differences between journal and poem concern what we might call 'gendered perspective'. Thus, William's measure of people is man ('She had a tall man's height or more') whereas Dorothy's is woman ('a very tall woman, tall much beyond the measure of tall women'). Secondly, Dorothy's setting is specific and localized ('the road to Ambleside ... beside a bridge at Rydale', etc.), whereas William's is unspecified ('I left her and pursued my way'). Thirdly, Dorothy emphasizes that the woman is 'native', part of the 'scene' – she may *look* 'foreign', but she isn't ('her face was excessively brown, but it had plainly once been fair'). William, by contrast, makes the woman seem exotic and 'other' ('*Egyptian brown* ... fit person for a Queen ... *Amazonian* files ... *Bandit's wife* among the *Grecian isles*') as all the phrases italicized here suggest. He says (presumably with a degree of irony – or not?) 'On our English land / Such woes, I knew, could never be'. Fourthly, as already suggested, Dorothy's diary language has that 'eye-witness flatness' of tone ('about a quarter mile further I saw two boys before me, one about 10, the other about 8 years old'); William takes these details and tends to 'colourize' them, so to speak (the butterfly becomes 'crimson', the yellow flowers become 'the gayest of the land') and, indeed, he somewhat sentimentalizes them ('Yet they, so blithe of heart, seemed fit / For finest tasks of earth or air; / Wings let them have, and they might flit / Precursors to Aurora's car'). Fifthly (and relatedly), Dorothy's prose uses basic 'intensifiers' (as linguists call them) like 'very' or 'extremely' ('a *very* tall woman', 'a *very* white cap', 'her face was *excessively* brown'); William, by contrast, often uses language based on metaphor or simile ('a cap *as white as newfallen snow*', 'Her skin was of *Egyptian brown*' ('Egyptian' probably meaning 'like a gypsy'). Finally, and coming back to the gender issue, the contrasting attitudes of Dorothy and William reflect different assumptions about gender and power. Dorothy gives the woman bread, but doesn't give anything when asked later by the children, as she has already helped the mother ('I served your mother this morning'). She doesn't comment on the children's assertion that their mother is dead and merely notes the tricks which they use when trying to beg ('creeping with a beggar's complaining foot'). William, by contrast, emphasizes his own generosity ('a boon I gave her', and later 'Your mother has had alms of mine') and has his own 'masculinist' reasons for being generous (... 'for the creature / was beautiful to see'). Later, when the boys pretend their mother is dead, his attitude is judgemental and authoritarian ('I looked reproof ... 'you're telling me a lie'). This is not intended as a pompous rebuke of Wordsworth for being careful with his pennies – the Wordsworths were poor at the time, by genteel standards, and had just enough income to live independently in a cheap part of the country, renting an ordinary cottage, doing without a live-in servant and getting their main entertainment from walking, reading, writing and talking.

Intertextuality and authorship

One further advantage of taking an intertextual approach is the light it can throw upon the matter of the relationship between poetry and experience. We usually assume that poetry is about the recording of intimate personal experience, but in this poem we see a degree of 'fictionalization' of what actually happened and the use and appropriation by the poet of another person's words and experience. Perhaps it follows from this that poems can sometimes be much more like stories than we are usually prepared to allow (that is, with invented dialogue, partly imagined situations and strategic modifications of 'straight' factuality). After all, we don't usually assume that stories are authentic records of the author's lived experience, and yet we do often seem to expect this of poems.

The precise relationship between poetry and personal experience is a matter on which popular opinion and the views of poets themselves are often very much polarized. T. S. Eliot in his 1922 essay 'Tradition and the Individual Talent' (included in his *Selected Essays*) insisted on the need for a separation between poem and experience. Many poets make use of a fictionalized, named 'persona' in their poetry – see, for instance, the 'dramatic monologues' of Tennyson and Browning in the nineteenth century – the best-known examples being Robert Browning's 'My Last Duchess' and Alfred Tennyson's 'Ulysses' – where the speaker is an invented 'character' who is a fictionalized being, just like a character in a novel. Even when the poet is not using a persona and instead employs the first-person pronoun, speaking as 'I', it is a critical convention to refer to this authorial presence as 'the speaker' in a poem, rather than attributing the sentiments expressed directly to the author, and this recognizes the possibility of a degree of fictionalization as a legitimate proceeding in all poetry. Thus, Wordsworth, as we know from our intertextual study, never did wander 'lonely as a cloud' and come across a host of daffodils, but this does not invalidate the poem.

All this, then, has a bearing on the question of the nature of authorship itself. We assume that 'authorship' means being completely responsible for both the conception and the verbal embodiment of a text, but here we see a complicated collaborative process extending over a long period of time. Dorothy's journal makes it clear just how sustained and complex that collaborative process was, and the result is that the origins (and ownership) of an idea or perception or experience become difficult to identify precisely. So the very notion of authorship is made problematic by the facts of intertextuality. One of the reasons for studying the network of intertextuality that in this case includes Dorothy's journal and William's poems is that it shows us writing *in process*, not dropping ready-formed from the sky or born in mysterious moments of inspiration, but arising from specific incidents, encounters and conversations, and ultimately proving very difficult to detach cleanly from its 'background', whether this be contextual or intertextual.

Dove Cottage, gender and intertextuality

Of course, the gender politics of the domestic arrangements at Dove Cottage, as revealed in the diary, will seem particularly cruel to readers today. When Dorothy says in her diary that she did 'work', or took her 'work' out into the garden, she always means *needle*work – darning and sewing socks and shirts, probably mostly William's. She bakes bread and makes pies and does the washing while William composes. She writes too, but when she says 'writes' she sometimes means writing out fair copies of William's poems. A parody in *The Virago Book of Wicked Verse* imagines the kind of difficulties Dorothy might have encountered had she gone upstairs to write the 'Daffodils' poem herself. It begins:

> *I wandered lonely as a ...*
> They're in the top drawer, William,
> Under your socks –
> *I wandered lonely as a –*
> Not that drawer, the top one.
> *I wandered by myself –*
> Well wear the ones you *can* find.
> No don't get overwrought my dear
> I'm coming.

Anyway, for whatever reason, for her own composition she usually chooses the less- ambitious form of the private diary. So the collaborative process which produced Wordsworth's poem clearly has behind it a specific gender politics: the man uses the 'high' genre of poetry while the woman uses the 'low' genre of the diary. The woman's observations and experience are taken over by the man, so the woman is playing a 'service' role in relation to the man. We might say that the man 'appropriates the seeing' of the woman. Dorothy freely makes her diary available to William as a quarry for the poetry which will make him famous. She also acts as his secretary, constantly 'taking down his stanzas', as she puts it. For instance, on Thursday 8 July 1802, 'William', she writes 'was looking at "The Peddlar" when I got up. He arranged it, and after tea I wrote it out – 280 lines.' When the poems are eventually set up in print and the proofs arrive for correction, she acts as proof-reader. As previously attested, her devotion to him is absolute: she lives a celibate, unmarried life, remaining a member of the household after William marries, and in due course also becoming nursemaid, babysitter and teacher to his children.

But lamenting now a gender situation which then seemed 'natural' and becoming (so belatedly) angry with the poet who benefited from it seems pointless, like stoking a fire which has nothing to burn. If you believe that Dorothy was herself potentially as good a poet as her brother and was lost to us because of gender politics, then you should read her surviving poems and make up your own mind on the strength of the remaining evidence.[2] Personally, I see no evidence in those poems of any unusual talent I as a poet: she was a brilliant diarist with an immensely sharp eye and a turn of phrase which could be thrilling and sometimes much more moving than the more high-flown poetic language of her brother. See, for instance, these descriptions in the journal of the nearby lakes, where the language swoops from the most mundane to the dramatic within a phrase or two: 'After tea went to Ambleside – a pleasant, cool but not cold evening. Rydale was very beautiful, with spear-shaped streaks of polished steel' (16 May 1800). There is a sudden epic grandeur in those 'spear-shaped streaks of polished steal', describing the appearance of the surface of the lake, before the tone immediately reverts to the mundane with 'No letters! only one newspaper.' The entry continues: 'I returned to Clappersgate. Grasmere was very solemn in the last glimpse of twilight; it calls home the heart to quietness.' Here again that last phrase, 'it calls home the heart to quietness', suddenly hits an unforgettable intensity of tone before dropping again to the mundane. Juxtaposing the diary and the poems shows that even poetic language as self-consciously down to earth as that of the early Romantics like Wordsworth and Coleridge

---

[2]Dorothy wrote about forty poems between 1805 and 1840, including 'Address to a Child' and 'Floating Island', which Wordsworth included in his own books, specifying them as 'by my Sister'. For a general appraisal, see Susan M. Levin, *Dorothy Wordsworth and Romanticism*, New Brunswick, 1987. Her poem 'Peaceful our Valley, Fair and Green' is included in the *Norton Anthology of Literature by Women*, 2nd edn, Sandra M. Gilbert and Susan Gubar (eds), New York, 1996, pp. 325–7.

was still pretty elevated when compared with the register of ordinary speech and writing, rather than being seen in contrast with the prevailing tone of the typical poetic writing of the time.

What is also evident from the juxtaposition is a relationship of interdependency: Wordsworth as a poet needs the material Dorothy supplies in her diaries, which is based on detailed, documented observations of people encountered in the village and on meticulous scrutiny of such things as the effects of light on water, or the precise appearance of wild flowers against rocks. Dorothy's eye is like a microscope, scrutinizing detail in close-up: William's eye is panoramic and broad sweeping, typically registering an overall atmospheric effect rather than a specific small detail. The two eyes – the 'short-sighted' eye of Dorothy and the 'long-sighted' eye of William – need each other. Together they form a literary ecosystem, a symbiosis, a relationship of mutual dependency. Rightly or wrongly, Dorothy feels that she cannot supply the final twist needed to make her material into poetry – she needs William for that. Rightly or wrongly, William feels the need and entitlement to help himself, with her consent, to the solid, documentary observations which Dorothy supplies. We don't, today, find that very appealing, but we cannot change the past, and there is nothing we can do about it now. A new approach to Romanticism is stressing notions of ecology, and it seems to me that the best way to think of Dorothy and William is as a system and a partnership that worked, as an ecosystem which sustained a vital balance and did its job. Our case-study of intertextuality, then, needn't end with an indignant denunciation of Wordsworth but in an appreciation of the ploys and subterfuges by means of which writing actually gets done. Seeing that situation in all its complexity is one of the main benefits of an intertextual approach to literary study.

Issues of gender, finally, have been given a great deal of attention in literary studies since at least the 1970s, and this tendency is especially strong among Romanticists.[3] The study of British Romanticism was dominated until the 1980s by the male 'big five' poets (Wordsworth, Coleridge, Keats, Byron and Shelley), but since

---

[3]An influential book in this movement is Anne K. Mellor's *Romanticism and Gender*, New York, 1988. See also Lilla Maria Crisafulli and Cecilia Pietropoli (eds), *Romantic Women Poets: Gender and Genre*, Amsterdam/New York, 2007.

then there has been an increasing interest in the once-marginalized female members of the major groupings of Romantic writers (such as Dorothy Wordsworth and Mary Shelley) and a re-discovery of the many women poets of the period (like Anna Barbauld, Joanna Bailie, Charlotte Smith and Felicia Hemans).[4] So the irony is that increasingly figures like Dorothy, who were once on the margins of Romantic-period writing, are being seen as important figures in their own right. From the point of view of Wordsworth's many eminent visitors as his fame as a poet increased, Dorothy may have been just a member of his household, but that is not how she is regarded by Romantic scholars today. For them, her writing is worthy of study in its own right, not just for the light it throws on her brother's poetry.

This section has concerned intertextuality alone. In the next, we will broaden out to look at another example, attempting to deal with what we might grandly call 'total textuality', that is, with all the different kinds of textuality which can be seen as (to varying extents) 'in play' in works of literature. An outline sketch of 'total textuality' would include:

1 *Textuality* (also known as 'the words on the page')

2 *Intertextuality* (roughly, the words on related pages)

3 *Contextuality* (the social, cultural and historical context of the work)

4 *Multitextuality* (the surviving textual variants of the work itself – see chapter thirteen)

The next section looks at the way in which these different kinds of textuality come into play in a reading of a well-known Victorian poem.

---

[4]The work of some of these women poets can be found in anthologies like Jennifer Breen ed., *Women Romantic Poets: 1785–1832 – An Anthology*, Everyman, 1994 and Duncan Wu ed., *Romantic Women Poets: An Anthology*, Blackwell, 1997.

Total textuality: 'The Lady of Shalott'

What follows is an attempt to show all the aspects of the text which might be considered in the case of a specific and well-known literary text – Tennyson's poem 'The Lady of Shalott', given here in full in its later (1842) version:

Part I

On either side the river lie
Long fields of barley and of rye,
That clothe the wold and meet the sky;
And thro' the field the road runs by
    To many-tower'd Camelot;
And up and down the people go,
Gazing where the lilies blow
Round an island there below,
    The island of Shalott.

Willows whiten, aspens quiver,
Little breezes dusk and shiver
Thro' the wave that runs for ever
By the island in the river
    Flowing down to Camelot.
Four gray walls, and four gray towers,
Overlook a space of flowers,
And the silent isle imbowers
    The Lady of Shalott.

By the margin, willow veil'd,
Slide the heavy barges trail'd
By slow horses; and unhail'd
The shallop flitteth silken-sail'd
    Skimming down to Camelot:
But who hath seen her wave her hand?
Or at the casement seen her stand?
Or is she known in all the land,
    The Lady of Shalott?

Only reapers, reaping early
In among the bearded barley,
Hear a song that echoes cheerly
From the river winding clearly,
    Down to tower'd Camelot:
And by the moon the reaper weary,
Piling sheaves in uplands airy,
Listening, whispers "'Tis the fairy
    Lady of Shalott."

                Part II
There she weaves by night and day
A magic web with colours gay.
She has heard a whisper say,
A curse is on her if she stay
    To look down to Camelot.
She knows not what the curse may be,
And so she weaveth steadily,
And little other care hath she,
    The Lady of Shalott.

And moving thro' a mirror clear
That hangs before her all the year,
Shadows of the world appear.
There she sees the highway near
    Winding down to Camelot:
There the river eddy whirls,
And there the surly village-churls,
And the red cloaks of market girls,
    Pass onward from Shalott.

Sometimes a troop of damsels glad,
An abbot on an ambling pad,
Sometimes a curly shepherd-lad,
Or long-hair'd page in crimson clad,
    Goes by to tower'd Camelot;
And sometimes thro' the mirror blue
The knights come riding two and two:

She hath no loyal knight and true,
    The Lady of Shalott.

But in her web she still delights
To weave the mirror's magic sights,
For often thro' the silent nights
A funeral, with plumes and lights
    And music, went to Camelot:
Or when the moon was overhead,
Came two young lovers lately wed:
"I am half sick of shadows," said
    The Lady of Shalott.

       Part III
A bow-shot from her bower-eaves,
He rode between the barley-sheaves,
The sun came dazzling thro' the leaves,
And flamed upon the brazen greaves
    Of bold Sir Lancelot.
A red-cross knight for ever kneel'd
To a lady in his shield,
That sparkled on the yellow field,
    Beside remote Shalott.

The gemmy bridle glitter'd free,
Like to some branch of stars we see
Hung in the golden Galaxy.
The bridle bells rang merrily
    As he rode down to Camelot:
And from his blazon'd baldric slung
A mighty silver bugle hung,
And as he rode his armour rung,
    Beside remote Shalott.

All in the blue unclouded weather
Thick-jewell'd shone the saddle-leather,
The helmet and the helmet-feather
Burn'd like one burning flame together,

As he rode down to Camelot.
As often thro' the purple night,
Below the starry clusters bright,
Some bearded meteor, trailing light,
    Moves over still Shalott.

His broad clear brow in sunlight glow'd;
On burnish'd hooves his war-horse trode;
From underneath his helmet flow'd
His coal-black curls as on he rode,
    As he rode down to Camelot.
From the bank and from the river
He flash'd into the crystal mirror,
"Tirra lirra," by the river
    Sang Sir Lancelot.

She left the web, she left the loom,
She made three paces thro' the room,
She saw the water-lily bloom,
She saw the helmet and the plume,
    She look'd down to Camelot.
Out flew the web and floated wide;
The mirror crack'd from side to side;
"The curse is come upon me," cried
    The Lady of Shalott.

Part IV
In the stormy east-wind straining,
The pale yellow woods were waning,
The broad stream in his banks complaining,
Heavily the low sky raining
    Over tower'd Camelot;
Down she came and found a boat
Beneath a willow left afloat,
And round about the prow she wrote
    The Lady of Shalott.

And down the river's dim expanse
Like some bold seer in a trance,
Seeing all his own mischance –
With a glassy countenance
   Did she look to Camelot.
And at the closing of the day
She loosed the chain, and down she lay;
The broad stream bore her far away,
   The Lady of Shalott.

Lying, robed in snowy white
That loosely flew to left and right –
The leaves upon her falling light –
Thro' the noises of the night
   She floated down to Camelot:
And as the boat-head wound along
The willowy hills and fields among,
They heard her singing her last song,
   The Lady of Shalott.

Heard a carol, mournful, holy,
Chanted loudly, chanted lowly,
Till her blood was frozen slowly,
And her eyes were darken'd wholly,
   Turn'd to tower'd Camelot.
For ere she reach'd upon the tide
The first house by the water-side,
Singing in her song she died,
   The Lady of Shalott.

Under tower and balcony,
By garden-wall and gallery,
A gleaming shape she floated by,
Dead-pale between the houses high,
   Silent into Camelot.
Out upon the wharfs they came,
Knight and burgher, lord and dame,
And round the prow they read her name,
   The Lady of Shalott.

Who is this? and what is here?
And in the lighted palace near
Died the sound of royal cheer;
And they cross'd themselves for fear,
    All the knights at Camelot:
But Lancelot mused a little space;
He said, "She has a lovely face;
God in his mercy lend her grace,
    The Lady of Shalott."

Let's make some preliminary comments. Firstly, the poem is a 'multi-text', which is to say that it exists in distinctly different versions – an 1832 text and the 1842 revised version, which you have just read. In the earlier version, one of the most striking moments in the poem is missing, for 'Lancelot does not appear in the final stanza; instead the "well-fed wits" of Camelot gather around the boat to read the puzzling parchment on the lady's breast: "The web was woven curiously, / The charm is broken utterly, / Draw near and fear not – This is I, / The Lady of Shalott."'[5] Secondly, the poem is not a free-standing 'words-on-the-page' lyric poem, for it is deeply embedded in a substantial British cultural tradition of myths and legends about King Arthur and his knights, a tradition which goes back to the Middle Ages, for instance to the unknown poet who wrote *Sir Gawain and the Green Knight* in the fourteenth century and to Sir Thomas Malory's epic poem *Morte Darthur* in the fifteenth. This tradition, then, started long before Tennyson and continued long after, with modern works like T. H. White's twentieth-century tetralogy (sequence of four novels) *The Once and Future King* and films such as Hollywood's *The Knights of the Round Table* of 1953, the musical *Camelot* of 1967 and even *Monty Python and the Holy Grail* of 1975. Thirdly, the poem is also embedded in Tennyson's own major contribution to this Arthurian tradition, namely his epic *The Idylls of the King* of 1859, which incorporates ten major episodes, one of which is 'Lancelot and Elaine'. It is clear that Elaine, 'the

[5]Footnote 6, p. 44 in Kathy Alexis Psomiades, '"The Lady of Shalott" and the Critical Fortunes of Victorian Poetry' in Joseph Bristow ed., *The Cambridge Companion to Victorian Poetry*, Cambridge, 2000.

lily maid of Astolat' who lives 'High in her chamber up a tower to the east', is a close analogue (or parallel) of the Lady of Shalott, for she dies of unrequited love for Lancelot and her body is placed on a barge, with the letter she has written explaining her plight, and floated down to Camelot. The image of the Astolat/Shalott lady and her barge became a major subject for Victorian painters, with notable examples by Waterhouse, Egley, Meteyard, Hughes, Grimshaw, Rossetti, Holman Hunt and so on).[6] There are at least three additional layers of 'textuality' to take into account, then, these being the 'multi-textuality' of the text itself, which exists in two substantially different versions, the cultural *con*textuality of the extensive 'cultural production' on Arthurian topics (poetry, fiction, paintings and film) and the specific intertextuality of another text by Tennyson on the same material.

Current trends in interpretation

How, then, can we come to an understanding of what the poem means? In it, a Lady is imprisoned in a tower which is located on an inland 'island' within the river that runs to the town of Camelot. A mysterious 'curse' prevents her looking directly out of the window of the tower and she labours at a tapestry depicting the world beyond the tower, which she sees indirectly via a mirror on the wall. She seems to feel a longing for the bustle of life outside and is finally tempted to look out directly when Sir Lancelot, an alluring figure in shining armour, passes by. As soon as she looks out the curse comes into operation and she knows she is doomed to die. She places herself in a barge on the river, having painted the words 'The Lady of Shalott' on the prow, and her body drifts down to Camelot, where it is seen by 'All the knights of Camelot' and (in the 1842 version) by Sir Lancelot, who (in the final lines of the poem) 'mused a little space; / He said, "She has a lovely face; / God in his mercy lend her grace, / The Lady of Shalott.' Lancelot's reaction seems perfunctory and, to modern readers, almost comically sexist, but as Kathy Psomiades

[6]See George P. Landow ed., *Ladies of Shalott: A Victorian Masterpiece and its Contexts*, Providence, 1979.

points out, it could have been worse ('it is not, for example, as inadequate as "Can I watch the autopsy?" or "Do you think I could have the boat after we bury her?"').[7] In the parallel story in 'Lancelot and Elaine', Lancelot's indifference to Elaine's fate stems from his continuing obsession with Guinevere, which is tearing him apart and will eventually destroy Camelot and what it stands for. Should we read this back into the much shorter poem, or must we try to read the two separately, even though they are two pieces by the same author on the same theme and material?

A response to this question might be to say that however we read the poem, our reading will be *partial* in both senses; firstly, it will not be able to take account of every element in the poem, and secondly it will be the product of a personal predisposition or prejudice of which we ourselves will probably remain unaware. Thus, the most traditional readings of the poem saw it as an allegory of the necessary isolation of the artist: the Lady engages in the practice of representing life in art (through the medium of the tapestry she is weaving), but artists can only do this if they are in some measure detached from life; the detachment is represented in the poem by the tower, the island and the prohibition on looking at life directly. But the Lady wants to be part of the flux and bustle of life, rather than being elevated beyond it in nun-like contemplation, so she is drawn to look out, thus breaking the spell, so that the tapestry flies apart ('Out flew the web and floated wide; /The mirror crack'd from side to side').

However, this kind of interpretation (with its attribution of heroic, supra-human qualities to the artist) is much out of favour in English Studies today, and it would be difficult to find academic critics who would take seriously the idea that artists and writers either can or should attain a kind of panoramic elevation of insight and viewpoint above and beyond life in general. It is easy, too, for them to point out the 'partiality' of this interpretation, especially the way it ignores the fact that the artist-figure in the poem is a woman. Pointing this out lays the ground for interpretations which foreground issues of gender, and these approaches are currently more highly favoured. Interpretation on these lines would see the imprisoned Lady as an emblem of the patriarchal restrictions placed on women in Victorian

---

[7] Bristow ed., *The Cambridge Companion to Victorian Poetry*, p. 29.

and later times. A general isolation from the flux of life results in a kind of vicarious or proxy living in which the woman identifies longingly with the life and achievements of husband, brothers or children (the 'Shadows of the world', perhaps, which appear in the mirror); she is confined to activities deemed 'suitable' (here the traditional 'woman's work' of weaving), repressing many aspects of her own nature, including her sexuality, for it is the alluring figure of Lancelot which finally causes her to defy the curse and look out. The Lady, then, becomes a kind of heroic resister of these implacable patriarchal norms and the poem a protest at the waste of human happiness and potential which they entail.

Four kinds of interpretation

Are these two basic interpretations (the one which is centred on notions of the artist and the one which is based on aspects of gender) mutually exclusive? The first is 'idealist' in tendency, seeing the role of the artist as requiring a stance beyond and above life, while the latter is 'materialist', in that it is rooted in notions of the earth-bound, socially determined limitations commonly placed upon a particular section of the population (here, capable and intelligent women). Do we have to *choose* between these two interpretations, or can they be combined in some way? Clearly, the notion of combining the two is attractive, and the argument for doing so here might be that Tennyson may well have *intended* the poem as an allegory of the artist, but he inadvertently produced a text in which his imprisoned muse-figure seems (to us) more obviously representative of patri-archal restrictions. This 'semi-combined' reading takes the view that the poet intended to say one thing but inadvertently expressed something else, and I call this 'semi-combined' because it makes use of both readings, but without actually reconciling them. A more truly combined reading might see the poem as exploring a notion of the artist as necessarily 'feminized' in outlook, retreating to the margins of life, in order to attain a viewpoint on it, and then observing rather than doing, characteristics of Victorian women rather than Victorian men. While he was not a conventional Victorian patriarch, a Tennyson primarily intent on undermining patriarchal norms still seems to me a little implausible. True, the man who designs poems as a way of life engages in a less obviously 'manly' undertaking than one who designs battleships, like his younger cousin Tennyson d'Eyncourt (though the poems turned out to be more durable than the ships), so there is a contextual plausibility in this kind of combined idealist/materialist interpretation.

All three of these levels of interpretation (that is, the idealist, the materialist and the combined) focus on elements that the poem itself clearly foregrounds. One further level concerns matters the poem either does not mention at all, or else features only peripherally: this seems characteristic of the 1980s and 1990s, when readings were very much shaped by aspects of the literary theory then in vogue. Thus, Alan Sinfield's short book *Alfred Tennyson* (in a series called *Re-Reading Literature*, aimed at students and featuring applications of literary theory to canonical authors) argued that:

> poetry which appears to be remote from political issues is in fact involved with the political life of its society: it disseminates ideas, images and narratives of the way the world is, and that is always a political activity. (p. 11, quoted by Psomiades, *Cambridge Companion*, p. 31)

This might at first seem just another kind of 'materialist' reading, but Sinfield sees it as 'a poem about the construction of the bourgeois self, and the anxieties attendant on this construction' (Psomiades, *Cambridge Companion*, p. 32). Seeing the poem as being about the *construction* of the social self and its attendant anxieties is not the same as seeing it as simply being about the social self. Sinfield isn't writing about society as an external phenomenon but about social identity as an on-going inner process. To repeat, the ideas he uses – 'constructing' identities rather than just having them (such as being a Mancunian or a six-foot basket-ball ace) and 'entering into language' rather than just learning language and the social practices that go with it – are very distinctly ideas which derive from the literary theory of the 1980s. Thus, when the web fails to give her 'a coherent sense of herself in the world', the Lady abandons it and sets off for Camelot in a doomed bid 'to enter language and social identity' (p. 32).

This approach takes its cue from the fact that it is impossible to use language which is 'first hand': the words and phrases we use can never be like new-minted coins which have never been circulated before; on the contrary, our words always have a history and a provenance. Roland Barthes in his much-quoted essay 'The Death of the Author' emphasizes this aspect of language when he writes that

> The text is a tissue of quotations drawn from the innumerable centres of culture … The writer can only imitate a gesture that is always anterior [pre-existing, belated, derivative], never original.

In the case of 'The Lady of Shalott', the reflexive, theorized reading seems a natural one because the word 'text' comes from the Latin *textere*, which means to weave. The Lady is very prolific of 'texts' in the widest sense, weaving her tapestry, writing her name on the prow of the barge, singing her ceaseless songs until the breath leaves her body and finally 'composing' her own corpse as part of a silent tableau which the onlookers seek to read and decode. This is distinctly, then, a fourth kind of reading: it is highly theorized, reading back into the poem the theoretical concerns of the critic's own era in a manner which seems defiantly anachronistic. Sinfield's reading is applied literary theory: it bypasses the lengthy chain of 'readings' of the poem produced over the years by the 'lit crit' industry and draws it into the (then) brave new world of theorized reading. The difficulty for this kind of reading is that it seems to abandon the *overt* content of the poem altogether and doesn't really explain anything about the purpose and effect of the Arthurian and medieval setting. While it would be immediately plausible to suggest that a Victorian novel like *Middlemarch* is about 'the construction of the bourgeois self' and its attendant anxieties, nothing that is specific about this poem seems to be accounted for by this very generalized reading. The notion of 'entering into language and social identity' is one which would not have been recognized by Tennyson or his readers, and while this is not in itself enough to invalidate this kind of interpretation (after all, it is commonplace to invoke the Freudian notion of the Oedipal desires and responses in a reading of *Hamlet*), it does mean that detailed, text-specific supporting evidence is required. It is significant, too, that Sinfield largely ignores the gender issue – for him the poem is about 'the bourgeois self', which subsumes a specific gender politics into politics in general.

'Synoptic' interpretation

So far, then, we have looked at four kinds of interpretation – the idealist, the materialist, the combined and the theorized. A fifth level of interpretation can be posited, this being a 'synoptic' approach which draws upon all four of these, aiming for what we earlier called 'total textuality'. This kind of reading – exemplified by Isobel Armstrong in her book *Victorian Poetry: Poetry, Poetics and Politics* (Routledge, 1993) – retains the political emphasis which is an element of all but the first of these, but is much more directly keyed in to the details of the poem, trying not to lose sight of the overt content in the way that the fourth (theorized) type inevitably does. Armstrong sees the poem as one 'which has no source' and is therefore 'a modern myth', a 'conflation of a number of mythic structures', such as the chivalric and fairy tale motif of the imprisoned lady in the tower, myths of the weaving lady, like Arachne and Penelope, and myths of reflection, like those of Narcissus and Echo. The lady, she says, 'dies a sacrificial death, failing to come into sexuality and language' (all these quotations from p. 83). The notion that the lady longs for inclusion in the turmoil of real life and is tired of her isolation is fully consonant both with the internal evidence of the poem ('I am half sick of shadows' she says at the end of Part II as she sees in her mirror 'two young lovers lately wed') and with Tennyson's own remarks on it, as quoted in his son's *Memoir*: 'The new-born love for something, for someone in the whole wide world from which she has been for so long secluded, takes her out of the region of shadows into that of realities' (quoted in Staines, *Tennyson's Camelot*, p. 10 [see note 8]).

However, it isn't quite true to say that the poem has no source: it was the first of a long succession of Arthurian works by Tennyson 'based, not on Malory's retelling of the Arthurian tales in his *Morte Darthur* (1470), but on a medieval Italian novelette entitled "*Donna di Scalotta*", which was reprinted in 1804 as Novella LXXXI (81) in a collection entitled *Cento Novelle Antiche* (*One Hundred Ancient Novellae*). A notebook entry of Tennyson's records this source, and he may have been introduced to this kind of Italian material by his friend Arthur Hallam.[8] Important aspects of the poem which are not found in the source are 'the mirror and the web it inspires, the curse, the geographical relationship of the island, the river and Camelot' (Staines, *Tennyson's Camelot*, p. 11), and the changes between the 1832 and 1842 versions show Tennyson moving the poem further from the Italian source (Staines, p. 11). When he wrote the poem he did not know the Maid of Astolat story in Malory, which he later used in the *Idylls*, as we saw, and details which are in Malory (the barge, the letter held by the dead lady in the 1832 version, etc.) are also in the Italian source (Staines, p. 12).

Armstrong sees the Lady, who is cursed to labour ceaselessly at her weaving, as a representative of 'alienation and work' (p. 85): Tennyson, she says, 'is manoeuvring together the constraints working on women and the compulsions working on other forms of labour' (Staines, p. 84), so this too has elements of the 'combined' reading, alleging that the poem combines a critique of patriarchal restraints with a kind of coded protest at the political, social and industrial conditions which had produced widespread unrest round the time of the first Reform Bill of 1832. This interpretation involves giving considerable centrality to the agricultural workers mentioned in the poem, like the 'reapers, reaping early' in stanza four. She writes,

The reapers and the Cambridge rick-burners reacting to the corn laws, the starving handloom weavers who were being displaced by new industrial processes, these hover just outside the poem and become strangely aligned with the imprisoned lady. (pp. 84–5)

The liminal presence in the poem of starving handloom weavers and Cambridge rick-burners (who set fire to hayricks which had been harvested with the new machinery that had made their own labour redundant – scenes Tennyson had witnessed [Sinfield, *Alfred Tennyson*, p. 30) seems to have become a widely accepted view, but the precise nature of the 'hovering' is difficult to define. The reapers

[8]All this information about sources is in David Staines, *Tennyson's Camelot: The* Idylls of the King *and its Medieval Sources*, (Wilfrid Laurier University Press, 1982), p. 9.

in the poem are 'reaping early' and are still there, and 'weary', at the end of the day 'by the moon', still hearing the eerie song of the lady in the tower. She does seem to be linked with them in the next stanza as 'There she weaves by night and day / A magic web with colours gay', but this doesn't really sound like alienated labour. Far from it, in fact, for it seems that her weaving is the one thing she finds pleasure in, for 'in her web she still delights / To weave the mirror's magic sights', so that it is difficult to see grounds for Armstrong's statement that 'For all its magical aesthetic quality, the weaving of the web is ceaseless work without escape and without *pleasure*' (p. 84). The other peripheral female figures in the poem do not seem especially oppressed (in Part II, market girls in red cloaks, a troop of damsels glad and the woman who is one of the 'two young lovers'), and this would seem to present another difficulty which cannot easily be disposed of. All the same, the reading is delicately poised, drawing on many different kinds of interpretive strategy: it has elements, for instance, of a 'theorized', deconstructive approach (in the way it draws peripheral details like the passers-by into a centrally signifying role in the text), it makes use of historicist data (like the plight of the hand-loom weavers) and it brings in broad layers of cultural intertextuality (for instance, weaving as a traditional literary motif).

It is not, however, an easy model to imitate and it tends to be reproduced in cruder and more diluted form, with some elements of the synopsis ignored. In particular, the desire to read the poem as an allegory of organized labour can lead to more drastic misreadings of the text. A book on university education complains about students' accounts of this poem in examinations, which seem to offer reductive versions of Armstrong's 'alienated labour' reading, attempting on spurious grounds to bring *into* the poem what Armstrong more cautiously sees as 'hovering' on the outside. Thus one student writes: 'Both the lady and the reapers are set outside the commercial capital city of Camelot, and ... indeed both may be the victims of industrial society.' On this kind of reading, Lancelot is roughly shoehorned into the role of capitalist exploiter, for 'Technology is shown as an intrusive force in the lady's life, in the form of Lancelot; she brings the curse upon herself by looking down at his shining armour and "coal-black hair"; Lancelot appears as a machine.' Finally, her abandonment of her web and loom and her sailing down to Camelot in a barge are seen as 'perhaps suggesting the weavers moving to factories in towns – urbanisation'.[9]

It may well be the case that elements authors themselves highlight as central to a literary work may not be the real centre and that scrutinising the parts of the text which are left in shadow by the authorial spotlight may well be a good idea. But clearly, again, it has to be possible to demonstrate the centrality of these shadowed elements without implausibly ignoring, or blatantly misreading, aspects of the text. If the word 'coal' in the phrase 'coal-black curls' at first makes us think of coal mines, from which it is a short step to converting Lancelot into a figure like Gerald Crich (the arrogant mine owner in D. H. Lawrence's novel *Women in Love*), then perhaps we ought to pause for second thoughts before we rush on to make something of this. The context of the phrase 'coal-black curls' is Part III, which is entirely devoted to presenting Lancelot as an alluring, sexually attractive figure who seems brimming with all the life and vitality from which the lady feels herself excluded; he is the image which finally breaks her resolve and makes her start up from the loom. In this context his curls are called 'coal-black' because, like every other aspect of him, they shine; the phrase, therefore, designates the youthful sheen of his copious black locks, a sheen which is precisely suggested by the phrase 'coal-black', for coal too has a sheen or a gloss which exactly suggests the effect Tennyson is trying to convey. Likewise, the armour obviously isn't of the kind produced by the nineteenth-century industrial workers of Vickers-Armstrongs (which turned out the battleships designed by Tennyson's cousin), but is the personal and hand-made kind fashioned by highly skilled medieval craftsman and therefore quite unsuited to be an emblem of nineteenth-century industrial production. As readers, then, we must find a reasonable balance between the claims of textuality on the one hand and of contextuality on the other, and we need to accept the textual restraints within which our interpretive strategies must operate. The synoptic approach, then, is our fifth kind of reading: like the third type, it is combinatory, but whereas the 'combined' reading seeks a reconciliation between *two* opposed

[9]These quotations from student scripts are from Duke Maskell and Ian Robinson, *The New Idea of a University*, London, 2001, p. 152.

lines of interpretation, the synoptic combines a whole range of varied interpretive approaches. The question we have *not* solved, however, in discussing Tennyson's poem, is the status of all that content which (in Armstrong's formulation) 'hovers' on the threshold of the poem. Bluntly, is all this 'hovering' material part of the poem or not? As I have indicated already, this question about the status of context is one of the momentous issues facing the discipline of English Studies today, and is later the subject of Chapter 10.

5

English and Creative Writing

Teaching elephants: creative writing in America

The organization of writing degrees in the United States is highly distinctive, not least because of the vast scale of the enterprise. Associated Writing Programmes, usually called the AWP, is the organization for the teaching of creative writing in higher education in the USA and Canada and according to the company's data, 446 undergraduate degree courses in creative writing were being offered by the approximately 1,500 colleges and universities in the United States in 2012.[1] To its detractors, this huge enterprise is the bizarre joint product of the counterculture of the 1960s and the business-enterprise culture of the 1980s and 1990s.[2] But creative writing programmes are much older than is popularly supposed. They originated with the English Composition course established at Harvard in 1873 (see Gerald Graff, *Professing Literature*, p.46), and a course in 'Advanced Composition' was also available at Harvard from 1884, with the emphasis on 'practice, æsthetics, personal observation, and creativity rather than theory, history, tradition, and literary conservation' (Fenza: see footnote 24). Students on this course, taught by

---

[1] See the AWP website at http://www.awpwriter.org/ [accessed 2 July 2013]
[2] This is the argument of a piece called 'Creative Writing in the Academy' by David Radavich, published by the Modern Language Association (the MLA) in *Profession 1999* and cited in 'Creative Writing and its Discontents' by D. W. Fenza (Chair of the AWP) in an article first published in the AWP's journal *The Writer's Chronicle* (March/April, 2000). I am drawing on Fenza's piece throughout this sub-section.

Barrett Wendell, had to hand in a piece of writing *every day*, but it still recruited 150 students in its second year. This may be a testimony to the negative qualities of the English courses that were the alternatives, for early 'Composition' was, among other things, an attempt to approach literature in the more student-friendly manner (as we would say) of the 'generalists' discussed in the next chapter. These early Harvard courses were taught from the 1880s through to the 1920s. In 1930 Norman Foerster, a noted pioneer university teacher of literature, became the director of the School of Letters ('Letters' means Literature) at the University of Iowa and started 'classes in creative writing and a new emphasis on literature as an art', so that this graduate school 'was the first to contain the basic components of today's creative writing programmes: a course of study leading to a graduate degree; seminars for writers on the issues of craft and form; the study of literature as an art; and a creative work for a thesis' (Fenza). The related Iowa Writers' Workshop was founded in 1942, specializing in 'the education and nurturing of literary artists' and leading to the Master of the Fine Arts (MFA) degree. Similar programmes followed, at Johns Hopkins University in 1946, at Stanford and Denver in 1947 and at Cornell in 1948. The creative writing movement, then, had close connections with a range of liberalizing tendencies in the history of the discipline of English, including the desire to broaden literary studies beyond the narrow, language-based approaches of the nineteenth century, and to study modern literature in general, and American literature in particular, with the same rigour and seriousness as was devoted to the study of the literature of the past. The movement involved, for instance, several of the 'New Critics' of the 1940s (see the next chapter) who were writers as well as critics (such as John Crowe Ransom at Vanderbilt University and Yvor Winters at Stanford) and it was also aware of the progressive educational philosophy of educators like John Dewey, who pioneered such ideas as 'learning by doing' rather than 'learning by rote'. Much of the residual antagonism against creative writing which lingers on in the early twenty-first century seems to replay old battles between 'theory' and 'practice' within the discipline, between those who seek to accumulate 'knowledge about' literature (dates, sources, variant readings, and so on) and those who 'merely' do it, whether that means writing it, enjoying it or finding ways of communicating the grounds of their enjoyment to others. When Harvard appointed the novelist Vladimir Nabokov to a professorship, the linguist Roman Jakobson famously remarked, 'What's next? Shall we appoint elephants to teach zoology?' Hence the title (which I have adapted for this sub-section) of the best-known book about the development of creative writing at American universities, D. G. Myers' *The Elephants Teach: Creative Writing Since 1880* (Prentice Hall, 1995).

The range of undergraduate writing programmes currently available in the United States includes those which enable students on an English degree to major in creative writing as well as those which are exclusively a BA in Creative Writing. Typically, both these require the study of the literature of the past and the present and also some study of the English language itself, as well as practical tuition in the writing of fiction, poetry, drama scripts and creative non-fictional prose. All are a world away from the outdated caricature which imagines that creative writing courses merely encourage self-expression, or teach a cynical and uncritical manipulation of 'market' preferences. The faculty staff members who teach these courses are invariably active and published writers whose tuition is often supplemented by readings and workshops taken by major writers who are more loosely affiliated to the programme. The permanent faculty staff members often have an MFA degree, which is becoming the main professional qualification for the teaching of creative writing at college and university level, equivalent to the PhD, which has long had the same status for English faculty members outside the creative writing programmes. These MFA degrees tend to be intensively taught, two-year, highly selective programmes, taking a small number of students each year – often around a dozen – and involving tuition in both the pedagogy and practice of creative writing. MA degrees in creative writing, usually with a larger enrolment and without the pedagogic element, are also widely available.

Creative writing in UK higher education

So the teaching of writing, both as 'composition' and as 'creative writing', has long been part of the curriculum in the United States, but this has until fairly recently not been the case in what publishers call 'RoW' (the Rest of the World). In the UK, indeed, the separation between English departments on the one hand and living poets and writers on the other often seemed to be enshrined in the constitution. Creative writing, therefore, did not formally become part of the higher education system until 1970, when an MA in Creative Writing was founded at the then-recently established University of East Anglia by the novelists Angus Wilson and Malcolm Bradbury. This famous enterprise remained a workshop-based course in the writing of fiction for a quarter of a century, with well-known contributing tutors like Angela Carter and Rose Tremain and an increasing list of highly successful graduates, including Ian McEwan, Clive Sinclair and Kazuo Ishiguro. As it was founded by novelists, the East Anglia course retained its exclusive concern with fiction until 1995 when the poet Andrew Motion became the director and a poetry strand was added, followed by one in script-writing.

It isn't surprising that university courses in creative writing in the UK should have started at what was then a new university, and that courses of a similar type did not become common elsewhere until much later. Other early entrants to the field were the MA in creative writing at the then Sheffield Polytechnic (now Sheffield Hallam University), the Creative Writing MA started in 1981 at Manchester Polytechnic (now Manchester Metropolitan University) and another MA course, at Lancaster University, started in 1983. One of the marked features of the field is that provision at postgraduate level (which is to say, mainly MA degrees in the early days) preceded the existence of BA programmes, which began to emerge only in the 1990s. Initially, these BA programmes were set up outside the traditional university sector, that is, in the post-1992 universities and at university colleges. Why should this have been so? In one sense, the answer is obvious – tradition is often the enemy of innovation, so the institutions most conscious of their status as guardians of traditional academic values have been slowest off the mark.

Yet another reason for the growth of creative writing provision outside traditional universities was that the teaching syllabus of the latter had always been somewhat remote from the creative arts, whereas the large polytechnics of the 1980s were usually amalgamations of several institutions within a region, often including a college of art and a college of (higher) education, which had probably started life as a teacher training college. Institutions of this kind usually had strong performance traditions in departments of art, movement and dance, and music, and even in their English departments, which had long been involved in the teaching of creative writing techniques for use in primary and secondary schools. Such institutions routinely included practitioners of various arts as members of their staff (my own colleagues at one such institution included composers, artists, potters, dancers, fabric-designers, poets and writers of children's books), and this produced an institutional ambience and mindset quite different from that of a traditional university. This, in a word, is the soil in which the teaching of creative writing took root in the UK.

At the time of writing (2013), the growth momentum of the discipline in the UK remains powerful. The equivalent UK organization to the American AWP is NAWE, the National Association of Writers in Higher Education, which lists 46 UK institutions teaching creative writing at undergraduate level, 48 at MA level and 46 at PhD level.[3] The long-term effects of this massive expansion are as yet difficult to determine, but one beneficial result may be to contribute something towards the survival of contemporary poetry. This depends upon the survival of contemporary poets, something that cannot be ensured merely on the proceeds of selling poetry books. In each generation in Britain, W. H. Auden once said, there are just two people who can live on the sales of poetry alone. Even well-known figures may routinely sell under a thousand copies of a title, so most poets survive by means of the 'reading circuit', which provides them with reading engagements at literary festivals and societies, schools and other educational institutions. The fees from these may just about add up to a working wage, but at the personal cost of leading a nomadic existence which (the poets say) is barely compatible with the maintenance of family life and relationships, let alone with securing the kind of stability and work-space a writer needs. One effect of the creative writing boom, then, has been to provide a large number of poets with a degree of security, regular contact with a seriously interested audience and a work routine built upon a reflective engagement with their craft.

---

[3]See the NAWE website at http://www.nawe.co.uk [accessed 2 July 2013]

Creative writing and English departments

The 1990s began to see some erosion of the traditional student base of English by newer degree subjects like media studies and theatre, film and television studies. The appeal of these subjects was partly the creative opportunities they offered, for example for film-editing, film-making, script-writing and so on, and it therefore seemed that offering this kind of creative opportunity as part of undergraduate study in English departments would be a sensible step. So what are some of the key characteristics of the creative writing course at undergraduate level? Firstly, the dominant teaching and learning format is the 'workshop', in which members of the group in turn read out a piece of work for discussion, or have it discussed after prior distribution to the class or (increasingly) receive online comments from the group on a previously-posted piece of work and then use these in some way in the further development of the piece. As the course develops, the tutor will stress the importance of making comments helpful, specific, thoughtful and supportive. Usually the writing will have taken place outside the session, but occasionally the tutor may ask students, individually or in pairs, to start a piece on the spot in response to an idea or a piece of writing presented in the session by the tutor. In these cases, the piece thus started may be worked upon during the following week, and then presented in a more developed state at the next session.

A second common feature is that material produced in the workshops will be collected in some way into a student's course 'portfolio', which will be presented for assessment when the module is complete. Typically, the aim of the portfolio will be to stimulate 'reflective practice', so that the material presented will be not just the completed 'product' (a poem, a story, a dramatic sketch) but also evidence of the 'process' it went through, in the form of a series of drafts with explanatory comments on the various stages through which the work passed. The comments will explain the reasons for some of the changes made and this kind of work will begin to produce the 'reflective practitioner', one who consciously reflects on the craft of writing. Thus, the creative writing course embodies the view that writers aren't just 'naturals' who either know or don't know how to do it; rather, the assumption is that we can teach and learn key skills, hone our methods and clarify our writing intentions. We can benefit from trying to explain to others what we are trying to do and we can learn how to keep working at an idea until we have refined and improved its execution. Becoming a writer, these courses assume, is a long-term experiential process, and they recognize that it is beneficial to serve an apprenticeship in a community of writers rather than waiting in a lonely garret for the onset of inspiration.

A final characteristic of creative writing courses is the assumption that creative writers need to be creative readers too, so they commonly involve the simultaneous study of literature alongside students not in the creative writing stream and they require, in particular, the reading of literary criticism and literary theory. Hence, the influences (between the English Department and the Creative Writing course) are mutual, and these degree-stream courses in creative writing are thus different from the classes in writing, which can be taken outside degree programmes in 'extra-mural' departments. Such courses do not usually entwine the practice of writing with the systematic study of literature. University courses, by contrast, present writing in an 'integrated' manner, as part of an established set of intellectual practices which includes literary criticism. Struggling to say what they mean, the creative writer and the literary critic face the same challenges, and this is why creative writing courses have so quickly come to seem at home in English departments.

I will end this chapter by giving an impression of the kind of activities a student might expect to undertake when enrolled on a creative writing course. It is of the nature of a creative writing course that students write regularly, all the way through the academic year, in response to specific set tasks. Some of the written work produced will be discussed, usually in groups of up to a dozen or so students, in the 'workshop' sessions which form the backbone of most courses, as we have seen. In my own teaching, I have long been interested in devising writing activities which encourage students to work in unfamiliar formats and on topics not directly based on their own personal experience. One common and fruitful practice is the form of writing usually referred to as 'ekphrastic poetry'. The word 'ekphrastic' comes from the

Greek 'ekphrasis', which roughly means 'out-speaking' or 'plain speaking', or just 'description'. Ekphrastic poetry is the kind which responds to a painting or photograph, or some other art object (such as a Grecian urn or a piece of sculpture). Such poems usually begin by simply (or not so simply) describing the object or image concerned, hence the appropriateness of the term 'ekphrasis'. After the descriptive bit, it can take off in any one of a range of possible directions. For instance, if the art object is a portrait, the poet might speak *to* the person depicted, or *as* that person, or *about* that person, the latter either from 'outside', as a present-day observer or commentator, or from 'inside', as an onlooker or observer within the picture, or perhaps as the artist who painted it, or the photographer who pressed the shutter. This is by no means an exhaustive list of the possibilities, but already several possible permutations have been indicated. This kind of writing might be undertaken in relation to the photograph reproduced below, with students not being given any prior information about the image, and perhaps following some initial discussion.

The discussion might respond initially to questions from the tutor, and I have started sessions based on this picture with such questions as these: 1) When do think this picture might have been taken? 2) What kind of equipment might have been used? 3) How long might the exposure have been? 4) Was the photographer male or female? 5) Is the sitter being herself or acting a role? 6) If so, how would you describe that role? 7) How would you imagine the sitter's own attitude to the role being played? 8) What might be the title of the picture? 9) Is this photograph a reference to, or 'quotation' of another kind of picture? 10) What sentiments or beliefs does the picture seem to express or embody?

The questions fall into three distinct groups: 1–3 are technical or historical and prompt a detailed conceptualization of the circum-stances in which the picture was made; 4–7 are about imagining the relationship between sitter and photographer and the feelings or attitudes each might have towards the other; 8–10 concern the relationship between this picture and other kinds of artistic repre-sentation that it may seem to evoke. A successful piece of writing might well focus mainly on just one of these three areas. Typically, the discussion would take up about 15 or 20 minutes in one session, and students would subsequently write their pieces and bring them to the corresponding session the following week.

I would call this an 'unseen' version of ekphrastic writing, in the sense of an 'unseen' examination – one in which the questions are unknown to the candidates before the exam and so cannot be researched in advance. In a 'seen' exam, by contrast, the questions are issued some time beforehand, and students can undertake specific research before taking the exam. So in a 'seen' version of the same ekphrastic writing task, the class might undertake, for example, specific research on the photographer or the circumstances in which the picture was taken, and this factual information would in some way be incorporated into the poem, giving the whole exercise what I would call a 'documentary' basis. In my own courses, I have called this kind of work 'docu-poetry', as a poem is produced which is based on specific research about factual material; so in the 'seen' version of the present exercise, the aim is to produce an ekphrastic docu-poem. Docu-poetry has two format-rules, which I developed in the light of experience with classes: the first is that the incorporated facts must be ninety per cent historically accurate, but a ten per cent element of poetic licence is allowed. Such poems need a shape which 'rounds off' the poem in a satisfying way, so that it doesn't just stop, but has a distinctive ending, as all poems should, and the ten per cent licence can be useful in achieving this. The second rule is that the docu-poem should be so crafted as to include all necessary contextual information within itself (by 'within itself' I mean within the poem and its title), so that no explanatory footnotes are required. In combination, these two rules mean that strong emphasis is placed on the need to edit, shape and craft the material in order to create a particular poetic effect.

Deciding what to ignore in the sources and what to include is crucial, and so is trimming away unnecessary detail and then juxtaposing elements to produce maximum impact. In writing such poems, my experience has been that a lot of labour is given to such apparently minor concerns as deciding the precise order in which a sequence of items of data should be released, and how the different items should be linked. What I like particularly about docu-poetry is the way the poet's ego seems to be removed to the periphery, so that the whole emphasis falls on the writing process itself.

Figure 5.1 Julia Jackson (1846–95), possibly by Julia Margaret Cameron.

Combining ekphrastic and docu-poetry based on the topic of the same photograph could begin from the same set of discussion questions given above, this time using them as points to research rather than as a stimulus to imaginative speculation. Students would be given basic information – that the picture was taken by the pioneer Victorian photographer Julia Margaret Cameron (1815–79), who made portraits of many famous figures of the day at her Isle of Wight home in the 1860s.[4] The long exposure times required mean that attitudes were carefully composed, props and costumes were selected to convey roles and characterization and emotions were dramatized visually, as in silent film. The sitter is Julia Jackson, mother of the novelist Virginia Woolf, posed in a style which resembles conventional religious images of the Virgin

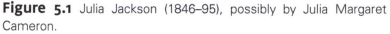

[4]The image is dated c.1865–6. The source is currently unidentified. The copyright holder is invited to get in touch with the publisher.

Mary, and (commentators say) represents Victorian ideals of saintly femininity, as embodied in the now-notorious epic poem *The Angel in the House* by Coventry Patmore (who in fact was a friend of the family). Woolf wrote, in 1931, that 'Killing the Angel in the House was part of the occupation of a woman writer'. Many readers will know Julia Jackson already, from reading Virginia Woolf's elegiac portrait of her mother as Mrs Ramsay in her novel *To the Lighthouse*. Cameron was a great artist whose portraits still look modern because the face usually fills most of the picture frame and is thus freed from the clutter and detail often found in Victorian photographs. Most of her pictures are of women, but hardly any of them are smiling (a difficult expression to capture when exposure times of ten or twenty seconds were needed), so conventionally feminized images are rare. But her views are not uniformly feminist, as the Jackson picture suggests, and the 'seen' approach to it might well bring out some of the frictions and contradictions evident in her wide circle of friends, relatives and sitters. It should be added, finally, that the same image, and the 'seen' approach to it, need not be limited to poetry writing – it could equally be used to write a piece of prose fiction based on these real-life materials, or as the basis for a feature article in factual–creative mode. On creative writing courses, the activities set should leave scope for the widest possible range of responses.

6

English Now and Then

Studying English seems to us such a natural thing to do that we probably never pause to ask ourselves when it started or how recently it came to be as it is now. There is, indeed, no reason why the development of our own discipline should be a constant preoccupation, but it is a distinct liability to be completely unaware of its history. There is also the danger that our ignorance might lead us to imagine that all present disagreements within the subject are entirely new threats to the stability of the discipline, whereas they are quite often re-plays of past conflicts. Hence, some knowledge of where English came from can be useful in understanding the cultural and historical roots of our own convictions. The view of 'early English' offered here first considers the USA and the UK separately in the nineteenth century and then the two together from the post-First World War period onwards. This joint national focus necessarily entails some neglect of the specific lines of development of the subject elsewhere, particularly in British Commonwealth countries, and in non-Anglophone countries in and beyond Europe. Also, the 'UK' view offered here is really the view from England, and there are different readings of this history from elsewhere within Britain. Robert Crawford, for instance, in *The Scottish Invention of English Literature* (Cambridge University Press, 1998), argues that English Studies (which we can roughly define as the formal study of vernacular literature) began in eighteenth-century Scottish universities (with the appointment of Professors of Rhetoric), and was exported during the next century to the United States and elsewhere. His book, and those listed in the footnote, will help to provide a broader national and institutional perspective on these issues.[1]

Early English in America

In the United States 'English' became a distinct academic discipline towards the end of the nineteenth century.[2] In the earlier part of the century the 'humanities' section of the college curriculum was based on the study of Latin and Greek, taught by daily 'recitations' in which brief passages were set for study, and individual students were called on in class to translate a few sentences and answer questions about any grammatical difficulties contained in the passage. Courses were taught from a single textbook and 'classes' and 'recitations' were the whole of it – there were no lectures in which a broader view of the literature and culture under study might be offered and no seminars in which the meaning and significance of the set texts could be discussed. Graduate study in the mid-century period was virtually non-existent (there were said to be only eight graduate students in the whole of the USA in 1850) and the idea of 'majoring' in a discipline did not exist, so there were no 'electives' (that is, options), this being a later Harvard innovation. As Gerald Graff remarks, when lectures and written examinations were introduced later in the century at Harvard and Cornell, they were regarded as dangerous innovations, not as the essence of conservative pedagogy that they would be taken as today.

As the century progressed, literature in English was allowed a peripheral presence on the curriculum, and the method of study was directly based upon the 'philological' model imported from German universities, which is to say that it was heavily language based, involving the teasing out of the grammar of the text, the etymology

---

[1] Gauri Viswanathan, *Masks of Conquest: Literary Study and British Rule in India*, Columbia University Press, 1989; Rajeswari Sunder Rajan ed., *The Lie of the Land: English Literary Studies in India*, Oxford University Press, 1992; Balz Engler and Renate Haas, *European English Studies: Contributions Towards the History of a Discipline*, The English Association, for ESSE, 2000.
[2] I am drawing in this sub-section on Gerald Graff's fascinating and definitive book *Professing Literature: An Institutional History*, University of Chicago Press, 1987.

of the words used in it, the provenance of its images and the naming and classification of the literary tropes and devices employed by the authors. Highly specialist and scholarly though this kind of thing is, as a teaching routine it is more a protracted form of aversion therapy to literature than a way of interesting undergraduates in reading and enjoying major authors. By the 1880s there were annotated editions of major writers – Shakespeare, Spenser, Bunyan and so on – to cater for this dreary market. But there was also the growth of a different approach to literature teaching, one which was based on 'rhetoric' rather than philology. These courses would be taught from a 'reader' containing extracts of famous passages from major writers. Students would read them aloud and be coached in doing so with suitable weight and expression, or would memorize them for public performance. From this approach evolved the Harvard Composition course, in which students would write their own pieces on the same themes, putting into practice the lessons learned from the models. This, of course, is useful vocational training for the professions many of the male students would later take up, as politicians in local, State or Federal government, as attorneys, or as ministers of religion. But the 'rhetorical' approach and its emphasis on public speaking fell out of favour as the century progressed and as it came to be seen as stimulating a rather vacuous and tricksy style of public speaking. So the Harvard Composition course lost its oral element in 1873 and became a course in writing.

The 'rhetorical' (or non-philological) mantle was inherited by the 'generalists', as Graff calls them – teachers like Henry Wadsworth Longfellow, Charles Eliot Norton and James Russell Lowell at Harvard, who taught a much more generalized kind of literary appreciation. Generalists and philologists often co-existed uneasily in the same department (a familiar situation), but the drive towards the professionalization of the discipline was already well underway and the generalists, in spite of their often charismatic and popular lecturing style, were seen as too unsystematic in their methods to prevail in the era of the MLA (the Modern Language Association, founded in 1883, which became the discipline's main professional body in the USA). So the balance was finally tipped against philology only after the First World War, when an upsurge of patriotism inaugurated the formal study of American Literature and the emergent

'New Critics' of the 1920s and 1930s established for the first time a coherent rationale for the study of literature 'as literature' rather than as language.

Early English in the UK

At Oxford and Cambridge, England's only universities in the early nineteenth century, the syllabus was dominated by the study of Latin and Greek, just as in the American colleges. When University College London was founded in 1828 a professor of English Language and Literature was appointed; likewise at King's College, London, founded the following year, a professorial appointment was made in 1835 (it was the same person, Thomas Dale, who moved from one to the other). This meant that English could be studied at the new London University, though not as a separate degree subject until 1859. So began the spread of university English nationwide and beyond, as London's degrees could also be taken externally at university colleges (the predecessors of today's large civic universities) in many of the large industrial cities throughout Britain and overseas in countries under British influence or control.

In many ways, these new English degrees can be seen as part of a movement against elitism, since they were a form of education available to those not born into the privileged upper classes, whose male members would study Latin and Greek at their public schools and then go on to Oxford or Cambridge before sliding into comfortable careers in government, the judiciary, the armed forces or the universities themselves. English degrees were not available to women, to those not members of the Anglican Church and to those whose backgrounds, while not necessarily impoverished, were not privileged either. This is the heroic 'humanist' story of English Studies, in which English is a factor in the long struggle for social justice, as told in the few sources available until around the early 1980s.[3] An opposing view, which became dominant in the 1980s

---

[3] Such as Stephen Potter's *The Muse in Chains* (Cape, 1937, rpt Folcroft, 1973); E. M. W. Tillyard's *The Muse Unchained* (Bowes & Bowes, 1958) and D. J. Palmer's *The Rise of English Studies*, Oxford University Press, 1965.

during the 'theory wars', sees the spread of English as a middle-class conspiracy to maintain social stability by duping the aspirant lower-middle classes into acquiescence with the system that oppresses them. Rather than being given a share in the material wealth to which they are entitled, they are offered cultural 'wealth' instead, in the form of access to Shakespeare, Milton and similar cultural 'capital', tricking them into a belief that they are thereby becoming 'stake-holders' in society as currently structured.[4]

When the subject of English was belatedly established at Oxford in the 1870s, the 'price' exacted by the University was that it should be accompanied by systematic study of the history of the English Language and its antecedents – Old English, Middle English, Old Norse and so on. This form of study included the translation by students of major Old English texts like the epic poem *Beowulf* and the assumption was that 'hard' content like this would prevent English degrees from becoming a 'soft option' that involved little more than 'chatter about Shelley', in the notorious phrase used in the faculty debates by Edward Freeman, Oxford Professor of History.[5] Clearly, close textual study for its own sake was not then envisaged or imagined; this could hardly be necessary, the assumption was, since the texts were in the students' own language.

All this, it should be added, gives a strictly *university* perspective on the UK history of English. But it must be emphasized that English had long been an important part of the higher education curriculum outside universities, for instance, at institutes for the part-time education of working people and at training colleges for teachers. The 1870 Education Act, which established a national system of compulsory elementary education, also provided for the setting up

---

[4]For this version of the history of English see Brian Doyle's 'The Hidden History of English Studies' in *Re-Reading English*, Peter Widdowson ed., Methuen, 1982; Terry Eagleton's chapter 'The Rise of English' in his *Literary Theory: An Introduction*, Blackwell, 1983; and Chris Baldick's *The Social Mission of English Studies*, Oxford University Press, 1983.

[5]In an article in the *Contemporary Review* in 1887, Freeman explained that what he meant was speculative biographical chatter about *Harriet* Shelley, Shelley's first wife (who drowned herself in the Serpentine in Hyde Park when he abandoned her). Freeman's article is reprinted in a fascinating collection of key documents on 'early English' in the UK, *The Nineteenth-Century History of English Studies*, Alan Bacon ed., Ashgate, 1998.

of colleges to train teachers for these new state schools, and English was from the start a major subject on the syllabus at these. Whereas English was only grudgingly accepted on to the university syllabus, at training colleges it immediately assumed something like its mature twentieth-century character, with the emphasis on literary criticism and close reading. As David Shayer writes in a valuable book about the history of English teaching,

> in fact from 1905 until the mid-twenties, when the universities caught up with them, one can say that for scope, variety, correct priorities and proper study attitudes, the training colleges were offering some of the best English courses in the country.[6]

Early English in practice

Early English degrees did involve (among other things) close work on literary texts, but in a form which would probably seem rather puzzling to a modern student, for this was indeed English, but not as we know it, and the object of attention in close textual study was the language of the text *as language* (that is, as simile, metaphor, rhetorical device and so on) rather than the text's literary and thematic significance. In other words, the approach was very much influenced by philology. The following example of a set of model questions about a poem gives us a glimpse into the discipline in the first decade of the twentieth century, when it was in a hybrid or transitional phase. These questions show evident unease about merely philological text-work, but the compiler obviously has no very clear idea of what might be offered instead. The example is from David Shayer's book (p. 34, see note 32), and the questions are being recommended for the teaching of literature in schools rather than universities. They are indicative, all the same, of a period of uncertainty about how to teach literature in the gap between the growing disillusionment (from the turn of the century onwards) with the old historical–biographical–grammatical approach of the nineteenth century and the arrival of the 'close reading' pedagogy in the 1920s

---

[6]David Shayer, *The Teaching of English in Schools*, RKP, 1972, p. 31.

and 1930s. So for a class on Tennyson's poem 'Break, break, break', the following questions are recommended:

1. Give the derivation and etymology of the word 'break' as used in the poem.
2. Scan the line 'Break, break, break' and compare the metrical effect of 'Ding, dong, bell'.
3. Discuss the influence of geological strata on poetry.
4. Express in good prose the thought that the poet would fain have uttered, and indicate the reason of his disability.

This confusing set of questions is indicative of a laudable desire to move away from talking about authors rather than texts – there is no question here about Tennyson's life, nothing about how in 1842 the poem was 'made in a Lincolnshire lane at five o'clock in the morning, between blossoming hedges' (as Tennyson himself had helpfully explained). Nor is there anything about the unstated subject of the poem, the poet's friend Arthur Hallam, who had died in 1833. Instead, the poem is to be treated more or less 'on the page', so this session is, albeit confusingly, about 'reading literature as literature', with (for instance) attention drawn to the effects of the poem's rhythm and imagery (the 'geological strata').

On the other hand, looking at the etymology of a key word in the poem (as required by the first question) is very much a 'residual' element, harking back to an approach which is essentially 'philological' and obsessed with 'the naming of linguistic parts' in literary texts. All the close work demanded of students and pupils in the nineteenth century (and lingering on in many places into the second half of the twentieth) amounted to this, with the meaning and significance of the lines taken for granted. The bizarre third question about rock strata is prompted, presumably, by the mention of the 'cold grey stones' on which the sea breaks in the poem – but this is clearly either the subject of a PhD thesis, or else no subject at all. But perhaps even this question shows a desire to focus 'internally' on what the poem is *about* rather than (for instance) on what prompted it. The final question (about what the poet would fain express if he could) manifests the same desire, but anyone who could answer it would have the answer to life, the universe and everything, and would obviously have no need of poetry. (I am reminded of a friend's embarrassment when she was asked, during an English class at school, to explain exactly what Cleopatra meant, in Shakespeare's *Antony and Cleopatra* when she said 'Oh, my oblivion is a very Antony'.) Such direct demands upon us to unscrew the inscrutable were explicitly condemned by the American New Critics in their doctrine of the 'heresy of paraphrase', which held that the sentiments expressed in a poem were not usually precisely expressible in any other medium, not even 'good prose'.

Two revolutions and a 'turn'

From the post First World War period onwards, it is possible to see a major convergence in the course taken by the discipline on the two sides of the Atlantic. Though with different inflections, English was radically re-shaped by two revolutionary breaks with its own past. The first, starting in the 1920s in the UK and the 1930s in the USA, involves a new kind of radically text-based study, and the second, about fifty years later, during the 1970s, involves a major shift towards literary theory. In the UK, in the 'Cambridge revolution' of the 1920s, the discipline (to put it crudely) junked much of its own past, a past which had been about such things as the lives of authors, the literary history of genres and 'influences', the quasi-nationalistic celebration of the literary canon as the 'soul' of the nation and the rhetorical analysis of devices such as metaphor, simile and allusion within texts. This range of concerns had amounted to a kind of conflation of the American 'philological' and 'generalist' approaches. Instead, under the crucial influence of Cambridge figures like F. R. Leavis, I. A. Richards and William Empson, it now turned to a rather more austere mode of study, condemning most of the approaches previously available as (in various ways) 'external' to the text, because they studied primarily the political and social context from which the writing emerged, or the philosophical positions embodied in it, or the genre history of which it is a part. The 'Cambridge' mode of thinking radically sidelined all this and sought to focus exclusively on the text itself. The text became, as it were, an object caught in a searchlight, plunging its surrounding context into darkness, a darkness which the very presence of the searchlight rendered all the more impenetrable. The key books which set out the new approach were Richards' *Principles of Literary Criticism* (1924) and *Practical Criticism* (1929), and Empson's *Seven Types of Ambiguity* (1930).

The New Critical revolution of the 1930s and 1940s in the USA had essentially the same aims and effects, insisting upon a rigorous, text-based focus for literary study, the key books being John Crowe Ransom's *The New Criticism* (1941) and *Understanding Poetry* (1938) by Cleanth Brooks and Robert Penn Warren, who had both been students of Ransom's. The effect upon students of literature classes taught in this new way could be immensely powerful, producing an unforgettable classroom experience, which those who subsequently became teachers themselves often sought to reproduce for their own students. Here, for instance, is an account of the impact of this kind of teaching (the writer has just asked himself the question 'Where did the New Critical revolution take place?'):

As far as I am concerned the revolution took place in a classroom during my sophomore year. A man walked in and suddenly, instead of taking notes on [Robert] Frost's trip to England, we were asking why 'nothing gold can stay' – in the poem, in our lives, everywhere. He was a new critic. The old critics had talked about history or biography or the sources, without ever getting into the stories and poems. They were dull. The new man offered us live reading. He was not dull. What kept him from being dull (outside of his natural talents) was his motto: read literature as literature. The motto, we heard later, came from something called the New Criticism. It was forcing a change in classroom after classroom, not only on our floor but up on the graduate floor.[7]

---

[7]From Harold Swardson, *Fighting for Words: Life in the Postmodern University*, Verlag Die Blaue Eule, Essen, Germany, 1999, pp. 42–3. The quoted passage is in Chapter 2, 'The Heritage of the New Criticism'.

Pedagogic revolutions begin like this, when a teacher walks into a classroom and does something different, and the effects on those in the room can last a lifetime.[8]

The second revolution, which followed in both countries roughly fifty years later, was the arrival of literary theory of the 1970s (as will be discussed in detail in Chapter 8). This represented another radical shift by the discipline into new ground. The ground in question is the fourth area in the following list of five possible areas of primary interest within English Studies:

Area One: Traditional scholarship – historical, biographical, linguistic

Area Two: Close reading, with an implicit human value discovered in the act of reading

Area Three: The study of literature in its social and cultural contexts

Area Four: An 'international' approach to literary study, invoking structuralist, poststructuralist and other foreign critical modes

Area Five: The aligning of literature with other, more popular modes of signification, notably television and films[9]

Of course, this kind of model has to leave out all the fine shading: for instance, the traditional scholarship of Area One obviously did not stop dead in the 1920s, when area two became the dominant, but continued to be a force, now often called the 'old historicism', as represented in such books as E. M. W. Tillyard's *The Elizabethan World Picture* and Basil Willey's *The Seventeenth Century Background.* Likewise, the precise relationship between this 'old' historicism of then and the 'new' historicism of today and

---

[8]Of course, these procedures too could degenerate into routine, as Valentine Cunningham notes: 'Anyone who was a student in the early 1960s (like me)', he writes, 'will recall the sheer dullness of the by-then established New Critical routines suffocating readings in their affectionate but strangulating grip' (*Reading After Theory*, Blackwell, 2002, p. 38).

[9]This useful list (attributed to John Beer) is given in Bernard Bergonzi's account of the 'theory wars' of the 1980s, pp. 15–16 in the chapter 'Bitterness in the Eighties' in his book *Exploding English: Criticism, Theory, Culture*, Oxford University Press, 1990.

between the traditional study of 'sources and influences' on the one hand and current interests in forms of intertextuality on the other are matters which are difficult to tease out and cannot be addressed at all in such a broad-scale model. All the same, the model does give us a useful thumbnail diagram of the shifting territory of English Studies and it has the virtue of highlighting the simplicity of the 'two revolutions' notion of the discipline's twentieth-century history. Using this model, we can say that 'English' begins with a focus on Area One ('traditional scholarship'); the 1920s and 1930s revolution then switches it to Area Two ('text'); and the 1970s revolution to Area Four. Since those two revolutions, the discipline has taken a 'turn' to history again. Area Five (for the record) has tended to drift out of the English Studies area and into a realm of 'Cultural Studies', which is loosely affiliated with Media and Communications Studies and Sociology. It is easy to say, and easy to see, that a fully adequate study of literature in an ideal world would need to combine elements from areas one to four. It is equally obvious that this simply cannot be done on an undergraduate syllabus, and that is the source of nearly all the shifts and disagreements which have occurred throughout the history of the discipline. My argument in Chapter 8 will be that the 'theory re-revolution' of the 1970s had many elements of continuity with the 'close reading'/New Criticism revolution of the 1920s and 1930s. In other words, these two major revolutions are, as it happens, related: thus, close readers are always closet theorists, and theorists are always closet close readers, each belonging to what they would see as the Devil's party without knowing it (as Blake said of the Milton of *Paradise Lost*).

Coda: English here and there

English degree courses today are not, of course, the same worldwide, and being aware of the range and diversity of English degrees can help us to understand and appreciate the special characteristics of our own local version of English. Potentially, the differences are infinite, but these are some of the main ones. Firstly, if you take an English degree in a country where English is a foreign language (rather than in Anglophone countries like the USA, the

UK or Australia), then 'English' will mean language study as well as literary study, probably in more or less equal measure, with courses in phonetics, semantics, grammar, contemporary usage, and so on. So your study will be multi-disciplinary, in the sense that you will be studying both literature and language in a sustained way. Whether it will also be *inter*-disciplinary – that is, with real integration of the language and literature elements – will depend on where you are studying and where your teachers did their own training.

Secondly, if you take your degree in the USA, then you will receive systematic training in writing techniques (in courses with titles like 'Freshman Composition') to a far greater extent than anywhere else in the world. This will mostly occur in the early, pre-specialist stages of the degree, when you will also be taking introductory courses in other disciplines. These pre-specialist stages are also more extended in Scottish universities, and to a lesser extent in Wales, than they are in England. Thirdly, opportunities to do your own original creative writing as part of an English degree will be much greater in the USA, and more recently in the UK, than elsewhere in the world. In Europe outside the UK, the distinction between critical and creative work remains very firm, and the kind of writing students are required to undertake often places more emphasis on acquiring sound scholarly procedures of research and application than on the encouragement of independent critical judgement. Likewise, the style of teaching in the UK tends towards the 'dialogic', placing open seminar discussion at the centre of the syllabus, whereas elsewhere the tendency is often towards the 'monologic' or 'transmission' model of teaching, with lectures being seen as the key element in the learning process. This can sometimes have the result that to overseas eyes the UK student can seem bizarrely ungrounded in some of the basics. These differing cultural practices can become matters of great importance if you take part (as many students do today) in exchange semesters at universities abroad. Fourthly, the course itself will be longer 'elsewhere' than the standard three-year length of the British under-graduate degree. And finally, the 'inner canon' of writers regarded as the cornerstones of the syllabus will vary greatly across the globe, with black and women writers, for instance, being given a much more prominent place in the USA than elsewhere, and the syllabus in Europe tending to give more emphasis to the British writers of

ENGLISH NOW AND THEN

the 'realist' school from the 1950s and 1960s (Graham Greene, John Braine, Kingsley Amis, for instance) than is currently the case in the UK, where many courses seem to jump straight from modernism to postmodernism, that is, from (say) Joyce, Woolf and Eliot to Toni Morrison, Angela Carter and Hanif Kureishi.

When we think of reading literary texts, our primary image is still that of holding a bound book, with pages we can flick through. If a passage seems important we might underline it, or turn down the corner of the page, or write something in the margin. If interrupted, we can drop in a bookmark, or a supermarket till receipt, and slip the book into a pocket or handbag. Books, especially paperbacks, are the most portable and humane of objects, so endearingly 'user-friendly', in fact, that the subjects of old-fashioned autobiographies and memoirs often speak of their books as their 'friends'. Increasingly, though, our 'bookmarks' are electronic, and an ever-greater proportion of our reading is done on the screen rather than the page. So doing English today means not just reading the words on the page, but scrutinising the script on the screen as well. These 'online resources' are the subject of the next chapter.

7

Online and Digital English

A backward glance

When the first edition of this book was published in 2002 the UK was still in the dial-up era and there were only 200,000 subscribers to broadband. By 2011 there were 20 million. So when I returned to the topic of online English early in 2013, I expected to find that electronic resources for English had continued to expand. Instead, it seemed that many lively, original and helpful sites had disappeared. Others, formerly based in well-reputed individual universities, had been absorbed into bigger and bigger consortia, making them more difficult to track down, diluting their academic credentials and identity and rendering them surprisingly vulnerable to the reductions in public and charitable funding which followed the global financial crisis of 2008. One notable casualty is the Electronic Text Center of the University of Virginia Library, one of the pioneer collections of 'ETexts', founded in 1992 and lasting until 2007, when it was absorbed into the University's '"VIRGO" system, (its general catalogue for electronic texts and images).' We tend to assume that bigger means better and stronger, but in education, publishing and many aspects of creative cultures, the opposite seems to be the case.

Some of the most significant online casualties have been in the 'gateway' sites – those that provided links to other sites. The latest edition of the *MLA Handbook*, published in 2007, gives as prime examples of the 'gateway' the American Voice of the Shuttle (discussed later) and the British *Intute* Consortium, which was maintained by a grouping of seven major British universities. It was formed in 2006, bringing together eight existing mega-sites, which together covered the full range of university subjects. The humanities hub in this grouping, founded in 1985, was based at Oxford University and called 'Humbul'. It reviewed and catalogued humanities websites, and when it joined the *Intute* mega-mega-site in 2006 it must have seemed like progress, not least because there was solid-looking joint funding from the UK's research councils and university funding bodies. Then came the drastic post-crisis cuts in university funding; *Intute* lost its financial backing and was suspended and frozen in July 2011. It was agreed that the mothballed mega-consortium would remain available for a further three years, but what will happen to it then is unknown. A book, once published, exists for centuries, perhaps even for ever, but galactic-scale mega-sites are fortunate, it seems, to be granted an afterlife of three years. Parts of the *Intute* wreckage which may seem to have untapped commercial potential are being cherry-picked by other consortia, often themselves outfits of fathomless complexity, but whether that will improve their life expectancy remains to be seen. Anyway, all that is a prelude to this: if you still can, take a look at the Virtual Training Suite, which is (for now) a rescued segment of *Intute* (http://www.vtstutorials.co.uk/) [accessed 3 July 2013]. It has been taken over by an organization called TutorPro, which announces that it will be 'moving the whole project forward into the world of smartphones, tablets and mobile devices': scroll down and click on English and start your reading of this chapter by taking the excellent tutorial on using the internet for English Studies. It was compiled in 2010 by Professor Matthew Steggle of Sheffield Hallam University.

Databases and topic sites

The aim of this chapter is to show how using online resources can enrich the way we think and write about literature. It does not seek to provide a comprehensive guide. Your own library or subject department will doubtless have a help sheet (or several) giving you details of the sources available to you locally. Indeed, well-endowed institutions will have vast amounts of specialized online data on tap for their students, but there is an even vaster array that retains the kind of global open-accessibility which is still the essence of the internet. The availability of these electronic archives can to some extent counter the effects of over-stretched institutional budgets, of remoteness from major copyright libraries and even of differences in wealth between nations, giving many of us some of the privileges once enjoyed only by the best-placed and most successful scholars.

I see two kinds of 'traditional' online resource as being especially important. Firstly, there are full-text databases, which (as the name implies) mainly offer complete texts of literary works online, sometimes with appended critical and contextualizing material. Some of these contain electronic versions of all the books or plays by a given author or a selection of texts of a stated generic type (such as writing by nineteenth-century women). Usually, each work has a separate searchable file, with a 'consolidated' file containing all the books as a single, searchable document. This can be used like a concordance (see below) to search for (say) individual words right through the whole of the author's works. Secondly, there are topic-and-period sites, in which the emphasis is the other way round. That is, they mainly supply contextualizing and critical materials, but sometimes with appended texts. Some of these topic-and-period sites contain materials which aim to broaden the scope of literary study, introducing texts and materials on neglected, non-canonical writers and/or providing a wider range of historical, theoretical and contextualizing data than was hitherto widely available for the literary study of a given topic or period. But many of them – equally useful in a different way – simply focus on major canonical authors who have long formed the bedrock of literary studies, but aim to deepen our study by providing radical and innovative materials for teaching and studying them. Typically, both kinds exploit the technical range and capabilities of the internet to the full, often with a multi-media element (using sound, photographs, facsimiles, film-clips, multiple texts and so on). The bulk of the present chapter is a discussion of these two major kinds of online material, that is, the databases and the topic-and-period sites. But first, some words of warning.

Being choosy online and referencing

The quality of open-access online materials varies a great deal. I would recommend that you always look these gift horses in the mouth. Some attractive-looking sites will have been set up by naively enthusiastic amateurs whose knowledge and understanding may be limited. In general, it isn't difficult to distinguish the good from the less good, and a touch of internet snobbery can be helpful in doing so. In other words, if a site is maintained by an internationally recognized cultural institution (the Folger Library, let's say, or the British Council, or a well-known university), then it is worth making the assumption that the material is probably going to be useful and reliable. On the other hand, sites with the words 'my' or 'favourite' (or both together) in the title are often bad news and should be treated with caution ('My Edgar Allan Poe Page', 'My Favourite Romantic Poems' and the like). Misspellings, colloquial English and erratic punctuation are always danger signals (you see how snobbish I am suggesting you should be). Be cautious, in any case (that is, no matter how illustrious the source), when downloading quoted material from sites, whether the material be poems, stories or quotations from critics. If you intend to write about a downloaded poem or story in an essay, then you should, where possible, check the text for accuracy against the most recent critical edition of the author available in your university or college library. If the site doesn't indicate which edition of (say) a Coleridge, Wordsworth or Tennyson text is being reproduced, then you should assume that an out-of-copyright nineteenth-century printing is probably being used to reduce costs. This may differ slightly from the text in an up-to-date modern edition and will be without any of the new insights and discoveries modern textual scholarship may have supplied.

Be warned, too, that while web pages of the 'My Favourite Romantic Poems' type often reproduce poems in full, they are nearly always transcribed inaccurately and should not be relied upon. The inaccuracies may seem minor: for example, capitalization may not be faithfully followed; punctuation may be randomly modernized or ignored; spellings may be inconsistently updated, elisions expanded ('o'er' rendered as 'over', and so on); and stanza numbers switched from Roman ('iv') to Arabic ('4') or vice-versa. All these inaccuracies are individually minor, perhaps, but cumulatively they mean that you are not reading the poem the author published. In these matters, nothing less than pure, 100-per cent pedantry will do.

The online version of a poem or other literary text may be accompanied by notes supplied in hypertext form, which is to say that when you click on a particular word or phrase in the text you are taken to an explanatory note. If the site is reputable, these may well be useful and authoritative. Obviously, though, if you make use of the annotation, you should also credit the source. Generally, it is worth noting, the reputable sites tend to provide mainly scholarly material of various kinds rather than just critical material (or, at least, they use the latter predominantly to complement the former). For instance, a site might make available a range of poetry and documents from a given historical period that have never been published in modern reprints, or it might present data on manuscript variations in the writings of a well-known author, perhaps using actual facsimiles of the author's hand-written originals. A site which simply provided critical essays and opinion on (let's say) Coleridge or Shakespeare would not be offering anything different from what is widely available in academic books and journals, and we might wonder why the author hadn't sought that form of publication. There is some risk, too, that such material might seem to invite being lifted at the click of a button into one's own essays. There are, it is true, eminent scholars whose websites include some of their own complete critical essays. Usually, these essays are subsequently included in books, so the author's aim is presumably to make them available in the public domain in the (often) two- or three-year gap between composition and appearance in book form. All the same, doubts have been expressed about the wisdom of this practice, in the light of widespread anxieties about possible plagiarism in assessed work on English courses. So I will emphasize here that the rule for web material is the same as that for printed material – you need to acknowledge the source of anything you use.

Tutors are often asked what form the citation of web material should take. In the USA, the best source of guidance is the MLA (the Modern Language Association), which issues internationally accepted guidelines on style for books, articles and essays. Its *MLA*

Handbook for Writers of Research Papers (7th edition, 2009) is used worldwide. For the referencing of online sources, the most significant change in this edition is that the inclusion of the URL is now optional, presumably because it has proved to be the least stable element in online references and because most online searches are these days conducted using the name of the site and searching via Google or similar. By contrast, in the MHRA (Modern Humanities Research Association) system, which is used in the English-speaking world outside the USA, the URL is still a required element. Below is a bibliography reference for Voice of the Shuttle, first in MLA style (with the optional URL included), and then in MHRA:

> Liu, Alan ed. *Voice of the Shuttle.* University of California, Santa Barbara, English Department. October 2001. Web. 15 Jan 2013. http://vos.ucsb.edu/

The elements in this MLA-style reference are:

- the name of the organizer of the site, with surname first if this is an entry in a bibliography, but if it is a footnote, first name comes first, followed by the surname

- the title of the site, italicized – as for a book title – and followed by a full stop

- the source or location of the site, followed by a full stop

- the date the site was constituted in its present form, if known

- the medium of publication (in this case 'Web' as opposed to 'Print') followed by a full stop

- the date when the site was accessed (because, unlike books, websites are frequently modified or updated)

- finally, the optional URL is given, enclosed in angled brackets, and followed by a full stop.

All the information you require should be on the site's entry page, but if any of these items are missing, don't worry – just record what you can, keeping this basic shape. The person here designated 'ed.' may be variously described as the Director, the Project Manager, and so on.

In MHRA-style, the same reference would be as follows:

Liu, Alan ed., *Voice of the Shuttle* (University of California, Santa Barbara, English Department, October 2001) http://vos.ucsb.edu/ [accessed 15 January 2013] (p. 4).

The guiding principle for MHRA referencing of an electronic source is to follow the style for print referencing as closely as possible. Also, the reference as a whole is considered as a single sentence, so the elements are separated by a comma, not full stops, but no commas come between elements enclosed in brackets (whether these be the round, square, or the angle type), and the whole reference ends with a full stop. So this time the elements in the reference are:

- the name of the organizer of the site, followed by a comma, with the surname first if this is an entry in a bibliography, but if it is a footnote, first name comes first, followed by the surname

- the title of the site, italicized, as for a book title, and followed, within round brackets, by the source or location of the site, followed by a comma, followed by the date the site was constituted in its present form, if known

- this is followed, within angle brackets, by the URL, which is obligatory in MHRA style

- then, enclosed in square brackets, comes the date when the site was accessed, with the name of the month not abbreviated, but given in full

- finally, if there is a page or section number, this is given in round brackets, as shown, and the reference concludes with a full stop.

Note that the MHRA Style Guide (3rd edn, 2013) can be bought as a print publication or downloaded free in the form of a pdf. file from http://www.mhra.org.uk/Publications/Books/StyleGuide/index. html [accessed 3 July 2013]. Likewise, a substantial part of the *MLA Handbook for Writers of Research Papers* used to be available free on the MLA website (as was the case a decade ago when I wrote the original version of this chapter), but for the seventh edition the electronic version is only accessible by purchasers of the print version.

Going through the gate

To get a general sense of what resources for English are available online, you need to use one of the main 'gateway' sites, which contain links to large numbers of domains. Perhaps the most widely used of these for humanities subjects is 'The Voice of the Shuttle', http://vos.ucsb.edu/index.asp [accessed 3 July 2013], which was set up in 1994 and is headed by Romantics scholar Alan Liu from the English Department of the University of California, Santa Barbara. The 'VoS', as everyone calls it, is without rival for its ultra-clear structure and its range of coverage.

On arriving at the VoS entry page you will see the scope of the enterprise from the three lists running down the left-hand side of the screen, headed respectively 'Contents', 'Resources' and 'Guide to VoS'. Under 'Contents' there is a succinct list of broad headings for the whole range of humanities disciplines, from Archaeology to Religious Studies. The most useful ones from the English Studies viewpoint are 'General Humanities Resources', at the head of the list, then the 'mega-heading' 'Literature (in English)' and also the much-used 'Literary Theory' link (so much used that some have imagined that VoS is solely a dedicated literary theory site). If you click on 'Literature (in English)' you have the options of either using the very broad literary categories in the summary panel at the top right of the screen – 'Anglo Saxon and Medieval', 'Romantics', 'Victorian', 'Contemporary (British and American)', 'Minority Literatures' and so on – or else browsing your way down the main list. If you click on (say) 'Victorian' in the summary panel you will be taken to another vast list, including both broad, generic sites (such as 'The Victorian Sonnet' and 'The Victorian Women Writers Project') and specific sites on individual writers from Arnold to Wilde.

Though it is no longer accessible via VoS, I would like to draw your attention to Dino Franco Felluga's popular Introductory Guide to Critical Theory, http://www.cla.purdue.edu/english/theory/ [accessed 3 July 2013]. I have long found this a very useful item, and the practical examples of theorized readings are succinct and convincing, even though Felluga's coverage of the field of literary theory is selective, being restricted to the categories of Gender & Sex, Marxism, Narratology, New Historicism, Postmodernism and Psychoanalysis. The virtue of the site is that it is based upon the simple, practical and effective formula of using the theoretical ideas in relation to two short literary texts (these being a pair of sonnets from Edmund Spenser's *Amoretti* sonnet sequence of 1595). For other theory resources, go back to the home page of VoS and click on 'Literary Theory' in the Contents menu on the left-hand side. In the screen this takes you to, click on the first item, which is 'General Theory Resources'; in the first sub-menu, click on 'Online Literary Resources' (a list maintained by Jack Lynch of Rutgers University), which is near the end; then click on 'Modern Literary Theory', which takes you to a site called 'Introduction to Modern Literary Theory' at http://www.kristisiegel.com/theory.htm [accessed 3 July 2013]. This is a useful resource set up by Kristi Siegel of Mount Mary College, Milwaukee. It is another undergraduate introduction to literary theory, and it too has the virtue of simplicity and good design. It doesn't do applications, but the overall coverage is broader than Felluga's, so it offers a useful complement to his material, giving clear definitions, a basic bibliography on each theory and a series of further links. In my experience, material of this kind, which is actually written for students, is more useful than the massive printed 'readers' on which many literary theory courses are based. Sites like these show the advantages of clarity, simplicity and good design over the gimmicky, graphic-heavy presentations which the very capabilities of the web itself often seem to stimulate.

In Chapter 10, I mention that the word 'silence', or 'silenced', is used thirty-four times in Jane Austen's *Mansfield Park*. It would be naïve of me to hope that you will be amazed at my industry and dedication to duty in re-reading the novel from cover to cover, listing occurrences of this single word in a notebook. Of course, I obtained the information by looking up the novel in a full-text online database. I used the Electronic Literature Foundation (ELF) version of *Mansfield Park*, which is in the 'Works of Jane Austen' section of the site, http://www.thegreatbooks.org/ [accessed 3 July 2013]. The statement on the entry page for the ELF announces that its mission is 'to produce advanced electronic texts to be used by students, scholars, and admirers of literature around the world. Our goal is to provide free access to a variety of texts from world literature available in several languages and/or editions, with forums for communication regarding these works, for all types of readers.' Works available (in 2013) include the whole of Shakespeare, Chaucer, Dante, Poe, etc. I simply entered the word 'silence' in the search box for *Mansfield Park*, and seconds later a list of the 34 occurrences came up on the screen, each complete with chapter and line number:

Search Results

Terms entered: **Silence**

34 Matches		
Chapter	Line	Text
2	96	Bertram's silence, awed by Sir Thomas's grave looks,
6	206	It did not suit his sense of propriety, and he was silenced,
6	297	but his determined silence obliged her to relate her
9	197	The chapel was soon afterwards left to the silence and stillness
9	374	A general silence succeeded. Each was thoughtful.
10	64	This was followed by a short silence. Miss Bertram
10	177	After an interval of silence, "I think they might as well
10	181	This could not be denied, and Fanny was silenced.
13	304	And Edmund, silenced, was obliged to acknowledge that the

34 Matches		
Chapter	Line	Text
14	125	A short silence followed. Each sister looked anxious;
14	243	A short silence succeeded her leaving them; but her brother
15	265	Miss Crawford was silenced, and with some feelings of resentment
17	95	She either sat in gloomy silence, wrapt in such gravity
18	147	but her diligence and her silence concealed a very absent,
19	195	where nothing was wanted but tranquillity and silence.
20	44	silenced as ever she had been in her life; for she
21	90	"And I longed to do it – but there was such a dead silence!
25	88	contrast to the steady sobriety and orderly silence of
26	36	some minutes' silence to be settled into composure.
28	251	want to be talked to. Let us have the luxury of silence."
30	105	As soon as her eagerness could rest in silence,
30	234	They will be angry," he added, after a moment's silence,
32	168	silence, "that you mean to _refuse_ Mr. Crawford?"
33	214	In spite of his intended silence, Sir Thomas found himself

34 Matches		
Chapter	Line	Text
33	234	for the strictest forbearance and silence towards
33	281	in the course of eight years and a half. It silenced her.
34	351	hoped to silence him by such an extremity of reproof,
35	238	silence and abstraction. Edmund first began again –
37	141	a great talker, she was always more inclined to silence
41	4	his silence, between which her mind was in fluctuation;
41	259	Fanny was doubly silenced here; though when the moment
44	11	and persuaded myself that you would understand my silence.
45	164	long silence, and behave as if you could forgive me directly.
47	119	was not to be silenced. The two ladies, even in the short

34 Matches found.

Source: http://www.thegreatbooks.org/library/texts/austen/mansfield/index.html

I can then see whether there is any pattern in the occurrences – for example, are they clustered in particular parts of the book? (They don't seem to be – the chapter numbers in which the word 'silence' occurs seem to spread fairly evenly). To look closely at any specific example, I have merely to click on the relevant line number in the second column, and the screen will show the word, highlighted in its textual context, so that I can look for any peculiarities or special features in the way the word is being used.

For major authors like Austen, comprehensive textual data has long been available in the form of massive print volumes called 'concordances'. A concordance of Shakespeare, for instance, would list all occurrences of specific words right across the Shakespeare canon. In pre-electronic days, concordances required massive labour to produce, and they only existed for the most major writers and texts (Shakespeare, The Bible, Tennyson and so on). Their great size and unwieldiness made them library-only items, and years of usage could reduce them to a sorry state of dilapidation. Their limitations were, in summary, their great cost, their zero portability, the difficulty of correcting or updating them for many years once they had been published and their general inflexibility – they could only supply the needs their compilers had anticipated.[1]

As an excellent example of a single-author, full-text database, we can take the Internet Shakespeare Editions site, http://internet shakespeare.uvic.ca/ [accessed 3 July 2013], which is run by the University of Victoria, Canada, and provides scholarly, fully edited and fully refereed texts of Shakespeare's plays and poems. Each play is a separate file, but by ticking 'All Plays' before making a search you can track occurrences of a given word right across the canon. However, working on the vocabulary of (say) *Troilus and Cressida* alone, we can insert (let's say) the word 'war' in the 'Search for' dialogue box, then click 'Selected works' and then *Troilus and Cressida*: the search tells us that the word occurs fifteen times in the play. But that is just raw data. What, you might ask, is the point of doing such a search (other than because we can)? How could data like this be used in the course of constructing a critical argument about the play? Again, the answer is that we are looking for patterns: for instance, which character in the play is the most frequent user of the word 'war', and is it always used with reference to military matters, or are there cases where it is used metaphorically, with love being seen as a kind of warfare? Hence, we would be using the full-text database to provide data for interpretive argument. Of course, this could have

---

[1] As an example, see John Bartlett's *A Complete Concordance to Shakespeare*. This is published by Palgrave and was last reprinted in 1997. At a little under 2,000 pages, it has remained in print for over a century (original publication was in 1894), and it was priced at £185 in 2001.

been done by a diligent reader using a printed text, but it would have taken much longer, and perhaps, having expended so much time on it, we would be tempted to over-invest in the results of the search. It would be interesting, too, to know whether the word 'war' is used as frequently in other Shakespeare plays which entwine the love and war themes as this one does, for example, *Othello* and *Anthony and Cleopatra*. A quick search provides the data and the examples: 'war' occurs seven times in *Othello*, fourteen in *Troilus and Cressida* and twenty-one in *Anthony and Cleopatra*. In the last of these, the only text is the First Folio of 1623, and therefore the text is in the original spelling, so a search on 'war' produces no results, as the Elizabethan spelling was 'warre'. By contrast, the word 'love' occurs seventy-three times in *Othello*, fifty-seven in *Troilus and Cressida* and thirty-nine (as 'loue' – no hits are recorded if you search for 'love') in *Anthony and Cleopatra*. The ratio of occurrences of 'love' and 'war' in these plays is potentially revealing, as is their distribution throughout the plays and among the various characters.

Four sites with foresight

In using online materials, many scholars are looking not just for something more but for something different – that is, for ways of combining and synthesising information and materials which were not available to us in the pre-electronic age. Those who came of age in the digital era (the 'digital natives', as they are sometimes known, though presumably not by themselves) take such possibilities for granted and expect more than just ease of access to material, which would be much the same in print form. So I will mention here four sites that in my working experience have offered possibilities and procedures which seemed distinctly futuristic when I first stumbled upon them and have retained their sense of novelty so that I still feel when I use them that I am merely exploring their possibilities.

The first of the four is the Victorian Web http://www.victorianweb. org [accessed 3 July 2013], which provides a wealth of material on Victorian culture, but based on 'intermedia' principles which pre-date the internet and go back to the site's origins in 1987. The idea is that it is based on the notion of making connections, so that instead of accessing entire books or complete articles, material from many such sources is 'digested' and then used in a wide range of different juxtapositions. For instance, I made use of the site in writing about Tennyson's 'The Lady of Shalott' for chapter four: searching on the title of the poem brings up a series of headings, beginning with the text of the poem itself, then 'The landscape around the lady's tower', with links to click showing Victorian representations of the scene, a heading for weaving and embroidering, and for the literary and painterly motif of the lady by a window, as well as other links to analogue motifs elsewhere in Tennyson's work (such as in 'Elaine') and to the influence and effect of the work elsewhere in Victorian literature. I also used the Victorian Web in a documentary poetry project, which drew upon accounts of the building of the railways in Dick Sullivan's book *The Navvies* (Coracle Press, 1983). At several points in the book Sullivan quotes his own father, who became a navvy in 1903. The book, and its marvellous photographs, is repro-duced in full, with added material, including a 2006 retrospect by the author. The book can be read on-line chapter by chapter, but links to individual chapters will also come up in response to various searches, for example, those about Victorian engineering, or the itinerant way of life, or funeral practices. So each search made on this site brings up a cross-section of themed materials, sources, images, sounds and performances.

Working on the Victorian period in a 'canon-breaking spirit might also take us to the Victorian Women Writers Project http://www. indiana.edu/~letrs/vwwp [accessed 3 July 2013], which is a highly rated and attractive resource set up in 1995 by Indiana University. The original aim of this site was to make more widely available the texts of 'lesser-known British women writers of the 19th century', but that brief has now been extended beyond Britain, and the material collected includes 'anthologies, novels, political pamphlets, religious tracts, children's books, and volumes of poetry and verse drama'. I click on the word 'Authors' on the entry page, and can now either scroll through the list, looking for something that seems potentially relevant to what I wish to write about, or else click on the appropriate letter of the alphabet if I am looking for a particular author. In this case, I click on 'L' to bring up 'Levy, Amy (1861–89)', having heard about this writer at academic conferences, but without finding much of her work currently in print. Four items of hers are available, so I go back to the entry page and click on the first, 'A Ballad of Religion and Marriage', and then I am through to this highly subversive brief text (twenty four lines in all), which was crudely printed in twelve copies for private circulation around 1915, probably by a suffragette group, more than a quarter of a century after the young author's tragic death:

A BALLAD OF RELIGION AND MARRIAGE

Swept into limbo is the host
    Of heavenly angels, row on row;
The Father, Son, and Holy Ghost,
    Pale and defeated, rise and go.
The great Jehovah is laid low,
    Vanished his burning bush and rod—
Say, are we doomed to deeper woe?
    Shall marriage go the way of God?

Monogamous, still at our post,
    Reluctantly we undergo
Domestic round of boiled and roast,
    Yet deem the whole proceeding slow.
Daily the secret murmurs grow;
    We are no more content to plod
Along the beaten paths—and so

    Marriage must go the way of God.
Soon, before all men, each shall toast
    The seven strings unto his bow,
Like beacon fires along the coast,
    The flame of love shall glance and glow.
Nor let nor hindrance man shall know,
    From natal bath to funeral sod;
Perennial shall his pleasures flow
    When marriage goes the way of God.

Grant, in a million years at most,
  Folk shall be neither pairs nor odd—
Alas! we sha'n't be there to boast
  "Marriage has gone the way of God!"

Facsimiles of the printed text are given, and the effect is to give the web-user a powerful sense of immediacy of contact with a long-ago struggle against oppressive social forces. Strangely, this most up-to-date of media can give us a strong feeling of being in direct contact with the literary past.

What of online study materials (other than full texts) on major canonical authors? What can online resources do for the most familiar canonical texts, the ones which are taught daily in schools and universities worldwide? Often these sites have an extremely precise focus, sometimes not just on a single author or even a single work, but on *part* of a work, perhaps centred upon a specific scene in a play, or on the different textual and manuscript versions of a single poem. I will take two renowned sites as examples. The first, called *Hamlet on the Ramparts* http://shea.mit.edu/ramparts [accessed 3 July 2013], is 'a collection of texts, images, and films related to Hamlet's first encounter with the ghost'. This resource is (says its home page) 'a public website designed and maintained by the MIT Shakespeare Project in collaboration with the Folger Shakespeare Library, and other institutions. The aim is to provide free access to an evolving collection of texts, images, and film relevant to Hamlet's first encounter with the Ghost (Act 1, Scenes 4 and 5).' The site, then, contains a range of materials, including the various versions of the text, early editions, prompt books, a century and half of paintings of the scene and much about the eighty or more extant film versions of the play – indeed, one of the first films ever made was a film version of *Hamlet*.

There are also detailed lessons and tutorials. One of these, for instance, contains a fine suggestion about Hamlet's 'dram of evil' speech (I.iv.13–38), which occurs just before the ghost's entrance in Act 1 Scene 4. In the speech, Hamlet (having heard the sound of drunken late-night partying floating up from the castle below) talks obsessively about defects of character, and especially about people whose character is ruined by 'the stamp of one defect' (I.iv.31). In such cases, whatever virtues the person has are tainted by that one vice, since (it ends) 'The dram of evil / Doth all the noble substance often dout / To his own scandal' (I.iv.36–8). Here, 'dout' may mean 'douse' or 'dim', or 'doubt' in the sense of 'call into doubt' or 'render doubtful'. The tutorial idea suggests that before starting to read out the speech to a class a dropper is used to release a single drop of red food dye into a glass of water, and as the speech unfolds (in all its slow, syntactic tortuosity) the red colouration will gradually suffuse the whole glass. The class is then asked to talk about the connection between the speech and the drop of dye in the glass. We don't have to do this, or see it done, to feel the force of this powerful image – this is effective even as a pedagogic theatre of the mind which finds a living image to illuminate the verbal image of the speech. Even if we still don't quite understand the *precise* meaning of every word in lines 36–8 about the 'dram of evil' (a 'dram', of course, is a small drop), we undoubtedly now understand the *significance* of what it says.

Another section of material on the site concerns the various films of *Hamlet*, especially in connection with the long tradition of the role of Hamlet being played by a woman. But in one film version Hamlet is played not just *by* a woman but *as* a woman, namely the 1920 film with the Danish star Asta Nielsen in the title role. Nielson was an international icon – the Shakespeare scholar Ann Thompson is quoted to the effect that 'by 1914, she was the most popular film star in Germany and was known all over the world. There were "Asta" cigarettes, pastries and hair-styles in Germany, and Asta Nielsen cinemas in San Francisco, Dusseldorf and Nagasaki. Her picture decorated trenches on both sides during World War I.'[2] This was a silent film, of course, and Nielsen played Hamlet as a woman forced to pretend she is a man for the sake of the crown. The interpretive written frames within the film explain that it uses Edward P. Vining's thesis in *The Mystery of Hamlet* (1881), that Hamlet was not only a 'womanly man' but 'in very deed a woman, desperately striving to fill a place for which she was by nature unfitted'. The material examines the implications of all this, using a series of stills from the film alongside quotations from film-theorist Laura Mulvey on the male

---

[2] In *Shakespeare the Movie*, ed. Lynda E. Boose and Richard Burt, Routledge, 1997, p. 216.

and female gaze. The full extract from the film (nine minutes) can be run using 'RealPlayer', and this is then broken down into a series of short clips with commentary – click on the image of Nielsen (http://shea.mit.edu/ramparts/collections/films/index.htm) [accessed 3 July 2013]. My own brief comments here have touched upon aspects of only two of the items on the site, but they indicate, I hope, how such online material can revitalize the study of a text so familiar that studying it may threaten to lapse into pedagogic routine.

The last site I wish to consider is an Oxford University resource called The First World War Poetry Digital Archive, available at http://www.oucs.ox.ac.uk/ww1lit/ [accessed 3 July 2013]. The best introduction to the enormous amount of material on this site is to click on the 'Archive Showreel' panel in the centre of the entry screen, which takes you to a six-minute introductory video on YouTube. I will focus here on just one element, the Tutorials, which are at http://www.oucs.ox.ac.uk/ww1lit/education/tutorials [accessed 3 July 2013]. There are several seminars in this strand, the first being a general introduction to First World War poetry, using the selection of poems provided. The second seminar is a close study of a single poem, Isaac Rosenberg's 'Break of Day in the Trenches', first published in 1916 in the famous Chicago journal *Poetry*. (Rosenberg was from the working-class Jewish community of the East End of London and was killed during a night patrol in April 1918.) The third tutorial is 'An Introduction to Manuscript Studies' and its aim is 'to introduce editorial practices and manuscript studies'. The student is asked to prepare a text of Wilfred Owen's poem 'Dulce et Decorum Est' for an edition of his work. Owen was killed on 4 November 1918, exactly a week before the end of the war (his parents received the news of his death on Armistice Day). The tutorial involves study of 'the primary sources (the manuscripts which contain the poem), the choice of a base manuscript, collation of manuscript variants, and the production of your own 'edition' of the poem. The poem survives in four different manuscript versions (two at Oxford, two in the British Library), and facsimiles of any two can be put on the screen at the same time, then scrolled down together so that the variations can be noted. We see, for instance, that in the first manuscript the poem is dedicated 'To a certain poetess', in the second it has no dedication, in the third the dedication is 'To Jessie Pope etc' (Pope had published some rather facile patriotic verse, which Owen had seen) and in the fourth the dedication 'To Jessie Pope' is deleted and 'To a certain poetess' is substituted. The first line, 'Bent double, like old beggars under sacks', was originally 'Hunched double' in one version, and the same version has 'rag & bone men' instead of 'beggars'. Line eight of the poem caused the most trouble. The soldiers in the poem are so tired that they are 'deaf even to the hoots / Of' falling shells', and the phrase 'Of' falling shells' is rewritten in various ways in the different drafts, the other three versions being 'Of tired, outstripped five-nines that dropped behind', 'Of gas shells dropping softly that dropped behind' and 'Of disappointed shells that dropped behind'. Of course, the effect differs greatly each time the line is changed: the precise description of the shells as 'five-nines' shows an officer's necessary technical knowledge of the calibre of shells and his ability to recognize them and take appropriate action when possible. The second version, in which the 'five-nines' are just 'gas shells', is very much a 'plain-language' rendering, with the repetition of 'drop' perhaps suggesting the tiredness referred to. The final version is distinctly more fanciful – the shells are 'disappointed' because they overshoot their targets and fail to achieve their death-dealing destiny. Which version is best? Which is the true voice of the poem? It is the editor's difficult task to decide, and the seminar takes us in the most vivid way into both the dilemmas of the editorial process and the creative struggle of the poet in the act of composition. Owen sent one of the versions of the poem to his mother with the intriguing remark that it was 'not finished, but not private'. It remains suspended in this limbo for evermore. Again, then, an imaginatively constructed website seems to bring back the past with extraordinary vividness, and that is one of the attributes of online English at its best.

PART TWO

Progressing in English

8

Literary Criticism and Literary Theory

A brief history of criticism

Let's begin by underlining a distinction between literary theory and literary criticism. The former asks questions about literature in very broad terms, questions like 'What is it?' 'How does it work?' 'What is it for?' 'Whose interests does it serve?' Literary criticism, on the other hand, is about the interpretation and appreciation of individual literary works, so these larger questions (necessarily) are often left to one side. Contrary to general belief in Britain and America, literary theory came before literary criticism. That is, since ancient times, literature has more usually been thought of from a broad theoretical perspective rather than in critical (that is, text-specific) terms. The heyday of criticism is really just a brief 'window' of about fifty years in the twentieth century (roughly 1920–70), interrupting a tradition of critical theory which had started with Aristotle's *Poetics* in Ancient Greek times, and includes works such as Longinus *On the Sublime* in the Roman period, Sidney's 'Apology for Poetry' in the Renaissance, Shelley's 'Defence of Poetry' in the Romantic period and T. S. Eliot's essay 'Tradition and the Individual Talent' in the twentieth century. All these are representative of a kind of writing which is best described as 'literary theoretical' rather than 'literary critical', since they discuss ideas about literature's purposes, effects, procedures, and status, but without primary focus on the interpretation of individual literary texts. However, in Britain and America in the period roughly from the 1920s to the 1970s, literary debate was dominated (though to a greater extent in the former than the latter) by the interpretive discussion of individual literary works, in other words by literary criticism. Then, from the 1970s onwards, the dominance in professional discussions of literature again shifted back to the theoretical, in debates instigated by such figures as Roland Barthes, Michel Foucault and Jacques Derrida, which tended to centre upon questions of a philosophical, historical or linguistic nature.

British and American criticism – key differences

The earliest examples of the literary-critical, or text-specific, approach were Samuel Johnson's *Lives of the Poets* and *Prefaces to Shakespeare* in the eighteenth century and Coleridge's discussion of Wordsworth's writing in *Biographia Literaria* in the early part of the nineteenth. It is usual to distinguish two main varieties of criticism in the fifty-year 'window' from the 1920s to the 1970s when text-specific or author-specific criticism of this kind was dominant, these being British 'close reading' (also called 'practical criticism') and American 'New Criticism'. The British practice stemmed from empirical work on the evaluation of literary texts at Cambridge in the 1920s, as described in I. A. Richards' *Practical Criticism: A Study of Literary Judgement* (1929). Richards' pupil William Empson in his book *Seven Types of Ambiguity* (1930) exemplified the practice of minute verbal scrutiny of literary texts, while T. S. Eliot's *The Varieties of Metaphysical Poetry* (the Clark Lectures at Cambridge, 1926–7) and F. R. Leavis's *New Bearings in English Poetry* (1932) began the process of revising and supplementing the existing canon of literary works on the basis of detailed textual re-assessments. The British variant of literary criticism, then, was characterized by, firstly, a predominant interest in the *evaluation* of literary texts, secondly, by its methodological implicitness – that is, it refused to spell out as general principles the reasons for its exclusion from consideration of matters concerned with historical or biographical contexts, or with the reader's response to the text – and thirdly, by its moralism, that is, its valuing of a literary work primarily for its embodiment of humane values rather than for aesthetic qualities in the narrow sense.

The American version of literary criticism, known as the 'New Criticism', takes its name from John Crowe Ransom's book *The New Criticism* (1941) and is also seen in Cleanth Brooks' *The Well Wrought Urn: Studies in the Structure of Poetry* (1949) and in W. K. Wimsatt's *The Verbal Icon: Studies in the Meaning of Poetry* (1954). It was characterized by the opposite of the British qualities, that is, firstly, it was predominantly interested in the *interpretation* of literary texts, secondly, it was methodologically explicit – that is, it valued explicit programmatic statements about method (such as notions like 'The Intentional Fallacy' and 'The Affective Fallacy' [see the essays with these titles in *The Verbal Icon*] which laid out the grounds for excluding from consideration the author's intentions and biography, or the reader's reactions to the text) – and thirdly, it valued a literary work primarily for formal and aesthetic reasons, such as the extent to which it maintained a fine balance of opposed qualities and brought them into a unity of synthesis.

The British interest in textual *evaluation* meant that key essays frequently took the form of comparisons between two texts which dealt with similar subject matter, the purpose of the comparison being to establish grounds for ranking one text as superior to the other. Well-known examples include Leavis's essay comparing Shakespeare's *Antony and Cleopatra* with Dryden's version of the same story, *All for Love* (in his book *The Living Principle* [1975]), and the essay 'Reality and Sincerity: Notes in the Analysis of Poetry' (*Scrutiny* XIX, 2, 1952–3, pp. 90–8), in which he compares poems on bereavement by Emily Brontë and Thomas Hardy. Likewise, the original experiments recorded in I. A. Richards' *Practical Criticism* were designed to expose the uncertainty with which even well-educated readers make such comparative literary 'judgements' (a key word for the British practitioners of criticism).

What Leavis as a critic most valued in literature was the quality of 'enactment', in which the words 'embodied' the sense, rather than simply indicating or 'describing' it. In the *Antony and Cleopatra* essay he asserts that 'Shakespeare's verse seems to enact its meaning ... while Dryden's is merely descriptive eloquence', and the same distinction is used to delineate the difference between Donne and the Romantics on the one hand and the work of the Victorian poets on the other. He praises Donne and Keats in *Revaluation* (1936) for 'the liveliness of enactment – something fairly to be called dramatic', contrasting this quality with the 'decorative-descriptive' style of Tennyson. But for Leavis, it should be emphasized, 'enactment' is a linguistic strength with a *moral* foundation, for it is not a matter merely of technique, but of a lived and 'felt life' embodied in the very texture of the language. Thus, it is because Hardy has *been* bereaved, combined with his excellence as a poet, that his poetic language has this quality – the latter alone could not ensure it. Thus (in 'Reality and Sincerity'), 'Hardy's poem is seen to have a great advantage in *reality* [which is to say] that it represents a profounder and completer sincerity.' By contrast, Brontë is 'dramatizing herself in a situation such as she has clearly not known in actual experience'. Yet the piece also illustrates the characteristic weaknesses of the 'closed' close reading approach (see below), for Leavis ignores contextualising issues, treating the two poems as if both were personal lyrics, whereas Brontë's is actually part of a historical saga, spoken by a 'character' and written in a manner appropriate to formal public declamation, rather than being presented as the product of private, meditative inwardness.

'Intrinsic' and 'extrinsic' criticism

The American tendency towards greater explicitness of methodo-logical principle led to a number of useful distinctions, such as that between 'intrinsic' and 'extrinsic' criticism. The former is text-based, intensive and analytical, while the latter is context-based, extensive and discursive, making use of (for instance) historical information, knowledge of generic conventions, biographical data and so on. F. W. Bateson's notion of 'contextual reading' (in opposition to 'close reading') aimed to synthesize the two modes of intrinsic and extrinsic approaches. A more recent formulation along similar lines distinguishes between 'unseen close reading' (or '*closed* close reading', as we might call it) and 'seen close reading' (or '*open* close reading'). The former is the textual practice that rules out of play the use of any external data, and limits the critic strictly to 'the words on the page'. The latter, by contrast, reads the text closely, but alongside and open to a range of necessary reference material. This formulation attempts to cope with the paradox that the interdict placed by dominant critical practice on the use 'external' data took root at precisely the time when the most prestigious literature (such as the modernist works of Eliot, Pound, Joyce and Woolf) increasingly required copious 'external' annotation to explain the significance of allusions, proper names, references to historical figures, mythological parallels and so on.

Other objections to the critical practice of minute and intense verbal scrutiny might be listed as follows: firstly, it really only works at its best for the short lyric poem – it cannot do so, even for poetry, when the scale is epic and the mode primarily narrative. Secondly, for obvious reasons, it can never be a sufficient tool for the novel, given the vast scale of the text in comparison with the nature of the critical method – a close reading of the average Victorian novel would be like trying to bring in a grain harvest using only a pair of nail scissors. In practice, the main critical resource used by close readers of novels is to 'poeticize' the text, giving exaggerated importance, for instance, to the novelist's use of verbal imagery. Thirdly, the method is inappropriate to drama, except verse drama, but even here the 'poeticization' of the text is, again, often very marked, so that plays tend to become a static tableau of images – Leavis's praise of *Antony and Cleopatra* involves treating famous speeches as if they were free-standing lyric poems rather than moments in a drama. Fourthly, the linguistic data identified in the close reading process often remains less than convincingly integrated into the flow of critical argument – identifying an alliterative or assonantal pattern in a poem is the easy part; linking this convincingly to a reading and interpretation of the poem as a whole is the real challenge.

'Theory has landed'

'Literary theory', or just 'theory', is a loose portmanteau term for a series of new approaches to literature which emerged strongly in the USA, Britain and elsewhere from the 1970s onwards, challenging the dominance of both UK 'practical criticism' and American 'New Criticism'. The term 'theory', when used in connection with literature, includes structuralism, poststructuralism, deconstruction, feminism, Marxism, New Historicism, Postcolonialism, Postmodernism, literary linguistics, 'Queer Theory' and ecocriticism.[1] By the 1990s the study of theory had become the most compulsory topic on English degree courses, but how exactly did this spectacular rise come about? Because several of the major literary theorists were French (by nationality and/or culture), literary theory is usually regarded as a kind of French 'invasion' of lands which had hitherto been content to practice literary criticism and close reading, without ever raising their heads from the 'words on the page' to look around at the wider intellectual and social context of literature and literary study. But this view is, at best, a caricature of the real situation, since before the outbreak of continental theory in the 1970s, there already existed well-established alternatives to the dominant form of criticism in both Britain and the USA.

When theory finally landed in the 1970s it was received differently in Britain and the USA. A simple way of expressing the difference is to say that in Britain the initial interest was chiefly in structuralism, whereas in the USA it was mainly in poststructuralism. Thus Jacques Derrida, the foremost theorist of deconstruction, was invited to Yale and became a leading member of Yale's 'famous five' theorists (Harold Bloom, Paul de Man, Geoffrey Hartman and J. Hillis Miller were the others, and they are the collective authors of the definitive collection of essays *Deconstruction and Criticism*, RKP, 1979). The five became the spearhead of deconstruction and poststructuralism in the USA. Hillis Miller (b. 1928) had already, from the 1960s, explored beyond the limits of New Criticism, showing a strong

---

[1] This book does not aim to provide you with a systematic introduction to literary theory, but the bibliography entry for this chapter has five books suitable for students seeking information on the topic for the first time.

interest in European approaches which emphasized consciousness rather than form, while de Man (1919–83), even before the final 'deconstruction' period of his career, always emphasized 'rhetoric' above 'reference' in the literary work. Bloom (b. 1930), brought up in the ambience of Talmudic scholarship (that is, in the Jewish tradition of scriptural interpretation), had a strong interest in broad-scale, neo-Freudian approaches to literature and had always been a high theorist whose intellectual ambitions were as great as those of Derrida himself. Hartman (b. 1929), finally, had been one of the first to question the 'formalist' exclusivity of the New Criticism, he too arguing for the relevance of the Jewish rabbinic tradition of inter-pretation and of psychoanalytic approaches (see his book *Beyond Formalism: Literary Essays 1958–1970*, published in 1970).

In the earliest 1970s period of theory, key theory texts were often only available in extracted or translated form, so the work of intel-lectual 'mediators' was crucial. One of the most effective of these is Jonathan Culler, author of *Structuralist Poetics* (Routledge, 1975). The uncompromising central point of Culler's book is its insistence that the proper object of literary study is not the appreciation and enjoyment of individual works of literature, but the quest for an understanding of what constitutes literature and 'literariness'. This recipe for a change of emphasis in literary studies might not have seemed terribly promising at first, but the appeal of such an approach to postgraduates and to younger academics was considerable, for general ideas had been artificially suppressed in English Studies for a long time, thereby inevitably creating a strong appetite for them. Thus, a whole range of questions were never touched upon at all, questions, for instance, concerning the purpose and potential of literature itself, the nature of literary language and literary represen-tation, the role of the reader in the creation of literary canons and so on. Theory offered to release this hidden, repressed 'sub-conscious' of English Studies, breaking the widespread taboo on ideas and generalizations which many decades of practical criticism had effec-tively imposed. Now 'close reading' was replaced by 'theorized reading', and 'critical practice' (the term derives from Catherine Belsey's highly successful New Accents book *Critical Practice* of 1980) became the catchphrase for an approach to literature which involved a newly theorized way of reading that aimed to replace the old method of 'practical criticism'. Belsey's book insisted that there is a single system of cultural meanings and representations with no privileged literary realm operating by separate rules and norms. Thus (to put it crudely) gold-rimmed glasses signify the intellectual in Hollywood movies *and* in highbrow Russian novels. It is, for Belsey, merely 'bourgeois mystification' to suggest that language and representation work in a special way in literature.

As this stage (that is, by the early 1980s) theory began to popularize its basic beliefs and there was a more general shift of interest from structuralism to poststructuralism, that is, from early Roland Barthes to early Jacques Derrida, so that instead of seeing verbal structures as intimidatingly ordered and rule based, we began to see them as (thrillingly, subversively) anarchic and unpredictable. This stage of literary theory is also the period of the 'theory wars', a time of bad-tempered rows between theorists and non-theorists at conferences and meetings and on TV and radio programmes. It was a strangely fraught time, dominated politically by Reaganism in the USA and Thatcherism in the UK, with the frustrations induced by the political scene spilling over into the academic sphere. The characteristics of the 1980s phase of theory, then, are, firstly, prolonged and bitter hostilities between traditional approaches to literary study (usually called 'liberal humanism') and 'theory', secondly, the continuation of the shift from structuralism to poststructuralism, and thirdly, the growing confidence of theorists through a vigorous culture of conferences and dedicated journals, leading to the spread of theory until it became established at the heart of the undergraduate syllabus.

Sonnet 73: reading with theory

Some of the procedures of critical close reading were set out in the first chapter as ten 'sub-skills'. These, we said, are indispensable, yet insufficient. So what is it that literary theory can provide in addition? What is missing from the practice of close reading? Well, the ten sub-skills mostly look inwards, that is, into the text itself, and we also need to look outwards. This necessary looking outwards from the text is why we have, and why we need, literary theory. The ten 'starters' do not contain much that would focus us, for instance, on the cultural contexts and intertextual connections of a literary work. Theory can help us, especially, in considering four major aspects of the relationship between literature and the world beyond, these being firstly literature and history, secondly literature and language, thirdly literature and gender, and finally literature and psychoanalysis. These will now be considered in turn, using as the textual example Shakespeare's Sonnet 73, which reads as follows:

> That time of year thou mayst in me behold
> When yellow leaves, or none, or few, do hang
> Upon those boughs which shake against the cold,
> Bare ruined choirs, where late the sweet birds sang.
> In me thou see'st the twilight of such day
> As after sunset fadeth in the west;
> Which by and by black night doth take away,
> Death's second self, that seals up all in rest.
> In me thou see'st the glowing of such fire,
> That on the ashes of his youth doth lie,
> As the deathbed whereon it must expire,
> Consumed with that which it was nourished by.
> This thou perceiv'st, which makes thy love more strong,
> To love that well which thou must leave ere long.

History

The speaker in the poem, to put it delicately, is not as young as he was, and he ingeniously uses this fact to place a kind of scarcity value on himself. He is not going to be around long, so she (or he) had better love him well while he is. There is something very odd about that second line, but for the moment it's the fourth line I want to concentrate on. What does it mean? At one level, the general meaning is clear. The speaker is old. He is like a bare tree in winter. The birds of summer which used to sit upon those boughs and sing have now gone. It's all very sad. He is feeling sorry for himself, and he wants his lover to feel the same. But that word 'choirs' is like the bullet that grows (as discussed in the first chapter). It's the point in the poem where the literal and the metaphorical begin to 'deconstruct' each other. For this isn't just a pretty way of referring to birds: it also means, literally, the choir-stalls in which the monks used to sing Vespers. And those choirs are indeed bare and ruined now, because the monasteries were closed by Henry VIII during the English Reformation and the buildings were abandoned. All this happened not very long ago (the word 'late' means 'recently') and the metaphor chosen by the poet (the branches of the trees on which the birds used to sing in summer being like the wooden choir-stalls where the monks once sang) evokes all this recent and highly contentious history. Is it a coded reference, a line in which a secret 'recusant' – that is, someone who refuses to accept the new Anglican religion: in other words, a closet Catholic – signals regret for the suppression of the old Catholic religion? This would be a fashionable interpretation today, for there are theories that the young Shakespeare spent part of his youth with a noble Catholic family in Lancashire.[2]

Things are now becoming complicated. Instead of being a free-standing literary jewel which we can hold up to the light and scrutinize with our ten principles of interpretation, this little poem suddenly seems to be deeply enmeshed in the history of its time. We could read up on Reformation history and find out all about the monasteries. But it isn't so simple. It isn't just a matter of acquiring knowledge: if the allusion is actually there, it teaches us that we do not understand what the relationship is between literature and history, for if it is an allusion, then it is very difficult to work out precisely what it is doing in the poem. I mean this literally – not just how and why it got there, but what *effect* it has on the poem. Puzzling yet fascinating questions of this kind are one of the reasons for using literary theory. Here, then, is a whole area much in need of discussion in broad theoretical terms. This is the kind of gap in our understanding of how literature works which theory can attempt to fill.

---

[2]The line had already been read in the nineteenth century as revealing a nostalgia, at least, for Catholicism. More recently, Shakespeare's Catholic and Lancashire connections were discussed in E. A. J. Honigmann's *Shakespeare: The Lost Years*, Manchester University Press, 1985, 2nd edn, 1998, and Park Honan's biography *Shakespeare: A Life*, Oxford University Press, 1998 accepts and incorporates these findings.

Language

We said a moment ago that there is something odd about the second line of Sonnet 73, and investigating that oddity brings us to the issue of literature and language. What is odd about the line, of course, is the peculiar order in which the words occur. In the memory (in my experience), the line is nearly always 'yellow leaves, or few, or none', but Shakespeare actually says 'yellow leaves, or none, or few'. This seems to violate the natural word order, which would follow the logic of a phrase like 'going, going, gone', where a process of gradual diminishing is followed through until there is nothing left at all. This is one example of the way English words occur in a pre-determined order; we put the 'knives and forks' on the table, not the 'forks and knives'. A phrase like 'going, going, gone' has the logic of a countdown – three, two, one, zero. That is the way the words 'collocate', as a linguist would say; so the phrase 'yellow leaves, or none, or few' violates an expected and logical pattern. It isn't done to accommodate rhyme or metre, since neither is a rhyme word and both have a single syllable, so swapping 'few' and 'none' round doesn't make any difference to the metrical structure of the line. So it seems that what is happening is that underneath the main current of the language another current is running in the opposite direction. The speaker is *saying* that he is sexually 'past it', but then hints, with a nudge and a wink, that he isn't quite, and this is indicated by the unexpected order of the words.

This underlying counter-current of language can often be sensed. Language seems to have a natural tendency to undermine and contradict itself, to be one thing on the surface and another beneath. When a teacher says to a child 'Is that your coat on the floor?' it isn't a question, in spite of its surface form. It's a command. It means 'Pick it up.' Reading literature well is often a matter of picking up these counter-currents, these points where language undermines itself, runs against its own grain, carries along its own opposite in its slipstream. An example I am reminded of is when the Duke of Edinburgh withdrew his royal patronage from Harrods department store. I'm told that the sign in the shoe department that used to say 'Shoe-makers to His Royal Highness the Duke of Edinburgh' was altered to read 'Cobblers to Prince Philip'. That phrase *says* one thing, but, of course, *means* something else. Beneath the surface-current of its meaning (which is respectful and reverential) another current runs in the opposite direction and is anything but. Deconstructive reading is a kind of dowsing tool designed to pick up that counter-current that runs beneath the linguistic surface. In the first line of the poem, then, the speaker says 'That time of year thou mayst in me behold'. Is there a hint of optionality, as it has been called, in that word 'mayst', so that he is saying, in a sceptical way, 'Well, you *could* look at me like that.'[3] This notion of the undercurrents and cross-currents of language, then, opens up another area where we seem to need theory; it is the area of the investigation of the relationship between literature and language and the often-strange character-istics of language itself.

Gender

Another area for theory is that of the relationship between literature and gender. In the case of this poem, the gender issue is pretty stark. We might ask the question, what are the signs in this poem that it is written by a man rather than a woman? (This is often a very good question to ask of a literary text.) One sign, I think, is the fact that as a ploy in the seduction process the speaker draws attention to his relatively advanced age. Would a woman speaker in a love poem associate herself with images of late autumn, sunset, approaching death and dying embers? It seems unlikely. The male speaker takes advantage of a set of implicit cultural stereotypes whereby age in men connotes experience, man-of-the-world ease and notions of depth of character. No such positive stereotypical associations would be available to an aging woman speaker. Once again, the problem of the precise nature of the relationship between literature and society – word and world – is problematized, in this case concerning how literature relates to gendered social norms. But clearly there

---

[3] My reading makes use of Roger Fowler's chapter 'Language and the Reader: Shakespeare's Sonnet 73' in his book *Style and Structure in Literature*, Basil Blackwell, 1975.

is a relationship of *some* kind and it is active in this poem. In this regard, we again seem to need theory, a theory which can look at the relation between literature and gender and explicate (meaning, literally, to unfold) some aspects of the connections between them.

Psychoanalysis

The final area of discussion is the relationship between literature and psychoanalysis, which we can open up by asking what exactly the speaker's strategy of seduction is in this poem. The answer, I think, is that the strategy seems to be what we might call 'pre-emptive': he himself says that he is getting old, to pre-empt anybody else saying it, boldly bringing the tricky question of age into full view himself. He does this especially in the dark and gloomy image of approaching night in the second quatrain, which mentions twilight, then 'after sunset', then the last glow removed by 'black night', then death sealing everything up as in a tomb. Surely, we think, it's all over for this man. But in the next quatrain (lines 9–12) he draws back from this sombre image of total extinction, and suddenly we have images which suggest a re-kindling – a glowing fire, youth, and being consumed by something. Suddenly the deathbed is suffused by images of residual passion, residual potency – and remember that for the Elizabethans, the words 'death' and 'dying' often carried a secondary sexual meaning connected with orgasm. The 'going, gone, going' pattern of line two is repeated in the larger pattern made by the three quatrains, where the last one actually steps back from the extreme statement of the second-to-last.

What is working here, then, is a psychological process: often, the best way to conceal something is to reveal it, to hide it in the open, as is sometimes said.[4] If both parties to an exchange are aware

---

[4]This paradoxical trope (of concealment by non-concealment) is the driving force of Edgar Allan Poe's famous detective story 'The Purloined Letter', a tale which fascinated Derrida and Lacan, and for which the literary theory establishment developed something of a fixation in the 1980s. See *The Purloined Poe: Lacan, Derrida and Psychoanalytic Reading*, John P. Muller and William J. Richardson (eds), Johns Hopkins University Press, 1988, which usefully rounds up and comments on this material.

that something is being left unsaid, then it will appear in everything which *is* said. The addressee of the poem, whether male or female, is thinking 'But he's too old for me.' The speaker knows this, so *he* speaks that thought, and then he plants a little doubt about the truth of it with his suggestive references to the few leaves which still remain, the sap which still flows, the fire which still glows, the passion which still consumes. These mental processes are ones that psychoanalysis knows all about, and here again is another area in which theory can operate – that of the relationship between literature and psychoanalysis.

Doing it deconstructively – 'HD' and Adrienne Rich

So far in this chapter we have made a general case for using literary theory, arguing its compatibility with many elements of our traditional literary training. I'd like to look at another example now and take just one of the four categories in more detail, namely the second – the one about the relationship between literature and language. The reason for this is that this example enables us to think about deconstructive reading which on the one hand has been a powerful tool in literary theory but on the other has clear affinities with the kind of intensive close reading which we have always practised.

So, what *is* deconstruction? In general terms, it can be thought of as a kind of anti-reading, originating in the work of Jacques Derrida in the late 1960s, the aim of which is to expose the meanings which the text never intended itself to bear. In Terry Eagleton's well-known definition, it is 'reading the text against itself' or 'reading against the grain', 'knowing the text as it cannot know itself' (see *Literary Theory: An Introduction*), thereby revealing fault-lines (a favoured word) of doubt and contradiction within it. For Barbara Johnson, in another often-quoted phrase, deconstruction is 'the careful teasing out of the warring forces of signification within the text' (see her book *The Critical Difference*). As J. A. Cuddon suggests in *A Dictionary of Literary Terms*, this may result in the discovery of multiple and contradictory meanings, so that a text 'may betray itself', to use the emotive, hyped-up language which is often found in deconstruction. Other terms that are often used to describe deconstruction are 'textual harassment' and 'oppositional reading'. The process of deconstructing a text often involves fixing on what looks like an incidental detail – such as a particular word, or a particular metaphor – and then bringing it in from the margin of the text to the centre. In this way the text is 'de-centred' by the reading process and the overall effect is often perverse, obsessive, manic, or even apparently malevolent towards author and text, reader and literature. If we think of the text as a cat, then old-style close reading involves stroking the cat so that it purrs and curls in upon itself contentedly. Deconstructive reading is like stroking the cat the wrong way, against the grain of the textual fur, so that the cat bristles and hisses, and the whole situation becomes less predictable. The close-reader of old aimed to show a unity of purpose within the text: the text knows what it wants to do and, having directed all its means towards this end, it is at peace with itself. By contrast, the deconstructor aims to show that the text is at war with itself and that it is characterized by disunity rather than unity. So the deconstructor looks for such things as, firstly, *contradictions*, secondly, *linguistic quirks and aporia*, thirdly, *shifts or breaks* (in tone, viewpoint, tense, person, attitude, etc.) and, finally, *absences or omissions*.

So how does this kind of reading look in practice? I will give a mini-example and then a longer example. 'Oread' is a tiny poem by the American Imagist poet 'HD' (Hilda Doolittle, 1886–1961). It reads in full:

Whirl up, sea –
whirl your pointed pines,
splash your great pines
on our rocks,
hurl your green over us,
cover us with your pools of fir.

'Oread' is a poem which has already deconstructed itself. The title word 'Oread' means a wood-nymph, but the poem is an emblem of the impossibility of reading and an embodiment of the Derridean dictum that there is nothing outside the text. The deconstructive

malevolence splits the title thus: 'O/Read' and then shows that it
is impossible to say *what* we are reading. Is it a description of a
stormy sea which presents that sea through the metaphor of a
wind-tossed pine forest? Or is it a poem about a wind-tossed pine
forest which describes it using the metaphor of a stormy sea? It's
impossible to say. Or rather, it's about neither. It's about an object
which is pure textuality, which only exists in language; it's a sea/
pine-forest, or a pine-forest/sea. Here is a poem, then, which
actively *resists* reading.

For a more sustained example of the 'reading-resistant' poem we
can take the poem 'Transit' by Adrienne Rich (1929–2012), which
reads in full:

When I meet the skier she is always
walking, skis and poles shouldered, toward the mountain,
free-swinging in worn boots
over the path new-sifted with fresh snow
her graying dark hair almost hidden by   5
a cap of many colors
her fifty-year-old, strong, impatient body
dressed for cold and speed
her eyes level with mine

And when we pass each other I look into her face   10
wondering what we have in common
where our minds converge
for we do not pass each other, she passes me
as I halt beside the fence tangled in snow,
she passes me as I shall never pass her   15
in this life

Yet I remember us together
climbing Chocorua, summer nineteen-forty-five
details of vegetation beyond the timberline
lichens, wildflowers, birds,   20
amazement when the trail broke out onto the granite ledge
sloped over blue lakes, green pines, giddy air,
like dreams of flying

When sisters separate they haunt each other
as she, who I might once have been, haunts me   25
or is it I who do the haunting
halting and watching on the path

how she appears again through lightly-blowing
crystals, how her strong knees carry her,
how unaware she is, how simple   30
this is for her, how without let or hindrance
she travels in her body
until the point of passing, where the skier
and the cripple must decide
to recognise each other?   35

Contradictions

Some *contradictions*, firstly, are easily picked out: there is a flat
contradiction between line ten, 'when we pass each other', and
line thirteen, 'we do not pass each other'. There is a perceptual
contradiction in the 'graying dark hair' of line five – can it really be
perceived as both at the same time, and in any case, if it's almost
hidden by a cap how can the speaker know either way? In line seven
the 'fifty-year old, strong impatient body' again seems a perceptual
contradiction, for the image of youthfulness implied by the 'strong
impatient body' sets up contradictory connotations to those of the
phrase 'fifty-year old'.

Linguistic quirks and aporia

Secondly, the *linguistic quirks and aporia* are those points in the
poem where the language itself (rather than the perceptions) seems
to be behaving oddly. For instance, in line nine, is 'level' an adjective
or a verb? If the former, the meaning is fairly mundane – the two
figures are roughly the same height – if the latter, the effect is more
dramatic; the other's eyes level and lock with those of the speaker,

tracking and maintaining the eye contact as she moves. In lines 24–5, are the two figures sisters or not? The line seems to mean that they are paired *like* sisters, but they are *not* sisters. The speaker's reference to 'she, who I might once have been' is also ambiguous; it could mean 'she, whom I once had the potential to become, or to become like', or 'she whom I might have been like, had I chosen to be'. On the other hand, it could mean 'she, who I perhaps once was (or was once like)'. Then in line 34, the phrase 'must decide' is a linguistic non sequitur: 'must' implies obligation and 'decide' implies choice. It makes sense to say 'You must decide' or 'You must leave him', but it doesn't make sense to say 'You must decide to leave him'. This is indicative of a deeper confusion in the poem between obligation and choice, which is compounded at the end by placing a question mark after something which isn't a question. Further, is the cripple in line 34 literal or metaphorical? The speaker is moving along paths on and by the ski slopes, 'halt(ing)' in lines 14 and 27, which, of course, implies movement. In what sense, then, is the speaker to be thought of as a cripple?

Shifts

Moving now to the *shifts in person, attitude, etc.*, in the first two stanzas the figure described seems to be a stranger to the speaker, someone unknown ('the skier'), though strangely the speaker knows her precise age and the colour of her hair even though she is wearing a cap. The speaker speculates about her, as one might about a stranger ('wondering what we have in common', line 11). In the third stanza, however, she seems to become a remembered person ('Yet I remember us together', line 17), with whom the speaker has shared significant moments in the past. Then in the final stanza she seems to have become an apparition, associated with haunting, and materializing in a quasi-mystical way through the snow ('she appears again through lightly blowing / crystals', line 28). The differences between these three versions of the skier are so fundamental that the word 'shifts' hardly does them justice.

Absences and omissions

Finally, the *absences and omissions*. Again, these are fundamental. Who *is* the skier? We are never told. At the centre of the poem, then, is something left out, something withheld. Are these two roles ('the skier' and 'the cripple', lines 33–4) two aspects of the same person? The reader should resist the temptation to 'recuperate' or 'narrativize' or opt for the simplest reading, in which two sisters' lives move on to different 'paths' when one is crippled in a climbing accident and her subsequent life poisoned by sibling envy. Rather, the skier seems to connote an alternative self, a self-that-might-have-been, by whom the real self is haunted. The potential self seems to have a degree of hostility towards the actual self (also the scenario of Henry James's ghost story 'The Jolly Corner') and the self's awareness of this being seems to deconstruct the confident boundaries of her own subjectivity. The deconstructive reading, then, seems to enhance the perceived strangeness of this remarkable poem. We are left with a poem that seems to be fighting a civil war with itself. There is no secure, overarching vantage-point from which it all makes sense. The cat of signification isn't purring anymore. Deconstruction, of course, believes that it is characteristic of all language to fight itself in this way, so that any poem, when subjected to deconstructive enquiry, would reveal such symptoms to some degree, though obviously not to the same dramatic extent as 'Transit', a poem I chose as my example because it lends itself so well to this approach.

So, in this chapter we have taken a broad look at theory, looking at theory in theory in the first half, and theory in practice in the second.

9

English as Language

The word 'English' in 'English Studies' often means not just English literature but English language as well, for many English departments, especially in the UK and Europe, are departments of 'English Language and Literature' (or equivalent). This means that their staff will comprise literary theorists, literary critics and literary historians on the one hand, and on the other those who refer to themselves as 'linguists', not meaning that they are speakers of many languages (which is the usual lay meaning of this word), but indicating that their field of expertise is the study of language itself. Hence, the syllabus set for study in such departments covers both language and literature, and the language side of this joint syllabus is the topic of this chapter.

Let's begin by considering the following definition of linguistics (that is, Language Studies) from a helpful website:

> In its broadest sense, Linguistics is the study of human language: how it is structured, how it is used to represent meaning, how it is used to communicate ideas, how it is formed, how it is decoded. Linguistics tries to look for commonality across all human languages, and shouldn't be confused with 'Language Teaching' which aims to teach a single language. It is confusing that an expert in languages is called a 'linguist', since it leaves no name for an expert in Linguistics – maybe he [sic] should be called a 'linguistician'!

The breadth of this definition makes it a useful starting point, but what are some of the main subdivisions of linguistics? The list below draws on the same source and on the very useful *Concise Oxford Dictionary of Linguistics* (P. H. Matthews, 1997):

Stylistics – the study of style in language, especially in literary texts

Sociolinguistics – the study of language in its (usually contemporary) social context

Historical Linguistics – the study of the origins and development of languages, and of historical change within individual languages

Syntax – the study of the relationship between words and phrases within sentences

Semantics – the study of the meaning

Phonology – the study of the pronunciation of words and sentences (what basic sounds are used by a language, what regular patterning occurs in words)

Phonetics – the study of the production of speech by the human vocal mechanisms (how are sounds made, how do speakers of different accents differ?)

Psycholinguistics – the study of the mental processes by which sentences are constructed and decoded by human beings.

I will not, of course, attempt to represent that whole spectrum here. In fact, almost nobody would claim to have competence across all of this: to do so would be like claiming to be, simply, a scientist, without indicating what kind of scientist and what areas of specialist expertise you possess. So I will concentrate on just the first three categories in the list.

Stylistics

Outside the changing rooms for the swimming pool on the campus where I work there is a large blackboard propped against the wall.

On it is chalked the instruction 'Please leave any footwear here'. 'Here' means 'in this room' (or so I have always presumed), but visitors sometimes seem in doubt, and occasionally (especially in the summer) you will find pairs of shoes clustered around the blackboard itself, indicating that the word 'here' has been taken to mean 'in the immediate vicinity of this blackboard'. The ambiguity stems from the fact that the word 'here' is what linguists call a 'shifter' (the term was coined by the influential Russian linguist Roman Jakobson, 1896–1982), meaning that its referent is contextually defined. If *I* say 'Come here' it means 'to where *I* am'; if *you* say it, it means to where *you* are. By contrast, if the utterance were 'Come to London' it would mean the same thing no matter which of us said it (discounting, for a moment, the existence of London, Ontario). Shifters operate in routine and predictable ways in day-to-day speech, but in poetry their use can be very subtle and complex. Tracking language-use in poetry using technical terms and concepts derived from linguistics (like 'shifters') is the kind of thing undertaken in the form of literary analysis known as stylistics. In this section I will try to give an impression of the 'flavour' of stylistics by illustrating how one specific set of terms and concepts might be employed, namely the cluster of devices known as 'shifters', 'deictic features' and 'orientational features'. I choose this cluster of items because analysing how they work is particularly illuminating in the discussion of poetry.

'Shifters' and deixis

As well as being a 'shifter', as just described, the word 'here' has what linguists call a 'deictic' function. 'Deixis' (pronounced 'day-ix-iss') comes from the Greek word '*deiknuo*', which means to point or to show. Its root is contained in English words like 'in*dex*', as in 'index finger', meaning the finger which points, or the part of a book which 'in*dic*ates' – another cognate word – the location of particular information. 'Deictic words', says Richard Radford, are 'orientational features', and they are 'particularly important in the criticism of poetry because the poem (unlike the reported speech acts of a novel or a play) is rarely attended by external evidence of its spatio-temporal or social context'.[1] In other words, in everyday life, the utterance 'He was here yesterday' is seldom ambiguous, because there is usually plenty of evidence of the 'spatio-temporal or social context' of the utterance. Rarely does someone phone with that message from an unknown part of the globe, making it necessary to ask '*Who* was, and what do you mean by "here", and who are *you* anyway?' A poem, however, might well begin with precisely that phrase, 'He was here yesterday', and be without any spatio-temporal indicators, so that *all* those questions would become relevant, including the last, since the speaker in the poem might well be a proxy persona rather than the author speaking autobiographically. Deixis is a linguistic concept of peculiar conceptual breadth on the one hand, and, on the other, of stark precision in application. Of their nature, orientational features of various kinds are a feature of poetic openings; once a poem is orientated the need for them progressively declines. Romantic and Victorian poetry in particular is often very keen to establish the spatio-temporal context of the utterance, fixing what becomes the locatory pivot (meaning the focal place) of the entire poem.

Taking a ghost for a walk

Take, for example, Matthew Arnold's 'Thyrsis', one of his best poems, written (as the epigraph says) to commemorate his Oxford friend and fellow poet Arthur Hugh Clough. It opens with the line 'How changed is here each spot man makes or fills!' But where is 'here'? The reader's problem is like that of the reader of the notice by the swimming pool. Does it mean here in general ('here on earth', say), or is it referring to a specific place (Oxford, for instance)? As the poem unfolds, it becomes clear that the poet is retracing a specific walk in the Cumnor Hills near Oxford, which he and Clough had often taken together as students, so that the sense of the word 'here' has again shifted when re-used in the penultimate line of the first stanza 'Here came I often, often, in old days'. In the first line of the second

---

[1] Richard Radford, *A Linguistic History of English Poetry* (London: Routledge, 1993), pp. 40 and 207. See also Bradford's *Roman Jakobson: Life, Language, Art*, Routledge, 1994, pp. 92–3 on shifters and poetry.

stanza it is used again, and again with a shifted sense: 'Runs it not here, the track by Childsworth Farm'. Since his student days, the terrain has become unfamiliar to him, though as he says in stanza three, line four, 'Once pass'd I blindfold here, at any hour' (in other words, 'there was a time when this track was so familiar I could have walked it blindfolded, day or night').

I won't track the word 'here' any further than this through Arnold's poem, but I think it is clear that the shifters have a *double* shift in poetry and that this has a strongly enriching effect. Thus the opening phrase 'How changed is here ...' has a double meaning within the context of the poem, one being 'subjective', indicating how the world itself, to the middle-aged speaker, does indeed seem transformed – nothing now *feels* the same – and the other being objective, registering the fact of specific physical and social changes which have altered this terrain since Arnold was a student. By making this commemorative walk Arnold is laboriously seeking to relocate and re-activate the youthful ideals he shared with Clough (symbolized by 'the single-elm that looks on Ilsley Downs', to which they used to walk). It is the internal change, of course, that is the more troubling. The poem's act of mourning and willed restoration of purpose takes the form of retracing a walk in the Oxford hills which Arnold and Clough had frequently taken together as students and ends with a defiant proclamation of inner continuity with their youthful idealism, as the voice of Clough says to the poet '*Roam on! The light we sought is shining still ... Our tree yet crowns the hill*'.

Yet, the deictic pointers have a further and crucial level of ambivalence when they are used in a poem. The word 'here' seems to locate the utterance on the ground itself, as if Arnold is 'speaking' these precise words, or, more accurately, sub-vocalising these precise thoughts, actually on the spot. Of course, the poem is more likely to have been composed retrospectively in the poet's study (or in many different places), so that the deictic pointers ought strictly to say 'there' rather than 'here'. But the convention is otherwise, for poems 'talk through' and 'walk through' a past event, re-vitalising it, re-visiting the spot, re-thinking the thoughts. The paradox embodied in poetry is that poems often re-create a 'past' moment of reflection which actually exists *only* in the re-creation.

This discussion may not seem different in kind from conventional close reading, and indeed, I don't think it is entirely. The defining feature of literary stylistics is simply that it uses concepts and terminology from linguistics as part of its repertoire, but it doesn't seek to use *exclusively* linguistic material, and will necessarily work in tandem with more familiar approaches to reading. There are, of course, hundreds of linguistic terms which this kind of analysis could potentially employ: here is a random list from a useful essay which sets out to exemplify the stylistic analysis of a poem in a systematic way. Stylistic investigators, then, might focus upon such elements as: the use of *stative verbs* (those which denote a state, like 'to own', rather than an action, like 'to buy'); *collocational clashes* (when words occur in unexpected combinations, as, for example, in the term 'an elegant rant'); the use of *cataphoric words* (words which refer forward to something which follows, like 'these' in 'The most important considerations are these:'); the occurrence of *cohesive chains* (groups of words, perhaps from different parts of a text, which have the same associations, for example 'battle-shouts' and 'death-cries' might both be associated with a scene of armed combat); the poet's choice of *premodification* (as in 'a red-hot poker') or *postmodification* (as in 'a poker which was red-hot'); the significance of the *head nouns* ('poker' is the head noun in both the previous examples, irrespective of whether the modification comes before or after); the occurrence of *lexico-semantic deviations* (all the deviations from normal usage a poet might employ – for example, the word 'rainbow' might be used as a verb – 'the sun rainbowed the window').[2]

The stylistician, then, examines the language of the poem using categories and terms of the above linguistic type. The aim is not to provide an exhaustive stylistic description, of course, but to use such data as part of a literary critical-argument. In my comments on Arnold's 'Thyrsis', the focus on 'shifters' serves to highlight the sense of 'precariousness' Arnold has, of his own world shifting

---

[2]All the terms listed occur in the essay 'To analyse a poem stylistically: "To Paint a Water Lilly" by Ted Hughes' (but the exemplification is mostly my own). This is Chapter 1 in *Twentieth-Century Poetry: From Text to Context*, ed. Peter Verdonk, Routledge, 1993.

and changing and his familiar moral landmarks being dislodged. The 'shifters' provide what is in effect a linguistic reinforcement or embodiment of this pervasive feeling. It should be added, finally, that stylistic analysis is not confined to literature. Any text can be analyzed in this way, and you might find yourself engaged in stylistic analysis of (say) newspaper stories, advertisements, sports commentaries, fashion catalogues and so on. I have chosen to stick to literary stylistics as the main example to emphasize that literary criticism and stylistics can (and often do) very usefully complement each other. In the past, the two approaches were often enemies, but there seems no reason to perpetuate a situation which resulted in lost opportunities for both sides of the divide.

Sociolinguistics

Stylistics, as just argued, has close affinities with long-standing practices of close textual scrutiny in English Studies, and this is also true, although to a lesser extent, of sociolinguistics. A common element in many English courses used to be that attention would be given at some point to such matters as the language of newspapers, popular culture and advertising, usually in a highly critical spirit which was keen to expose the use of cliché in newspapers and the pandering to shallow, populist assumptions.[3] Among other things, sociolinguistics too scrutinizes the language of newspapers, advertisements and of social and professional groups, but in a spirit which is generally more openly descriptive and investigative rather than relentlessly prescriptive and condemnatory. We can define sociolinguistics, then, as the study of language and language use in its social context.

---

[3]This kind of work perhaps has its ultimate source in Q. D. Leavis's PhD thesis and later book, *Fiction and the Reading Public*, and in student texts like Denys Thompson's edited collection *Discrimination and Popular Culture*, Penguin, 1964, which has essays on advertising, radio and TV, the press, film, magazines, pop music and design.

Reading the papers

The focus of sociolinguistics may be of various kinds. For instance, it might be *lexical*, that is concerned mainly with 'lexis' (what lay people usually call 'vocabulary'); we might note, for instance, the way certain words seem 'tied' to a specific context, for instance 'wed' (meaning 'to get married') occurs in newspaper headlines, but isn't used in day-to-day speech – nobody says 'He's going to wed next week'. However, in newspaper headlines, the word is favoured for its shortness, so we might see the headline 'Rock star to wed', in which context it looks quite normal. A sociolinguistic study could also be *syntactical*, that is, concerned with what lay people usually call the grammar and structure of sentences. Thus, a headline, again, might say 'New school to close', which contains no unusual lexis, but structurally it is immediately recognizable as a newspaper headline. Why, exactly? Well, think of how one person might convey this news to another in actual conversation. The utterance might take the form 'The new school's going to close.' The usual telegraphic concision of the headline eliminates many of these words: '[The] new school ['s going] to close.' If we now 'audit' what is omitted, we have (1) The definite article ('the') and (2) the auxiliary parts of the main verb ('is going'). Performing this kind of analysis on a corpus of newspaper headlines would enable investigators to produce a list of the linguistic features which constitute the recognizable 'register' (that is, style) of newspaper headlines (omission of definite articles and auxiliary parts of verbs, preference for short words, etc.). Even from these brief comments, it will be clear that sociolinguistic investigations lend themselves very well to practical, investigative work of an enjoyable kind. It will be clear, too, that the main emphasis in such work would be *de*scriptive rather than *pre*scriptive.

Language and gender

Apart from the language of the media, what other aspects of language in society are commonly investigated from a socio-linguistic perspective? Well, one topic is that of language and prejudice, for instance in relation to gender: areas investigated might begin with such apparently innocent matters as the 'rank ordering' within gendered pairings of words – pairs like 'men and women', 'husbands and wives', 'sons and daughters'. Do these terms seem to have a 'natural' running order, just like 'fish and chips', 'sausage and mash', 'roast beef and Yorkshire pudding', where the first word in each phrase is the main element of the meal – the protein – and the second is the secondary, accompanying element? Is the analogy correct, and if so, how do we explain it? Likewise, consider the prevalence in the English vocabulary of 'praise' compounds bearing masculine elements, like masterpiece, MasterCard, master bedroom, master's Degree, and so on. Try to make a similar list with feminine elements. Consider which list is longer, and ask why.

Yet another level of sociolinguistic investigation within the ambience of gender might be an attempt to investigate differences in language use between men and women. This kind of work was characteristic of the 1980s, and at the time common findings were that:

(a) Men tend to use 'unqualified' statements ('It's too late to go now'), whereas women more often had 'question-tagged' statements which allowed the possibility of other views, as in 'It's too late to go now, isn't it?' Here, 'isn't it?' is a 'tag' in question form which is added to the statement 'It's too late to go now.'

(b) Male speech tends to have 'falling intonation' (that is, the tone drops at the end of the sentence – (*Let's' go* $_{now}$), whereas female speech (especially that of younger women) often has the rising intonation characteristic of questions, even when questions are not being asked (*Let's' go* $_{now}$).[4]

(c) Male speech tends to have more slang and neologisms than female.

(d) In the case of male and female speakers of the same social

---

[4]Since the 1980s, the phenomenon of rising end-intonation has become very marked, especially among younger English speakers worldwide, and particularly in certain national language communities, such as Australia.

    class, the regional accents of the male speakers are more marked.

(e) Male speakers seldom ask questions (notoriously, male drivers totally lost in a strange city will drive round for hours rather than stopping to ask directions).

(f) Male speakers use fewer 'phatic' features (these are the brief verbal signals which indicate to someone speaking that you are taking in what they are saying – phrases like 'Yes', 'I see what you mean', 'Really?' and so on).

(g) Only women speakers use 'disclaimers' – these are 'prefacing' elements like 'I don't know if you'll agree with this, but what I think is happening is ...'

My impression is that these differences are generally less marked now than then and that there has since been a move towards greater homogenization of speech patterns, reflecting much wider social trends. It will be clear, I think, that sociolinguistics is likely to stray from its aim of being purely descriptive when it begins to deal with topics like gender or prejudice. I don't think there is anything wrong with this. All the same, in such cases the potency of the investigation can be increased by suspending evaluative judgement for as long as possible.

Jargon

Another typical area of sociolinguistic investigation is that of jargon, especially the characteristic usages of particular social and professional groups. In considering the language of governmental and commercial spokespersons, for instance, we might notice a strong preference for 'aesthetic euphemisms', that is, for terms which 'dress up' the mundane. Thus, in a report on the countryside we may hear of 'single-purpose agricultural structures' rather than 'barns', or of 'organoleptic analysis' rather than smelling things to see what they are. These verbal preferences may be a harmless way of giving an air of learned professionalism to otherwise trite observations. But the use of 'semantic euphemisms' (that is, euphemisms which seem to want to *disguise* meanings, dressing them down rather than up, so to speak) may be less so. Many of these are connected with warfare, the most notorious perhaps being the use of the term 'collateral damage' as a way of avoiding mention of the killing of civilians. At the time of the war in Afghanistan, there was discussion of the possibility of allowing the use of 'physical interrogation'' of terrorist suspects in that country (*The Guardian*, 27 November 2001, p. 17). Being 'physically interrogated' doesn't sound very pleasant, but it sounds a lot better than being tortured. It is difficult to imagine discussing language use of this kind in a neutral and purely descriptive way. But again, suspending judgement for as long as possible does give us a greater chance of understanding what its users want this language to do for them. Those who use this kind of euphemistic language know, of course, that *we* know what the words actually refer to (they know, in other words, that the euphemistic veil is transparent). But the effect of using controlled language is to give the impression that *they* are in control of the effects of their actions. The jargonistic trick can still work on us, even though we have seen through it.

Brave new words

Another fascinating area for sociolinguistic investigation is 'lexical innovation', that is, the entry of new words into the language. These, of course, directly reflect social trends and technological change, and again they lend themselves very well to investigative activities. A key practice is simply to keep a log of 'first sightings' – writing down in a designated notebook precise details of the first time new words or catchphrases or technical terms are encountered. Sometimes these moments will stick in the mind – I can recall vividly the moments in the early 1970s when I first heard the terms 'bio-degradable' and 'hassle' – but usually a conscious effort is required to record the details. I kept such a record for teaching purposes in the early 1990s, and the following are some of the entries.[5]

---

[5]The record is subjective, of course, but keeping it trains us to register the presence of new words before they become a taken-for-granted element in our verbal environment. Also, the value is as much in the list as a whole, and the 'snapshot' it gives of a specific year or part of a year, rather than in the details of individual words.

Word	Meaning	Source
A Hold-Jockey	A disc jockey who chats and plays records for those 'on hold' waiting to get through to the offices of large organisations	BBC Radio Four, September 1991
ETOPS	A term in the aviation industry, meaning 'Extended Twin-engined Operations', that is, the trend towards building long-range commercial aircraft with two engines rather than four	TV travel programme, December 1991
Spin doctors	Political consultants who advise politicians about news presentation	March 1992
Float-operated valve	Reputedly now the preferred term in the building trade for the plumbing device previously known as a 'ball-cock'	BBC Radio Four, March 1994

Even a sampling as brief as this gives an immediate sense of the period, and the record is still valuable when the full occurrence details are not to hand. A useful language-based task would be to classify the various ways in which such new words are formed. Many, for instance, are so-called '*back-formations*', that is, words or phrases which are based on the model of already existing words or phrases – for example, 'hold-jockey' is a back-formation from 'disc-jockey'. Others are based on *acronyms* (like ETOPS).

At the time of writing (2013), interest in and anxieties about the changing vocabulary of English seem widespread, with newspapers and websites regularly featuring lists of new words admitted to the latest editions of important dictionaries (such as the *Merriam-Webster Unabridged*, the *Oxford Concise* and the *Collins Concise* dictionaries). Words recently featured in such listings include 'sexting' (the sending of sexually explicit text messages), 'bucket list' (a list of things one wants to do before dying), 'fauxmance' (a fictitious romance between celebrities, contrived in order to generate publicity and so benefit their careers), 'frenemy' (a friend who is also a rival for media attention or career success), 'tweetheart' (a person who has many 'followers' on Twitter) and 'Zumba' (the world-wide fitness craze based on franchised gym classes with thumping disco music). Typically, these new words are back formations (like 'sexting' from 'texting'), word-splices (like the blending of 'friend' and 'enemy' to produce 'frenemy') or puns (like 'tweetheart' and 'fauxmance'), mainly deriving from the culture of celebrity, social networking, the internet and computers. The Collins digital site invites suggestions from the public for new words that should be included in the latest editions of their dictionaries, and according to a spokesperson they have been 'blown away' [sic] by the scale of the response. Oddly, new words can also be superseded and drop out of the dictionary ('cassette recorder' has been dropped by Collins, now that this technology is obsolete, so perhaps 'fax' is living on borrowed time). Some words which sound up-to-the-minute actually waited a long time for their fifteen years of fame to arrive – an 'aha moment', formerly known as a Eureka moment, was first recorded in 1939, and an 'earworm', meaning a song or tune you can't get out of your head, has been around since 1802. If you feel more wearied than blown away by all this incessant linguistic invention, I suggest you revive yourself with an 'energy drink' (first occurrence 1904) and then join in the fun. Sociolinguistics, then, is a popular area of language study which provides many opportunities for practical work. It investigates language 'synchronically', that is, across the whole spectrum of usage today, rather than 'diachronically', which means 'through time', or historically. It is interested, especially, in language variation – variations, for instance, between different national varieties of English, between 'standard' and 'regional' forms, between the language-usage patterns of different generations and between that of men and women. It is interested, too, in the jargon associated with various professional groups, in the language registers typical of various trades and professions, and in recreational slang. It is, for many, the most attractive and the most contextually rooted form of language study.

Historical linguistics

If sociolinguistics is mainly 'synchronic' (that is, it's about 'language now'), then historical linguistics is mainly 'diachronic' (it's about 'language then') and concerns the history and development of language. Eighteenth- and nineteenth-century linguists studied inter-relationships between languages, aiming especially to work out the origins and sources of the languages of Europe and India. The study began with the imperial expansion which brought westerners into contact with the languages of India, the Middle East and the Far East, leading to the perception of similarities and parallels between them. The founding figure was the Orientalist William Jones (1746–94), whose presidential address to the Bengal Asiatic Society in 1786 included the seminal statement about the ancient languages of Latin, Greek and Sanskrit – that 'no philologer could examine them all three without believing them to have sprung from some common source, which, perhaps, no longer exists'. This, says David Crystal, is 'generally quoted as the first clear statement asserting the existence of Indo-European'.[6] 'Indo-European' is the ancient common ancestor language of most of the modern languages of Europe and India – it is the extinct 'missing link' between them. Realizing the common origins of most of the languages of India and Europe was a major breakthrough in this kind of study, and there was general acceptance of the hypothesis that there exists an 'Indo-European' language 'family', one of the thirty or so major language families worldwide.

The detailed picture reconstructed by the linguists of the nineteenth century is the result of painstaking linguistic detective work involving close scrutiny of the forms of many words across many different languages. The story they tell is that around 3000 BC the civilization now called Indo-European developed in Eastern Europe, with its own language, which was the common ancestor of most present-day European and Indian languages. Around 2500 BC this civilization broke up (perhaps because of climate changes) and the peoples migrated towards many different regions, including present-day

---

[6]David Crystal, *The Cambridge Encyclopedia of Language*, Cambridge University Press, 1987, p. 296.

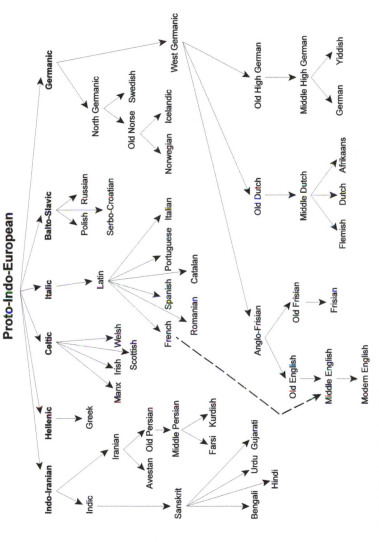

Source: Jack Lynch, Rutgers University

Figure 9.1 The Indo-European language family tree

Greece, Germany, Russia and India. In each place of settlement the language spoken continued to evolve, and it evolved differently in each of these new locations, so that what had been one language began to split into several new ones. In particular, seven main branches of Indo-European developed, these being Celtic, Germanic, Latin, Balto-Slavonic, Hellenic, Sanskrit and Iranian. From these seven major Indo-European branches of the ancient world have developed the language groups of today: the *Celtic* group includes Gaelic, Welsh and Breton; the *Germanic* group the languages of north-west Europe (English, German, Dutch) and the Scandinavian languages (Swedish, Danish, Norwegian, Icelandic); the *Latin* (or 'Romance') group includes French, Spanish, Italian, Portuguese and Romanian; the *Balto-Slavonic* group includes Russian, Polish and Czech; modern Greek is the descendent of the ancient *Hellenic* branch; the *Sanskrit* branch has Hindi, Urdu, Bengali and Gujarati and many other Indian languages; while the *Iranian* branch, finally, has modern Farsi (Persian), an Indo-European language which happens to be written in Arabic script. This kind of information seems to open up a whole new vista of knowledge – there is something about its panoramic reach, across vast epochs of time, across continents and ice ages – which is awesomely impressive, as if a whole area of human experience and interconnections has suddenly been revealed. This is how Keats felt, perhaps, 'On first Looking into Chapman's Homer'.[7]

Clandestine relationships

There is also something especially intriguing about the nature of the evidence which supports the picture of language relationships just given, and this links back to the basic attractions of English as a discipline, as sketched out at the start of this book. This is to do

---

[7]This account of language 'families' follows the traditional 'nationalist'bias of the early formulations: in other words, it privileges the development of national 'languages' rather than regional dialects, or language forms which cross national boundaries. In reality, the distinction between a 'dialect' and a 'language' is a political one – a well-known Yiddish saying, attributed to Max Weinreich, expresses this neatly, maintaining that a language is a dialect which has an army and a navy (see a note in *Language in Society* 26:3, 1997: my source for this information is Adrienne Bruyn, formerly of the Linguistics Department of Manchester University).

with the fact that some of the evidence is concerned, not with the *overt* similarities between words in these different languages, but with *covert* connections between them. 'Overt' connections are the kind which are evident in the present form of words; for instance, it is evident at once that it cannot be coincidental that the word for 'mother' in English must be related to the German *Mutter* or the Dutch *moeder* or the Swedish *moder*. But consider the words in the following list:

ENGLISH	FRENCH	ITALIAN	GERMAN	LATIN
father	père	padre	Vater	pater
fish	poisson	pescatore	Fisch	pisces
foot	pied	piede	Fuß	pes/pedis
hill	colline	collina	Hugel	collis
hundred	cent	cento	hundert	centum
heart	coeur	cuore	Herz	cor/cordis

There is, for instance, little overt similarity between the word 'father' and its French equivalent, *père*, or between the English 'fish' and the French *poisson* – these words do not look as if they could be 'cognate' (words are said to be cognate when they derive from the same source-word). However, we do notice that in both these cases an English word beginning with 'f' has a French equivalent which begins with 'p', and if we noticed (as did nineteenth-century philologists compiling lists of word equivalents across various languages) that this happens quite often (there is another example in the list), then we would have to conclude that it can't be an accident. Likewise, we notice another pattern of this kind – words which begin with 'h' in English and German ('heart' and *Herz*) begin with 'c' in French, Italian and Latin (*coeur, cuore, cor*). On this basis alone, we might conclude that, while all five languages ultimately come from the same source, English and German are more closely related to each other than they are to the rest, and are like 'first cousins', forming one group of close relatives. The same is true of French, Italian and Latin, which form another distinct group of close relatives within the languages mentioned. But the relationship between, say, English and French is more distant, perhaps resembling that of second or third cousins.

The complex patterns of sound equivalences in Indo-European languages (like these indicated in the diagram above), which disguised the close relationships between these words, are explained by 'Grimm's Law', which was worked out by the philologist Jakob Grimm (1785–1863) in his Germanic grammar of 1822 (Grimm, with his brother, was also famed as a compiler of fairy tales). The 'law' explains a pattern of nine different interlocking sets of consonant shifts, which also covers other equivalences, for instance, between Germanic 'd' and Romance 't'; hence, the apparently unrelated words 'hundred' and 'cent' declare the fact that they are really the same word when we know Grimm's Law and can see that the roots 'hund' and 'cent' correspond quite closely to each other, once we take into account the correspondences between the initial 'h' and 'c' and the concluding 'd' or 't'. This kind of work reveals the close connection between two words which now belong to different languages and have very little surviving *morphological* similarity (that is, their current external forms show few affinities).

Meanings on the move

If the major characteristic of philology is its interest in investigating language 'diachronically', then another important area of philological interest is the study of *semantic change*. 'Semantic' means 'concerned with meaning', and the focus here is not the words themselves as spoken sounds or written marks, but on the changes in what words signify. The fact that words change their meanings is evident when we read almost any document from the past: thus, when King James II first viewed the new St Paul's Cathedral in London, he expressed his profound admiration of the building by saying that it was 'amusing, awful, and artificial'. Today, this would be a pretty devastating verdict on any work of art, but all these words have undergone 'semantic' change since the time of James II: 'Amusing' then meant 'pleasing', 'awful' meant 'awe-inspiring' and 'artificial' meant 'skilfully wrought'.[8]

---

[8]This example is from Simeon Potter's book *Our Language*, Penguin, 1950, which is packed with information about the history of English. Potter was the first in an

Like so much else in language history, semantic change isn't random, but follows predictable patterns. We may think of words as being 'anchored' to their meanings – the word *aeroplane* isn't suddenly going to drift off all over the place and come to mean *flower pot*. But a ship at anchor doesn't remain rigidly still – a certain amount of 'play' is observable around the point of anchorage. Semantic shift or 'play', then, can be envisaged as having two main axes: along one axis, words can take on a meaning which is either more *restricted* or else more *extended* than it used to be. Along the other axis, words can gather overtones which are either more negative (or *pejorative*) than before, or else more positive (or *meliorative*) than before. We can arrange these two axes to form what I call 'the semantic cross', as below:

RESTRICTION

PEJORATION   +   MELIORATION

EXTENSION

The centre of the cross marks the meaning of the word at a given moment in the past (this being roughly the time of Shakespeare in the case of the examples given below). If the arms of the cross are taken as compass directions, we can say that northerly semantic drift, towards *restriction*, is more common than southerly, and that westerly drift, towards *pejoration*, is more common than easterly. The following words are examples of each kind of semantic change:

RESTRICTION
Meat: this word used to mean any kind of food (see the expression 'It was meat and drink to her'); now it means just one kind.
Starve: used to mean to die in any way (e.g. to starve for love); now it means just one kind of death.

---

illustrious line of British linguists able to write effectively about language for a large audience. His successors have included Randolph Quirk (*Language in Use*, Longman, 1990), Jean Aitchison (*Language Change: Progress or Decay?* 3rd edn, Cambridge University Press, 2001) and the many books of David Crystal, such as *The Stories of English*, Penguin, 2005.

Deer: used to mean any kind of animal (see the German word *Tiergarten*, which means a zoo, literally an 'animal-garden', and King Lear's remark in Shakespeare's play about 'mice and rats and other small deer'); now it means just one kind of animal, not animals in general.

Wed: used to be any kind of contract (e.g. you could be 'wed' to deliver goods by a certain day); now it means just the marriage contract.

EXTENSION

Hazard: used to mean a specific game of chance played with dice; now it means any kind of risk or danger.

Virtue: used to mean just strength, potency (from Latin *vir*, a man); now it means any admirable quality in anybody, whether male or female.

PEJORATION

Counterfeit: used to mean any likeness, not just one intended to deceive – Hamlet says to his mother, showing her the pictures of his uncle and his father, 'Look on this likeness, and on this, the counterfeit presentment of two brothers'.

Silly: used to mean 'happy' or 'fortunate' – when Troilus has successfully wooed Cressida (in Chaucer's *Troilus and Criseyde*) he is called 'silly Troilus'.

Lust: used to mean just 'vigour' or 'enjoyment' – a head-teacher might encourage lusty hymn-singing from the school choir.

Crafty: used to mean 'skilful', 'well made', the sense which survives in expressions like 'country crafts'.

MELIORATION

Success: used to mean any outcome, not just a happy one – you could have 'good success' or 'bad success'; the word literally just means 'what follows', as in 'successor'.

Enthusiasm: used to mean fanaticism, especially religious fanaticism – a seventeenth-century bishop famously remarked 'If religion is ever to perish it will be because of enthusiasm.'

Semantic change is a fascinating topic which offers many opportunities for discussion and debate. *Why*, for instance, should northerly and westerly drift predominate over their opposites? What is it (in human nature?) which brings about that change in the meaning of a word like 'success'? Whatever it is, a similar change seems to affect related words, like 'result'. When football managers say 'We came here to get a result' they don't just mean that they are hoping to be included in the results round-up on the Saturday evening sports programmes – to 'get a result' means to win, just like success.

Borrowed words

Another important aspect of language change which is of great interest to historical linguists is the phenomenon of so-called 'loan words', which are words 'borrowed' by one language from another (with no intention of ever returning them, in spite of the name). An interesting form of this kind of lexical study is to consider the early growth of English, as it absorbed words from adjacent languages to build its own characteristically 'layered' vocabulary, in which there is often a choice of words, each with a slightly different 'flavour', to designate a single thing. (See, for example, the trio *blessing* from Anglo-Saxon, *benison* from French and *benediction* from Latin.) If we think of the English vocabulary as being like a cake made up of several layers, then the bottom (or earliest) layer consists mainly of the 'West-Germanic' or 'Anglo-Saxon' words brought in by the Germanic invaders of the fifth and sixth centuries who displaced the indigenous Celtic peoples of Britain. These words are often monosyllabic, concrete and basic – words like *man*, *wife*, *house*, *meat* and so on. Some characteristic sounds are 'ch' (as in *church*) and 'sh' (as in *shirt*).

The second layer is North-Germanic, these being words of Scandinavian origin brought in by Viking invaders from the eighth century onwards. These are also short, basic words, often recognisable by the initial 'sk' sound (the word *sky*, for instance, which displaced the West-Germanic *welkin*, though in *Hamlet* Claudius's drunken revels 'make the welkin roar'). Other common 'sk' words are *skin* and *skull*. Other characteristic sounds which indicate words of Scandinavian origin are the hard 'g' (as in *go*, as contrasted with the

soft 'g' in *gin*) and the 'k' sound, as in *kirk* (the Scandinavian version
of *church*) and *kin*. That hard 'g' sound is in words like *leg* and *egg*:
the latter word began to replace the West-German equivalent word,
eyren (meaning 'eggs'), but the process was gradual. The printer
William Caxton, writing as late as 1490, has a story of merchants in
his own day sailing from the Thames to Holland and going ashore,
when becalmed off the south-east coast, where they knocked at a
house door to ask for food (the passage is given here in the original
spelling – 'goode wyf' means 'housewife'):

> [He] axed for mete; and specyally he axed after eggys. And the
> goode wyf answered, that she coude speke no frenshe. And
> the marchaunt was angry, for he also coude speke no frenshe,
> but wolde have hadde egges, and she understode hym not. And
> thenne at laste a nother sayd that he wolde have eyren. Then the
> gode wyf sayd that she understod hym wel.[9]

The confusion was due to the fact that there were two forms of
the word 'egg' then fighting it out for supremacy in the English
vocabulary: the country woman uses the older Anglo-Saxon word
'*ey*', which is '*eyren*' in the plural, this being one of the Anglo-Saxon
'weak' plurals, made by adding 'en' rather than 's' to the singular
form (the surviving examples of the weak plural form are the words
oxen, *brethren* and *children*). The London merchants, by contrast,
use the newer form 'egg', derived from Scandinavian, with that
characteristic hard 'g' sound. Sometimes two competing words
made a kind of truce, as it were, each taking a slightly different
sense. Thus, the Anglo-Saxon word *shirt*, with the 'sh' sound
characteristic of West-Germanic, had its North-Germanic equivalent
skirt, with that 'sk' again. Instead of one replacing the other (the
egg/*ey* scenario), both underwent a semantic shift in a 'northerly'
direction, towards a more restricted sense: a *shirt* became a
garment for the upper part of the body and a *skirt* one for the lower
part, with both words later acquiring additional gender-specific

---

[9]The anecdote occurs in Caxton's preface to a translation of a French version of the
Aeneid. It is quoted in many histories of English, for instance in Lincoln Barnett's
History of the English Language, Sphere Books, 1970, pp. 104–5.

connotations. A similar demarcation 'pact' was made between the words *church* and *kirk*.

The third major lexical layer of the vocabulary 'cake' is Norman French, these being words from French which were brought into the language by the Norman invaders of the eleventh century. Many of these words concern aspects of culture, such as religion, government, the law and cooking. It is well known, for instance, that the French words for common farm animals were incorporated into English to designate that animal when it had been cooked as food: English *pigs* when cooked become French *porc* (later *pork*); *cows* become French *beouf* (later *beef*); English *deer* become French *venison*; and English *sheep* become French *muton* (later *mutton*).

The fourth major layer of vocabulary is represented by the incorporation into English of many words derived from Greek and Latin at around the time of the Renaissance. These are typically longer, polysyllabic words, with a 'learned' or abstract feel. Again, there are characteristic spellings: longer words with 'eu' probably come from Greek, representing the Greek root which means 'good' or 'well'; another indication of Greek origins in longer words is the letter combination 'ph', representing 'phi', the Greek letter 'f' (so a word like *euphemism* is from Greek *eu-pheimi*, literally meaning to 'good-speak', and *philosophy* is from Greek *philosophos*, a lover of wisdom, and so on). The Latin words include many with the characteristic 'um' ending of Latin nouns, like *equilibrium*, *pendulum*, *auditorium*, *maximum*. Sometimes Latin prefixes were used to generate words (like 'in', meaning 'not', as in *inconsiderate*, *inconvenience*) and suffixes like '*able*' (from Latin *habilis*, meaning easily held or handled) were added to words of whatever origin (as in *understandable*, *manageable* and *laughable*).

The fifth layer, finally, contains words from the many languages from which English has 'borrowed', especially during the period of British imperial expansion. Often these words are recognisable by their obviously un-English spellings – *yacht* from Dutch, *guru* and *pundit* from Hindi, *kiosk* and *yoghurt* from Turkish and so on. Of course, the layers don't stop at five, but this basic five-layer model of lexical acquisition is a useful way of conceiving the basic loan-word process.

There are, of course, many other topics which are studied within the approach known generally as historical linguistics, such as the study of place names and surnames, and the consideration of the development of languages in terms of their syntax and structures as well as their vocabulary. But in my experience, matters of vocabulary and meaning are usually perceived as being much more immediately interesting by non-specialists than aspects of structure and form. Hence, we will end this brief survey of three major aspects of linguistics here, without venturing into the more demanding territory of structural linguistics.

10

English and History

At the end of the last chapter it was suggested that balancing the claims of text and context is one of the main problems encountered in literary study today. An approach to literature which focuses primarily on the text itself is often described (always disapprovingly) as 'formalism'; the opposite of formalism is historicism, which we can define as the approach to literature which focuses primarily on context. Currently, in the early years of the twenty-first century, historicism seems to be the 'default' approach to literature, so this term is usually employed without the disapproving connotations of the word 'formalism'. You may well conclude that the historicist approach is indeed the right one, and my aim in this chapter is simply to encourage you to critique the term 'historicism' so that it becomes, at least, open to question and is obliged to set out and defend its position in a rational manner. Our way into this topic will be to pose the question 'How much context is there in text?' Answering it will require us to examine the basis of our critical beliefs and practices, even if we take it for granted (as we must, of course) that those beliefs are right and good.

How much context is there in text?

To put the question this way round (rather than asking how much text there is in context) prioritizes text over context, making the assumption that our primary interest is in the text rather than the context. However, this cannot be taken for granted: for many of our most influential critics and theorists today, to be primarily interested in the text is to be guilty of 'formalism', this being a general term of disapproval for all forms of literary study which focus primarily on the formal, structural, linguistic and generic properties of the text rather than on its social, political and historical contexts.

The emerging problem, however, is that outlawing formalism and allowing contextualism a free rein effectively relegates literary study to the level of a sub-branch of history, one which merely happens to have a strongly 'textual' inflection. Literary study reduced in this way can have little claim to disciplinary independence, for it will simply have become literary-flavoured history. It's rather like taking milk with coffee – if we keep adding more and more milk we eventually reach the stage where we are drinking hot milk with a slight coffee flavour. That isn't illegal, of course, and we are all at liberty to drink whatever we like, but it isn't reasonable to assume that henceforth milk is the new coffee. Getting the balance right between text and context is of fundamental importance in this regard, especially at a time when there are signs that so-called 'traditional' disciplines (like English) are coming under some pressure from supposedly more 'vocational' alternatives. Students sign up for English, by and large, because they want to study literature: the study of context is a necessary adjunct. But it is only that, and if we want it to be our main object of study (whether as students, teachers or writers), then we ought to be in history departments.

Perhaps we can arrive at some notion of a sustainable balance between text and context by considering a well-known example of a critic 'importing' a new context into the study of a major literary work. The literary work is Jane Austen's novel *Mansfield Park* and the critic is Edward Said, whose book *Culture and Imperialism* (Vintage, 1995) discusses this novel in the part-chapter 'Jane Austen and Empire' (pp. 95–116 in the original book, and much reprinted in readers on critical theory). The estate of Mansfield Park in the novel is owned by Sir Thomas Bertram, whose income is partly derived from 'his West Indian property'. At a crucial stage in the book he has to absent himself for some months to attend to problematical business affairs in Antigua, and Said's view is that 'Sir Thomas's property in the Caribbean would have had to be a sugar plantation maintained by slave labour (not abolished till the 1830s)' (p. 107). So the handsome country house in the English shires with its surrounding park is maintained by a far less gracious estate overseas.[1] The political, on this kind of reading, is part of private life, and the fact that 'by the early nineteenth century every Britisher used sugar' (Said, p. 108) is the invisible chain that binds the two estates together.[2] The morality of this linkage is not questioned by the novel, and the English house and its ways stand for an approach to life which is genteel, humane, ordered and civilized, and in which due regard is given to the require-ments of all the inmates. This is in contrast to the dire and cramped Portsmouth home of the heroine Fanny Price, where peevishness and selfishness rule, symbolized in the way her taciturn father selfishly positions the only candle in the room between himself and his newspaper and carries on reading while ignoring the newly arrived Fanny's presence altogether. *Mansfield Park*, then, is read by Said 'as part of the structure of an expanding imperialist venture', and having done so, he says, 'one cannot simply restore it to the canon of "great literary masterpieces"' (p. 114).

My own experience of reading the Said piece is certainly something like that: once it has been read, the novel is changed, and can never again be viewed 'innocently'.[3] All the issues of personal conduct and social morality dramatized in the novel are re-contextualized within the intimate relationship that Said shows to exist between the two contrasting estates: the elegant English country estate and the Caribbean sugar plantation. Austen does

---

[1] The idea was first put forward in Avrom Fleishman's *A Reading of Mansfield Park: An Essay in Critical Synthesis*, Johns Hopkins University Press, 1970, but it was Said who expanded and popularized it.

[2] We should add, perhaps, that not quite *every* Britisher used sugar: many of those who supported abolition boycotted this commodity. William and Dorothy Wordsworth sweetened their tea and porridge with honey rather than sugar as a protest against the slave trade on which the supply of sugar to Britain depended, just as opponents of apartheid in our own time refused for many years to buy South African fruit or wine. (For the Wordsworth detail, see Penelope Hughes-Hallett, *The Immortal Dinner*, Viking, 2000, p. 227).

[3] As John Wiltshire points out in *Recreating Jane Austen* (Cambridge University Press, 2001, p. 162, footnote 33), the influence of the Said reading was quite evident in the 1999 Miramax/BBC film of *Mansfield Park*. If it has reached the 'heritage' film industry, perhaps we can expect it soon to feature even on the tea towels and china mugs sold to tourists at the Jane Austen properties.

not dwell on Antigua,[4] but she does mention it a number of times, and in such a way as to justify our further enquiry into it. Said's treatment of the issue is actually quite broad-brush: only one passage in the novel is read 'closely', namely the description of Sir Thomas, on his sudden return to Mansfield, putting matters there to rights like an absolute monarch, a Robinson Crusoe in total charge of his island, as Said puts it. Said mentions in passing the well-known moment in chapter twenty-one of the novel when Fanny raises with Sir Thomas the topic of slavery. Sir Thomas is not generally averse to talking about the West Indies. On the contrary, Fanny tells Edmund 'I love to hear my uncle talk of the West Indies. I could listen to him for an hour together.' Edmund tells her how well-disposed Sir Thomas is towards her, and adds 'I only wish you would talk to him more. You are one of those who are too silent in the evening circle.' Fanny denies this with, for her, considerable warmth: 'But I do talk to him more than I used. I am sure I do. Did not you hear me ask him about the slave-trade last night?' Edmund acknowledges this: 'I did – and was in hopes the question would be followed up by others. It would have pleased your uncle to be inquired of farther.' Fanny's response is to turn the accusation of silence on to her cousins:

> And I longed to do it – but there was such a dead silence! And while my cousins were sitting by without speaking a word, or seeming at all interested in the subject, I did not like – I thought it would appear as if I wanted to set myself off at their expense, by shewing a curiosity and pleasure in his information which he must wish his own daughters to feel.

The emphasis here is a little surprising: the 'dead silence' does not come from Sir Thomas's sternly indicating that the slave trade is not a suitable topic of conversation for the drawing room at Mansfield Park. On the contrary, Edmund assumes he would have been pleased to

---

[4]The final chapter has the famous opening 'Let other pens dwell on guilt and misery. I quit such odious subjects as soon as I can, impatient to restore everybody, not greatly in fault themselves, to tolerable comfort, and to have done with all the rest.' In the present context, this may seem somewhat incriminating.

be asked more questions about this matter, and Fanny is convinced it would have gratified him if his own daughters had shown more interest than they evidently did in serious topics of this kind.

So the whole topic of silence and its interpretation is crucial here, as it so often is in matters concerning literary context. In his popular collection of literary 'puzzles', John Sutherland takes *Mansfield Park* and the slave trade as his first 'case'.[5] He is – at best – politely respectful, but unenthusiastic, about Said's thesis: he is unconvinced that Sir Thomas's Antigua 'estate' (in Said's words) 'would have had to be a sugar plantation maintained by slave labour' and points out that the novel has very little indeed to say on the subject of Antigua ('Dead silence pretty well describes *Mansfield Park*'s dealings with Antigua generally', p. 4). Said, of course, sees the 'dead silence' on the matter (from nearly all previous critics, as well as from the author) as highly significant, and as indicating an aspect of colonial exploitation which is deeply engrained in the social fabric. The English gentry of the time (the first decade of the nineteenth century) were finding that the English country estate could not yield the returns which their expectations and way of life required, especially if they had several children, so the ownership of estates in the West Indies had become a way of supplementing their incomes. This briefly enabled them to compete with the emergent class of factory-owning industrialists, whose wealth and social importance would soon leave them behind. *Mansfield Park* is poised at this moment of transition, when many social attitudes and practices are those of the residual eighteenth century rather than the emerging nineteenth.

But the matter is complicated by two factors. Firstly, there are a number of tricky issues concerning dating: Said says that slavery was 'not abolished until the 1830s' (p. 107). In fact, Wilberforce's bill for the abolition of slavery was passed in 1807 (Sutherland, p. 8), but slavery continued in the West Indies until 1838. Though the bill was ineffective for so long, it officially came into force in two stages – between May 1807 (when no ship could be cleared for sailing from a British port with slaves on board), and March 1808, from which date no slaves could be landed at a British port. The long period of uncertainty between 1807 and the 1830s is partly explained by the fact

---

[5] *Is Heathcliff a Murderer? Puzzles in 19th Century Fiction*, World's Classics, 1996.

that the Act abolished the slave *trade*, not slavery.[6] Hence, slavery was an issue of moral and legal ambiguity for a period of thirty years in the early part of the century.

Furthermore, there is no general agreement about precisely when the novel was written and the exact years in which it is set, but the earliest suggested date is 1805 and the latest 1813. For most of this period, the Abolition bill had passed into law, but Sir Thomas's ownership of slaves (if that is indeed what he did in Antigua) was not illegal, although the morality or otherwise of slave labour was a very hotly debated issue. It might be expected that after 1807 Sir Thomas would be slightly warier than before of discussing the slave trade, thus implying that the book was written *before* abolition, but other indicators in the text seem to suggest a later date. One frequently mentioned date marker is Fanny's collection of books, which includes Crabbe's *Tales,* published in September 1812 (Southam), though Sutherland suggests that possibly the initial 't' of 'Tales' is lower case, which could mean that the texts referred to are actually the verse narratives in Crabbe's *Poems* of 1807 (Sutherland, p. 6). Another text mentioned is the *Quarterly Review* – in chapter ten, time is passed with the help of 'sofas, chit-chat, and Quarterly Reviews'. This journal was founded in 1809 (Southam, p. 13), and, he says, it carried 'the planter cause', so we might expect to find a copy lying around on the sofa in Sir Thomas's house. All the same, the pluralization is odd, and it may be that the term is being used in a loose generic sense simply to refer to journals of the kind which are published every quarter.

A second complicating factor is the precise social status of Sir Thomas, the question being, crudely, is he a representative of genteel old money or vulgar new money? Said sees him not as belonging to an ancient landed family whose income is merely supplemented by the Caribbean plantation, but as a representative of 'the colonial planter class' (Said, p. 112) whose wealth was founded

---

[6]These dates and details are taken from another essential piece on the issue, Brian Southam's 'The Silence of the Bertrams: Slavery and the Chronology of *Mansfield Park*' in the *TLS*, 17 February 1975, pp. 13–14. See also Frank Gibbon, 'The Antiguan Connection: Some New Light on *Mansfield Park*' in *The Cambridge Quarterly* 11, 1982, pp. 298–305 and Moira Ferguson, '*Mansfield Park,* Colonialism, and Gender' in *The Oxford Literary Review* 13, 1991, pp. 118–39.

on this source and who formed a distinct social group with their own well-known public activities – 'large houses, famous parties and social rituals, well-known commercial enterprises, celebrated marriages' (Said, p. 112). Southam places him socially in similar terms, remarking that

> there is something distinctly 'modern-built', *nouveau*, and West-Indian about Sir Thomas and his social standing, a point worth making since some commentators wholly misplace Sir Thomas, writing about him as a member of the old and established landed gentry who bears an ancient title. (p. 14)

As a 'second generation absentee [planter]' (p. 14), he is now keen to consolidate his position by giving his sons a genteel education and securing advantageous marriages for the women of the family. Hence, perhaps, his horror at the planned amateur theatricals, which he thinks likely to be talked about in the district and so lower the tone and reputation of the household, making it seem that the family are not the real social thing after all. Sutherland, however, is inclined to question 'Said's contention that Sir Thomas's wealth comes primarily from his colonial possessions and that his social eminence in Britain is entirely dependent on revenues from Antigua' (p. 6). At this period, he says, large landowners like Sir Thomas made substantial fortunes from agriculture at home, and if everything depended on the Antigua estate we would expect Lady Bertram to show a little more concern about the situation, but as he says, she brushes off Mrs Norris's enquiry with 'Oh! *that* will soon be settled.' This certainly undermines Said's notion of Sir Thomas being 'entirely dependent' on the Caribbean property and implies that he is an English landowner of the more traditional kind.

Assuming that we see the Antigua issue as an important factor in how we read the novel, perhaps the most interesting question is which side Jane Austen and Fanny Price are on – are they abolitionists or not? Sutherland sees Fanny Price as at the forefront of opposition to slavery, since in his view 'the novel contains clear indications that Fanny Price belongs to the Clapham Sect of evangelical Christianity, which hated plays and light morality only slightly less than it loathed slavery' (p. 8). Southam agrees, concluding that in spite of living in the lion's den (and looking about to inherit it) Fanny 'is unmistakably a "friend of the abolition"' (p. 14). Austen's own family had some implication in the trade ('In 1760, Jane's father, the Revd George Austen, was appointed principal trustee of a plantation in Antigua' – p. 14), so that 'the Austens too had a dependence, however slight, upon the prosperity of a plantation in Antigua'. For Said, in Sutherland's view, Fanny emerges as 'a pre-Victoria, empress (and oppressor) of a dominion over which the sun never sets' (p. 2). Since the novel, says Said, is

> part of the structure of an expanding imperialist venture, one cannot simply restore it to the canon of 'great literary masterpieces' – to which it most certainly belongs – and leave it at that. Rather, I think, the novel steadily, if unobtrusively, opens up a broad expanse of domestic imperialist culture without which Britain's subsequent acquisition of territory would not have been possible. (p. 114)

This conclusion seems to see the novel as very much implicated in the process of empire-building and exploitation, for its discreet drawing of a veil over what Antigua represents colludes with the process of simultaneously proclaiming moral human values, and seeing no contradiction between doing so and condoning slavery.

Let's now try to draw together what we have so far on the issue of contextual information in literary study, both in general and in relation to this novel. Firstly, we have followed Said in seeing Antigua as highly relevant to the novel, even though none of it is set there – indeed, it is only mentioned in passing nine times, and all the plot requires is that Sir Thomas should be absent for an extended period, not that he should be absent in this particular place. We see the novel's debate about personal morality as expanded to a political and international level by the fact of the estate in England ultimately depending (wholly or partly) on a sugar plantation in the West Indies. Secondly, we note the textual and historical precision which this kind of discussion requires – the silence at the mention of the slave-trade in chapter twenty-one doesn't necessarily seem to be Sir Thomas's, and we take this into account; we accept that he could conceivably have had non slave-owning business in Antigua, and so on. Thirdly, we are highly conscious of the complicated issues surrounding the dating of both the abolition of slavery and of the novel itself (where even the matter of a 't' being lower case or upper case may have a bearing). Fourthly, we are aware of the ambiguity of Sir Thomas's precise social-class status and how this again opens up another area of undecidability within the text. Fifthly, we re-consider both character and author in the light of the moral issues raised by the areas of context which this kind of enquiry opens up. For Said, though, the novel remains a 'great literary masterpiece' in spite of what he sees as its implication in the process of empire-building.

Where, then, does this leave us on the question of context in literary studies? I think that a way of focusing the question is to say that in literary study the problem of context in its most acute form is usually that of deciding how we interpret silence. *Mansfield Park* says almost nothing about Antigua – it is pretty well silent on the issue, and we have to decide how to interpret that silence. Of course, it is also silent on many other issues, such as the extreme harshness of discipline in the Navy, which Fanny's brother William is to join, or the conflict with the American colonies, which was taking place at the time. Clearly, we cannot take just any contemporary issue on which the novel is silent and promote it to a central place in our interpretation. Somehow, the acid test is that we need to show that what we have is not just *any* contextual silence, but a *pregnant* silence. And what are the signs of the 'pregnancy' which we could look for in another instance? Well, firstly, the fact that the silence isn't *total* – Antigua *is* mentioned in the novel, and not just once. Secondly, the relevance of Antigua is *pervasive*, affecting not just a single incident, but the foregrounded moral and thematic core of the novel, which concerns issues of conduct, questions of how we can live the (morally) good life at the same time as living the (materially) good life. It is also much concerned with acknowledging and meeting the claims of others. Remember, for instance, the telling moment in chapter twenty-seven when Fanny decides to wear for the ball all the gifts she has recently been given – both William's cross on Edmund's chain *and* Miss Crawford's necklace –, on the grounds that (although she now disapproves of Miss Crawford) 'She acknowledged it to be right. Miss Crawford had a claim.' This taking into account of everyone's claims is what Mansfield Park as a repository of moral values supposedly stands for, and this justifies our own taking into account of the claims of Antigua to due attention in the novel.

Thirdly, taking into account something the novel is largely silent about is justified also by the great weight the novel gives to the significance of silence itself. The word 'silence' or 'silenced' is used thirty-four times in the book, often designating moments which occur naturally in conversation as tone or implication is assimilated (chapter nine, 'A general silence succeeded'; chapter ten, 'This was followed by a short silence', and 'After an interval of silence'; chapter fourteen, 'A short silence followed' and 'A short silence succeeded'). At other times, the silence is more momentous – the forbidding silence of Sir Thomas shortly after Fanny's first arrival at Mansfield Park, his promised silence on the matter of Mister Crawford's proposal and the 'dead silence' which follows Fanny's mention of the slave trade. Fanny's own progress from awed silence to confident self-expression is one of the major lines of development in the book, and the related word 'quiet' and its derivatives are even more frequently used (48 occurrences), often designating the idealized reflective calm of the place and the way of life Mansfield Park represents. Fanny sees beyond the quality of mere 'agreeableness' (one of the attributes, inevitably, which Sir Thomas approves of in Henry Crawford), this being another much-used term in the book (seventy-three occurrences). She demands something deeper than this, and thereby, I think, gives us licence to do the same.

These are some of the factors, then, which enable us to admit the claims for a particular context in this case, and they may allow us to formulate criteria for assessing contextual claims in literature in general. We have looked, then, at an instance in which the claims made for the relevance of a specific context are well made and convincing. In the next section we will look at an example in which similar claims for the relevance of a specific context seem (to me) to be on weaker ground.

Is Keats's 'To Autumn' about Peterloo?

It was suggested in the last section that the problem of context in literary studies is really the problem of how to read silence. Indeed, John Sutherland argues that how we read what isn't there is a crucial dividing point between academic writing and 'lay' writing about literature. He cites Warren Roberts' book *Jane Austen and the French Revolution* with the comment

> Roberts' line goes thus: as is well known, Jane Austen never mentions the French Revolution. Therefore it must be a central preoccupation, and its silent pressure can be detected at almost every point of her narratives. (Sutherland, p. 5)

Such assumptions, he says, mark 'a new gulf which [has] opened up between the advanced literary critics of the academic world and the intelligent lay reader' (p. 6). Roberts' book, as Sutherland says, came out 'at the high tide of the theory-led "re-reading" of classic texts' (p. 5) and deconstruction was especially keen on interrogating the 'gaps', 'lacunae', 'faultlines' and 'slippages' in texts (all ways of denoting absences in texts). Although lay people in general probably still assume that doing English is about the close reading of 'the words on the page', the dominance of poststructuralism in the 1970s and 1980s meant that it had actually become just as interested in the words *off* the page.

But these days academic literary criticism and theory are not generally read by anybody outside the discipline, so the situation hardly ever comes to the attention of a wider public than the one which has grown quite accustomed to it. Occasionally, however, books with a hybrid readership (part 'lay', part academic) bring the issue into the open, and since literary biography comes into this category, the publication of major biographies sometimes has this effect. Hence, when Andrew Motion's biography of Keats appeared some years ago (*Keats*, Faber & Faber, 1997), reviewers seemed shocked at the extent to which the poet was seen so much in terms of the politics and the cultural politics of his day. Motion's discussion of 'To Autumn', Keats's most celebrated poem, seemed to cause particular affront. Perhaps reviewers had expected that a fellow poet would praise the 'balance' and 'perfection' of the work, and Motion does at first seem to be taking this line, as he informs us that 'Because "To Autumn" holds its balances so expertly, it has often been called Keats's "most ... untroubled poem." This, combined with its great fame and familiarity, can make it seem unassailable' (p. 461). He then begins to assail it, for balance, expertness and untroubledness had become suspect qualities in the critical climate of the 1990s: 'The surfaces of the poem might seem painterly and therefore static,' he assures us, 'but in fact they too are disturbed' (p. 462). Some of the disturbing factors are 'the social anxieties which had dogged him all his adult life', now unexpectedly in crisis since his recent visit to London [see below]. Then came the lines reviewers found especially shocking, as Motion linked the poem to a political event which had happened the month before it was written, when soldiers killed eleven people at a political demonstration at St Peter's Field, Manchester, an event immediately dubbed (in mocking reference to the then recent Battle of Waterloo) the 'Peterloo Massacre':

> It would oversimplify the case to say that because the poem was written in the aftermath of Peterloo, it is precisely concerned with the Massacre ... At the same time, it cannot and does not want to escape its context – which it registers in a number of subtle but significant ways. It has been suggested that the word 'conspiring', in the third line, both embraces and deflects the plotting that Keats knew surrounded Henry Hunt's recent activities [the soldiers' attempts to reach 'Orator Hunt' and prevent him speaking had led to the Peterloo Massacre in August; Keats was present a fortnight later, in a crowd of about 30,000, at Hunt's triumphal arrival in London.] The reference to the gleaner is more certainly charged with contemporary references. Gleaning [the practice of gathering in stray ears of corn left by the reapers – a traditional 'perk' for locals] had been made illegal in 1818 ... and ... the figure ... also refers to his sympathy for the denied and the dispossessed. So does his description of the bees. They are a reminder of the miserable facts of labour that Keats had condemned during his walking tour in Scotland ... (p. 462)

The whole poem, then, is turned into a kind of encrypted political statement, and all its favourite features – the 'conspiring' mists, the bees, the gleaner and so on – acquire hidden political meanings. Somehow, the exercise was all the more galling for being couched in Motion's characteristically suave prose style rather than in the more openly provocative verbal complexities of deconstruction.

Yet from within the discipline, Motion's political reading of the poem in 1997 seemed almost routine, for it had long been taken for granted that those 'stubble-plains' touched with 'rosy hue' represented not the fields Keats saw while walking by the Water Meadows in Winchester but the blood-stained ground of the previous month at St Peter's Field in Manchester, whether or not it would 'oversimplify the case' to say so. Though the poem is in fact silent about the Massacre and the 'miserable facts of labour', an 'interpretive tradition' had grown up from the 1980s onwards which reads a poem's silences as highly significant – 'it cannot and does not want to escape its context', says Motion of 'To Autumn'. In effect, though poets have the theoretical right to remain silent, anything they *don't* say may well be taken down and used against them.

A more uncompromising version of the Motion reading of 'To Autumn' had appeared (as chapter nine, 'To Autumn') in Andrew Bennett's *Keats, Narrative and Audience: The Posthumous Life of Writing* (Cambridge University Press, 1994). Bennett bypasses the poet's silence on political matters at the start: 'The *apparent* silence of "To Autumn" on the subject of politics tends to be read as evidence of a Keatsian desire to abstract poetic language from history' (p. 159, my italics). He follows the lead of Jerome McGann. who 'has analysed "To Autumn" as "an attempt to 'escape' the period which provides the poem with its context"'. He again spells it out that 'To historicize Keats's poem ... would be ... to listen to the fractious intertextual cacophony of history, politics, economics, noises which "To Autumn" *seems* to silence' (p. 161, my italics). What follows in the essay is an elaborate reading of a poem which (in my view) isn't there, a poem about the repeatedly mentioned topics of the essay – 'history', 'politics', 'economics', 'agrarian politics', the 'topographical violation of boundaries', 'agricultural labour relations', 'financial accumulation', 'subtextual economics', the 'legal limitations of enclosure', the 'discourse of gleaning'. In place of Keats's poem, the critic stages a melodrama about 'fracturing', 'suppression', 'illicit incursions', 'transgression', 'repression', 'invasion', 'violation' and 'intrusion'. And whatever *isn't* in the poem counts as further evidence against it: it is a poem which 'suppresses the cacophonous noises of history' (p. 160): the goddess Ceres isn't mentioned in it either, yet 'Ceres is the pervasive unstated presence in "To Autumn"' (p. 164) and 'the unstated figure of the goddess Ceres activates the discourses of labour, property, lawful exchange, and legal bound-aries, it is possible to hear in "To Autumn"' (p. 165). There is also 'a displaced representation of financial accumulation' which 'activates the subtextual economics' of the poem (p. 166), this being part of the 'silent barring of money from "To Autumn"' (p. 167); furthermore 'the stanza's silence over the political question of gleaning' (p. 169) is yet another offence which must be taken into account.

The critic says that 'we must refuse to be figured within, or by, the bounds of the text', and he certainly practices what he preaches. He is eminent, and work like his is widely practiced and admired, but it demonstrates (in my view) the dangers of professing our determination to read literature 'in context' and then admitting no *textual* restraints in deciding what the *con*text is. If we truly desire to be literary critics and literary theorists, rather than speculative historians, then we *must* do precisely what Bennett says we *mustn't* do – that is, we must 'agree to be figured within, or by, the bounds of the text'. Otherwise (and in spite of the heavy-industrial scholarship which historicist readings require), there can be little skill or intel-lectual challenge (or fun, even) in doing literary criticism and theory. Such writing (which allows the text no voice, except for the one the critic hears in its silences) is not the same thing as doing criticism, just as repeatedly kicking a football into an empty goal net is not the same as playing football.

One other striking aspect of such readings of Keats's poem is the dislike and distrust they express for the qualities which so many poets strive hard to achieve: Bennett writes, oddly, of the poem's '*notoriously* mellifluous harmonics' (p. 167, my italics) and is suspi-cious of the line 'barred clouds bloom the soft-dying day', because in the draft the wording is 'a gold cloud gilds the soft-dying day'. This mediocre line was rejected by Keats in favour of words which are vivid, accurate, tough, concise and innovative, and instantly recognizable as the real poetic thing. But for Bennett, changing the line is merely part of the psychic melodrama of concealment, and the poet makes the change because of his 'silent barring of money from "To Autumn"'.

I should add that I am not arguing that poems exist in a vacuum separated from all else a poet may be experiencing. On the contrary, I don't doubt that there are some links between aspects of the poem and the post-Peterloo social agitation. For instance, the surprising word 'conspiring' near the start of the poem was quite probably put into Keats's mind (subliminally or otherwise) by the intense discussion of conspirators and conspiracy in connection with 'Orator Hunt' and others in the weeks after Peterloo.[7] But this is quite different from saying that the poem is really about Peterloo and social injustice, or that Keats culpably tried to evade these matters by writing about an 'innocent' topic like the changing seasons and so was constantly 'ambushed' psychologically as he wrote the poem by the return of what he was trying to repress.

You will have noticed, finally, that we have now considered two examples of historicist readings of literary texts and have found Said's 'slavery' reading of *Mansfield Park* broadly acceptable while rejecting the 'Peterloo' reading of 'Ode to Autumn'. Are we, then, applying inconsistent standards and just picking and choosing on personal whim? I hope not, but you will have to make a decision on this point for yourself. For the record, in my view, some of the main differences between the two cases are these. Firstly, *Mansfield Park* isn't *completely* silent on the topic of Antigua and slavery – they are mentioned in the text – whereas 'Ode to Autumn' is completely so on the matter of Peterloo and labour relations. Those topics have therefore to be *read into* the text by the critic. Secondly, in the case of *Mansfield Park* the slavery issue and the matter of the West Indies estate have an evident relevance to the issues of morality, conduct

---

[7]The same point is made by Vincent Newey in his essay 'Keats, history, and the poets' in *Keats and History*, Nicholas Roe ed. Cambridge University Press, 1995, p. 186. Newey writes that if we accept the 'Peterloo' reading of 'To Autumn' (which he traces back to Jerome McGann's essay 'Keats and the Historical Method' in his [McGann's] *The Beauty of Inflections: Literary Investigations in Historical Method and Theory*, Clarendon Press, 1988), we 'collude in making of Romanticism a bankrupt ideology of evasion'.

and silence which are the overt themes of the novel, whereas in the case of 'Ode to Autumn' it is difficult to see any such 'fit' between the claimed content (social unrest and injustice) and the overt matter of the poem (seasonal transition, coming to terms with loss and change, and so on). Finally, the Said reading of *Mansfield Park* explicitly does not accuse the literary work of being culpably evasive and attempting to disguise the socially unacceptable by dressing it in high art. It *adds* a dimension to the work, whereas the 'Peterloo' reading seeks to *subtract* from the work's standing and is dismissive of the qualities readers have previously admired in it, reducing it to a new mono-dimensionality. Something like these three grounds, suitably adapted, ought to provide a general basis for evaluating historicist readings of literary texts.

Is History the new English?

The problem illustrated by the case of 'To Autumn' is the problem not just of how to identify context but of what to do with it when we have identified it. The approach we have been critiquing originated in McGann's work (as already mentioned) and in that of other major figures (such as Marilyn Butler[8] and Marjorie Levinson[9]) and it is usually described as 'New Historicist'. In these heavily historicized approaches, context tends to overwhelm text, so that we begin to find that historical work progressively replaces textual work. The text is disenfranchised (we refuse to be figured by its bounds), and our standards and procedures become those of history. This is fine if we believe that History is the new English, but not otherwise.

One thing we need is clear terminology which can highlight the nature of the dilemma for us and perhaps useful terms can be found in Stephen Greenblatt's essay 'Resonance and Wonder'. Greenblatt (a scholar of Early Modern literature, not Romanticism) is the founder of New Historicism, and what was new about the New Historicism

---

[8] *Romantics, Rebels and Reactionaries: English Literature and its Background*, Oxford University Press, 1981.
[9] See her co-edited collection *Rethinking Historicism: Critical Readings in Romantic History*, Basil Blackwell, 1988.

when it started in the early 1980s was its way of making vivid and thought-provoking juxtapositions between a literary text and a contemporary (or near-contemporary) historical document of some kind. The document might be a personal memoir, part of a travel narrative or an account of court proceedings. The document would be closely discussed for the light it throws upon (say) the attitudes of its era towards notions of personal or national identity, or sexuality. The reading of the document might take up over half the essay and the findings would then be used to illuminate a key aspect of a Renaissance play.[10] Work like this at its best had an exciting specificity and freshness, but this fascinating essay captures the moment when Greenblatt begins to pull back a little from the current of the movement he himself founded.

In the essay 'Resonance and Wonder', Greenblatt tries to explain his own approach to works of art by using these central concepts of 'resonance' and 'wonder'. He says, 'by resonance I mean the power of the object displayed to reach out beyond its formal boundaries to a larger world, to evoke in the viewer the complex, dynamic cultural forces from which it has emerged and for which … it may be taken to stand' (p. 276). So the 'resonance' of a work of art is an echo within it of the 'cultural forces from which it has emerged'. 'Resonance' is the quality that connects the art object to the social and political world. Thus, for example, a stylized and formally staged scene in a play may evoke formally staged events in politics (like the inauguration of a president or a state opening of parliament) or in religious ritual (like the formal procession to the altar for a High Mass). This kind of juxtaposition makes us see all three areas (theatre, politics and religion) as part of the same cultural 'economy'. We are aware that these procedures are intended to evoke a kind of awe in us, to impress upon us an image of power, and to think in this archetypally

---

[10] For work in this style see Greenblatt's book *Shakespearian Negotiations*, Clarendon Press, 1990. Greenblatt's anecdotal 'co-texts' often have the effect (or is it the side-effect?) of 'Americanising' the Shakespeare text under discussion: for instance, in the famous essay 'Invisible Bullets' (the second chapter of the book), Shakespeare's *Henry IV* and *Henry V* are read in the context of Thomas Harriot's *A Brief and True Report of the New Found Land of Virginia*; in another influential essay, 'The Cultivation of Anxiety: King Lear and His Heirs' (in Greenblatt's *Learning to Curse: Essays in Early Modern Culture*, Routledge, 1990), the anecdotal co-text is a piece about dealing with a difficult child, from the *American Baptist Magazine* of 1831.

New Critical way is to become aware of the play's 'resonance' – its 'active context', in other words.

'Wonder', by contrast, is the power of the art object in itself, in isolation, so to speak, 'the power to evoke an exalted attention' (p. 277). To expand this a little: all works of art have an enclosing 'frame' of some kind which *separates* them from the world – there is a literal frame around a picture; there is white space on the page around the words of a poem; there is a proscenium arch (or some equivalent) around the staged play. The 'exalted attention' which the work of art is able to evoke is partly the product of the frame. Of course, the frame is porous – the resonance operates through it – but it is always there, and should not be wished away by ditching formalism and 'wonder' totally and opting for contextualism and resonance.

New Historicism's concern has been very much with 'resonance'; it has wanted to 'reduce the isolation of individual "masterpieces"', says Greenblatt (p. 277). But Greenblatt seems to feel in this essay that the 'resonance' approach has now gone a little too far ('textual contextualism has its limits', p. 278), and he wants to give a slight steer back towards 'wonder'. He uses the example of museums and galleries, and the parallel is a fruitful one: imagine, for instance, the display of a major painting like Monet's 'Water Lillies': a display format based on principles of resonance might juxtapose with the picture such items as photographs of the place depicted, contemporary descriptions of the place (a gardener's, a relative's and so on), other paintings of the same scene, the artist's own account of the painting, contrasting views of other kinds of garden (a medieval garden, a Japanese garden, etc.). All this contextualising, of course, would make us think about the work as an object of representation *within* the world rather than as an object that *transcends* the world. On the other hand, to display the work with the emphasis on 'wonder', it would probably be isolated from other pictures, perhaps on a plain white wall, maybe visible down a vista from adjoining rooms, and with nothing to accompany it but a discreet label giving the artist's name, the title of the painting and the year it was completed. This form of presentation emphasizes purely formal properties – size, the massing of shapes within the composition, the disposition of colours across the canvas … It is not striving to tell us anything at all about the social conditions of privilege that produce art, or about the sources of an artist's ideas or methods of working, or whatever an artist might be thought to be (sub)consciously avoiding by painting massive pictures of gardens all the time.

New Historicism turned us towards 'resonant contextualism' so decisively, Greenblatt fears, that we may be losing the capacity of wonder altogether – we seem to be interested in nothing but social conditions and methods of working suffused by a kind of retrospective resentment of the social privileges enjoyed by the artist. But if we are not interested in shapes, colours and composition *at all* for their own sakes (which is to say, if we have cast off formalism without even a twinge of regret), then the whole process of discussing the poem (or any other art object) is curiously pointless, since ultimately it won't really matter what we have to say about all the rest. Context, then, has its claims, but if we allow its unlimited expansion without ever formulating criteria which put *its* claims in context, then we may find that little is left which can properly be called literary studies.

It may seem a little mysterious, finally, that literary studies has made such major u-turns as that represented by the shift from nearly exclusive formalism to nearly exclusive historicism. It seems like switching from one extreme position to its opposite extreme without passing through any intermediate state – as if a St Francis were suddenly to become a Vlad the Impaler.

11

The Essay: Crossing the Four Frontiers

Description

It is possible to identify four basic levels of literary discussion, which can be called, in ascending order of complexity, *description*, *commentary*, *discussion* and *analysis*. They can be illustrated by extracts from a hypothetical essay on Charlotte Brontë's novel *Jane Eyre*, all taken from the point in the essay where the matter under consideration is the relationship depicted early in the novel between the heroine and the Reed family. Firstly, then, in the kind of literary-critical writing which I am calling description, a sentence of the following kind might occur:

> Jane is mistreated by the Reed family, and although she is solely dependent on them to secure her livelihood, she speaks out against her harsh treatment. [*The essay then moves on to a different point.*]

Self-evidently, this is just a statement of what happens in the book. It simply describes events in the narrative. It merely indicates that the writer has read the novel and knows its plot, but there is no indication of whether anything has been understood about the significance of the events depicted. Such writing retells the story, or a section of it, usually sticking to the plot order of the events as they occur in the book, and when encountered in extended form, it is characteristic of the weakest kind of student essay.

It is universally agreed that 'story telling' of this kind in extended form is a bad thing, but it is worth adding here that the sentence quoted above as an example of description in an academic essay would be quite acceptable as a way of introducing a more in-depth treatment of a particular aspect of a novel, as demonstrated in the next sub-section. Thus, it is not the case that a really good essay writer will operate all the time in analytical mode, and perhaps the four 'levels' discussed here are best thought of as being like the different gears used in driving a car. A driver makes use of all the gears as appropriate, moving from one to the other as driving circumstances change. Of course, every reader of the novel, including the tutor who is marking the essay, knows that Jane is mistreated by the Reed family, on whom she is totally dependent, but making such a statement is a way of focusing, a way of homing in on the area of the novel on which you intend to concentrate and indicating to the reader what you see as the essential skeleton of meaning beneath the multifarious surface of the text.

Commentary

So an essay on the same novel which is predominantly *commentary* might begin a section in the same way, using that sentence as a way of indicating what is to be focused on, but would then take matters a little further:

> Jane is mistreated by the Reed family, and although she is solely dependent on them to secure her livelihood, she speaks out against her harsh treatment. This shows that she is becoming something which society disapproves of – a woman with a voice and opinions of her own. [*The essay then moves on to a different point.*]

Here, the factual description of what happens at this stage in the book is supplemented by comments on the significance of those events (as in the final sentence). Such comments are often fairly limited in scope, especially in student essays, and typically an essay which is written mainly at this second level would go on to cite or describe several other incidents from the book, each time attributing more or less the same significance to them. Hence, the overall structure of such an essay is often that of a list or catalogue of cited incidents, none of them examined closely, and without much 'thematization' beyond the reiteration of a single point of significance.

The comment in this case is rather stark and absolute, and it has certain quite common failings: firstly, 'society' is seen almost as a character, one capable of collectively holding certain attitudes. It is a term best avoided in writing about the Victorian period, which is often stereotyped and caricatured in student essays, as if everybody, irrespective of social class, personal circumstances and private convictions, held the same views and thought in the same way. Secondly, the period seems to be viewed very much from a present-day standpoint, as seen, for instance, in making the assumption that the most essential thing is that a woman should have 'a voice and opinions of her own'. But what if those opinions were ill-informed, or narrow-minded, or prejudiced – would it still be OK to hold them just because they are 'her own'? I am trying to indicate, simply, that we have to go beyond the commonplace and show evidence of unpacking our thoughts, questioning them, illustrating what we have in mind, being sceptical about received views, and so on. That is what a student working predominantly at the next level would begin to show evidence of doing.

Discussion

Perhaps the limitations of commentary can best be seen by comparing it with the next level, which I am designating *discussion*:

> When she protests against her treatment by the Reeds, Jane, of course, engages in a laudable act of rebellion and self-assertion in the face of injustice. But the emphasis of the passage is not really upon this, but upon the heroine's realisation of her own powers, which are tested in this episode for the first time. ('What strength had I to dart retaliation at my antagonist?' she begins by asking herself). When she makes her verbal assault ('I gathered my energies and launched them in this blunt sentence') she is herself

shocked at the force of her own words, as Mrs Reed is silenced
and rebuffed ('Mrs Reed looked frightened ... she was lifting up
her hands ... and even twisting her face as if she would cry')

Here the essay moves from commentary, which is essentially a
series of more-or-less isolated points on some aspect of a book,
to *discussion*, which is made up of a *sequence* of points linked
together and having a single focus. In the example just quoted what
is said concerns just one aspect of the scene, which is the heroine's
acquiring for the first time a sense of the force of her own personality.
This is an underlying facet of this literary text which the essay picks
out and highlights. It gives us, in other words, that vital ingredient
– thematization. By this I mean the identifying of recurrent strands
of significance and concern which shape and organize the on-going
torrent of incident, dialogue and circumstantial detail we encounter
when reading a full-scale Victorian novel. If the essay writer had
merely praised Jane for her self-assertiveness, or blamed her for her
failure to restrain her outburst, then the writing would probably have
remained at the level of commentary, for it would merely be part of
a catalogue in which the protagonist's actions are approved or disap-
proved of with reference to a fixed moral or social point of view. So
the defining quality which promotes the passage from commentary
to discussion is that it resists simple closure of that kind; it picks up
on a less-than-obvious facet of the text and then takes time to tease
out its implications in greater detail. Commentary passes rapidly over
the textual terrain at high level, flying a predictable course and quickly
moving on elsewhere. Discussion, in contrast, involves doubling back
over the territory in question and moving in for a much closer look.

Notice that in the essay extract above we have that essential kind
of deceleration, of slowing down, so that the writer isn't immediately
leaving the scene mentioned and hurrying on to somewhere else. The
most useful marginal comment I have ever seen made by a tutor on a
student essay was just the two words 'Slow down' inserted three or
four times at different points in the margin. Here, the slowing down
is achieved by inserting the brief quotations from the text which
demonstrate the presence of the theme of 'self-discovery', which
is being identified as a key factor in the protagonist's growing self-
awareness and self-confidence. For a child to have such a powerful

effect on an adult, and to realize that this has happened, makes for a truly formative moment. What Jane Eyre acquires as the novel progresses is very much *strength* of character – that is what determines her actions at key points in the remainder of the novel, and this scene shows the beginning of that process.

Analysis

So what, finally, does the fourth level, *analysis*, look like? Well, it takes up elements from the discussion level and incorporates them into something more wide ranging:

> When she protests against her treatment by the Reeds, Jane, of course, engages in a laudable act of rebellion and self-assertion in the face of injustice. But the emphasis of the passage is not really upon this, but on the heroine's realisation of her own powers, which are tested in this episode for the first time. ('What strength had I to dart retaliation at my antagonist?' she begins by asking herself). When she makes her verbal assault ('I gathered my energies and launched them in this blunt sentence') she is herself shocked at the force of her own words, as Mrs Reed is silenced and rebuffed ('Mrs Reed looked frightened ... she was lifting up her hands ... and even twisting her face as if she would cry'). The outburst here prefigures the moment near the end of the novel when she again has the undoubted satisfaction of releasing the full force of her tongue and telling others exactly what she thinks of them: this happens at the moment when she rejects St John Rivers, telling him 'I scorn your idea of love ... I scorn the counterfeit sentiment you offer; yes, St John, and I scorn you when you offer it.' In this later exchange, the matters at issue are the same as in the scene with Mrs Reed; on both occasions she refuses to take part in a masquerade of love – 'I am not deceitful', she tells Mrs Reed, 'if I were I should say I loved you' – and on both occasions she resents the assumption by the other party that she can repress her feelings in an inhuman way: 'You think I have no feelings, and that I can do without one bit of love or kindness', she says to Mrs Reed. In that sense, taking up St John Rivers'

offer of marriage in adult life would involve re-imprisoning herself in the red room of Mrs Reed's childhood neglect.

This, then, is analytical writing. The main difference between this and discussion is that in analysis the sustained scrutiny of one aspect of a text, which is characteristic of the discussion level, is combined with the making of links and connections with other parts of the text. So in the example, there is both detailed discussion of the early scene in the book, and a series of suggestions which link that scene with other crucial episodes which occur later on. Thus, the example is using the incident under immediate discussion (Jane's early mistreatment by the Reeds) as a springboard to a series of connections with other parts of the novel. The essay is not simply moving chronologically through the events depicted in the book (the most common mark of writing at the description and commentary levels). Rather, it is establishing its own order, based on an underlying integrative thematization, that is, a thematization which integrates key details of the scene under discussion with other sections or aspects of the novel. Here, the two incidents, one early, one late in the novel, are linked by the overarching themes of being expected to live without love, while at the same time pretending to love.

A further list of some of the other important characteristics of analysis would include the following. Firstly, the last extract isn't just making simple assertions; points are being qualified, amplified, re-stated, and this is indicated by the nature of the connecting words and phrases 'of course', 'but', 'not really', 'she is, almost', 'partly', 'all the same'. These words indicate that a debate, or a 'dialogue with the self', is going on. Secondly, the passage has slowed the pace of the discussion: the writer has paused and then homed in on a specific episode. That episode is being looked at closely, yet in broad connecting terms too, so that its implications for the rest of the novel are being teased out. Thirdly, the passage is working in close-up with the text, picking out specific phrases – not quoting huge chunks, but on the contrary, working mainly at what might be called 'phrase level', so that the sections quoted from the novel seldom amount to more than a single sentence, which is often the sign of real engagement in a literary essay. Of course, there are many different kinds of analytical writing. Some kinds, for instance, use sophisticated critical or theoretical vocabulary, but that is not a necessity, and it is not the case in the kind of analytical writing exemplified here.

When I try to describe (to myself and to students and teachers of literature) the rudiments of the traditional Anglo-American approach to literary texts, I arrive at taxonomies, or classification systems, like the one just set out. My motive is that I am constantly seeking some kind of synthesis and balance between old and new, between text-based and theory-based approaches. In practice, of course, a good literary essay will tend to move in a strategic way between these four levels – some element of description is essential in literary-critical writing, if only to speed up the process and facilitate the movement from one focus to the next. Likewise, it is possible to posit, beyond the four levels so far described, further levels in which connections are made with extra-textual issues of a literary–historical kind (level five), a social–political kind (level six) and a philosophical–linguistic kind (level seven). French theoretical writing about literature has a strong preference for abandoning levels one to four almost completely and staying at these 'higher' levels of discourse, especially six (the social–political) and seven (the philosophical–linguistic). In my own writing, and with my students, I am usually trying to encourage the crossing of the divide between the first four and the rest, so that the writing covers levels three, four, five and six especially (I am conscious that my taste and talents at level seven are fairly limited). As a writer, I find this kind of discursive taxonomy of essay writing very helpful, and I hope that others may do so too.

12

The Undergraduate Dissertation

On many English degree courses the culmination of a student's work in the final year takes the form of a dissertation, or, for creative writing, a final portfolio. The dissertation is usually around 10,000 words, on a topic chosen by the student and then approved by the department, often with agreed modifications. The typical pattern is that topics are chosen towards the end of the second year, finalized in the first semester of the third year and actually written in the final semester. At many UK universities, a number of general sessions are provided in lecture format in the early part of the final year, looking at ways of approaching a topic and research methods, and students are then assigned a tutor who will meet them individually to look at drafted sections on a specified number of occasions. Typically, a student could expect about four individual half-hour sessions with the tutor during the final semester, and for each of these a segment of around 2,000 words of drafted material will have been sent to the tutor beforehand. You can expect that the tutor will be a recognized expert on some broadly relevant aspect of the period you are writing about, but probably not a specialist in your particular chosen author(s). Assessment practice in relation to the final piece of work varies from one university to another: in all cases where I have been an examiner, every dissertation has been read and graded independently by two tutors, with the two then meeting to agree a joint final grade. Usually, one of those tutors will have been the supervisor of the piece in question. If these internal grades differ by a small amount, it is usual to split the difference without further discussion, provided both grades are within the same degree classification. If the difference crosses a classification boundary, the discussion can be detailed and quite prolonged, even if the gap is just a matter of a couple of marks. By academic convention, uneven numbers are always rounded up, not down, so if one tutor said 63 and the other 64, the result would be 64. The student should receive two sets of detailed comments, and usually the agreed final grade only, though some institutions will also show the two individual grades originally given, as well as the final one. In the (rare) cases when two tutors suggest very different grades and cannot agree a final result, a third adjudicator will be asked to read the dissertation and assign a grade without reference back to the other two, but taking their views and comments into account. In the UK system, a selection of dissertations will also be looked at by an external examiner from another university. Usually the dissertations sent to externals are those of students who might be on an overall borderline between classes, or who have been given what is for them an unusually strong or unusually weak grade. But a lot of effort and sustained work goes into the dissertation, so a grade attained here is often an individual's highest. This elaborate and lengthy process of assessment will probably seem rather quaint and eccentric to those who teach or learn at universities in other parts of the world, and in any case, the above information may well tell you more than (as a student) you would really want to know. My main purpose in discussing the marking process has been to emphasize that the grade for this major piece of work is never determined by a single examiner.

Shaping the dissertation

The most fundamental problem about the dissertation is working out how it should be structured. There is no universally applicable structural model, and the ultimate shape of your dissertation will depend on the kind of topic you choose to write about. From the structural viewpoint I would say that there are three main kinds of topic: the first is the '**X in Y**' type, the second is the '**Comparison**' type, and the third is the '**Open Field**' type, and I will say a little about the shape of each of these.

The '**X in Y**' type looks closely at a single theme or element in a chosen author, genre or period. Here are some examples: 'Fathers in the Novels of Jane Austen', 'Adultery in Eighteenth-Century Drama', 'Gardens in Medieval and Early Modern Literature', 'Illness in the Victorian Novel'. 'X in Y' dissertations can be structured in three main ways – the arrangement can be either **chronological**, or **factual** or **thematic**. I will illustrate these three arrangements using 'Illness in the Victorian Novel' as the example. In the **chronological** approach, firstly, we would aim to show a process of development or change in the treatment of this topic over the designated period. So we might take as our central body of work three novels all featuring illness, with one each from the early Victorian period (the 1840s), the mid-Victorian period (the 1860s) and the late Victorian period (the 1880s). We could cover a range of aspects of each of our chosen novels, and would try to cover all three novels in a similar way, perhaps in each case looking in turn at plot, characterization and authorial commentary, and then perhaps in each case looking in detail at (for example) a 'first-onset' scene, a scene of recovery and recuperation, and a death-bed scene. We would choose this chronological approach if we felt that over the course of the period there is a noticeable change in attitudes towards illness and ways of representing this.

If we had chosen the **factual** arrangement, we could look at different aspects of illness and the various ways in which the three novelists treat the topic, perhaps considering child illness, adult illness and chronic illness, using a different novelist for each. So for child illness we might consider the illness and death of Little Nell in Dickens' *The Old Curiosity Shop*, or that of Paul Dombey in his *Dombey and Son*; for adult illness, the illness and death of the heroine's mother in Elizabeth Gaskell's novel *North and South*, or Philip's illness and death in the same author's *Sylvia's Lovers*; for chronic illness, that of Ralph Touchet in Henry James's *The Portrait of a Lady*, or that of Clement in the same author's novella *A Passionate Pilgrim*. Six large Victorian novels would make quite a reading-heavy dissertation, but having a clear and solid overall structure makes it easy to break the 10,000-word total into manageable writing segments – in this case, three 3,000-word chapters on Dickens, Gaskell and James respectively, leaving about 500 words each for an overall introduction and an overall conclusion. You will already be accustomed, by the late stages of the final year, to writing essays of about 3,000 words, so these chapters will seem psychologically manageable, whereas thinking about the 10,000 word target as a single entity may seem very daunting. Of course, the three chapters have to be connected by running themes and by a certain uniformity of treatment, and not just be three separate essays placed end-to-end – but more of that later.

In the **thematic** arrangement, the idea is to look at the chosen topic as a set of 'sub-themes' which consider the broader topic from various angles. For instance, illness might be presented in a novel as a time when physical sickness can bring about the recovery of psychological or spiritual health, so that a couple estranged by strife, or misunderstanding or infidelity may finally rediscover their truer feelings and be reconciled (as happens in *Sylvia's Lovers*); or, in another novel, illness may be seen as a divisive force which sows the seeds of future strife within a family, as a feud develops over a disputed will, or a death-bed revelation, or a legacy bestowed (like Ralph's to Isabel Archer in *The Portrait of a Lady*, which has a decisive and negative effect on her life by making her the target of a ruthless fortune hunter). In other cases, a serious illness may function as a transformative conversion experience in the life of a character who recovers from it. In this kind of thematic arrangement, the major chapters or sections of the dissertation might have titles that indicate the 'sub-themes', such as (for the three instances just mentioned) 'Illness as social healer', 'Illness as the bringer of strife' and 'Illness as transformer of the self'. Notice that these are three sub-themes, so that again we arrive quickly at a symmetrical shape which divides the whole dissertation into essay-length segments of about 3,000 words, without presenting any tricky problems of distribution. If we had four sub-themes and six novels the structure would immediately become unbalanced, and we would have to spend time trying to decide how best to divide four into six. This may sound trivial, but actually it can prove very troublesome in a lengthy piece of writing, probably leading to one chapter being much longer than the others. Generally, it is better to have the core chapters all approximately the same length, unless there are excellent and easily stated reasons for doing otherwise. So those are three ways of tackling the 'X in Y' kind of topic.

In the '**Comparison**' type of dissertation, the primary aim is to compare the treatment of a specific theme or topic in the work of two or more writers, and we can take as an example a dissertation with the title 'The world of work in two post-war women novelists: Muriel Spark and A. S. Byatt'. We may decide that we are interested in three aspects of the topic: firstly, the representation of rivalry and conflict at work; secondly, in aspects of success and achievement at work; and thirdly, at the consequences of friendship and romance at work. This kind of dissertation can be structured in two main ways, which I will call the '***down***' method and the '***across***' method. The 'down' method structures the work into two halves, the first half discussing all three topics in turn in relation to Spark, and the second half doing the same thing in relation to Byatt, as indicated in this diagram:

Introduction	500 words
A) Spark	
1. Rivalry/conflict	1,200
2. Success/achievement	1,200
3. Friendship/romance	1,200
4. Overview of Spark	600
B) Byatt	
1. Rivalry/conflict	1,200
2. Success/achievement	1,200
3. Friendship/romance	1,200
4. Contrastive overview of Byatt	600
Conclusion	500

Approximate word counts are given for each section, and again they break down into manageable and familiar 'writing chunks'. However, the danger of the 'down' model is that the dissertation as a whole can seem broken-backed, so the two 600-word 'overview' sections are intended as 'hinges' which join the two halves together, the first summarising the characteristics and attitudes of the first writer, and giving the opportunity to 'cue in' or anticipate some of the differences which will be in seen in the second writer. The second overview can then be 'contrastive' in emphasis, aiming to highlight key differences between the two writers in terms of the three chosen themes. The 'across' model would be as indicated in the next diagram:

Introduction	500
A) Rivalry/conflict	
1. Spark 2. Byatt	1,200, 1,200, 600
B) Success/achievement	
1. Spark 2. Byatt	1,200, 1,200, 600
C) Friendship/romance	
1. Spark 2. Byatt	1,200, 1,200, 600
Conclusion	500

The management of this model is a little more complicated, and three 600-word hinges, rather than two, are needed, making nine sub-sections rather than eight in the central core of the dissertation. Although the 'across' model is less in danger of breaking into two separate extended essays, this is achieved at the price of constantly crossing to and fro between the two authors. The result can be that the dissertation never seems to settle into an in-depth analysis of either author, meaning that it can feel more superficial. Of the two models, it seems to me the more difficult to manage, and I have usually advised students to use the 'down' model.

Of our three major dissertation types, that leaves only the '**Open field**' variety, which is the broadest of the three, as the name implies. These are topics whose titles merely designate a field of enquiry, like these; 'Poetry of the Second World War', 'British Women Poets, 1980–1990', 'The stage-plays of the major Romantic poets', 'The epistolary novel in the 18th century'. In all such titles, the phrase 'Aspects of ...' is understood at the start, and the dissertation should not attempt to be an overall survey – indeed, comprehensiveness isn't required, and isn't possible or desirable. What is expected is an examination of a plausible cross-section of the designated field, one which acknowledges its own selectivity and explains the rationale behind the selection of the specific writers and sub-topics chosen. For instance, for the topic 'Poetry of the Second World War', a suitable approach might be a first chapter which discusses some of the differences between the poetry of the First and Second World Wars, an overview second chapter on the character of Second World War poets and poetry, and a third chapter which presents a set of 'case studies' of prominent poets in this category, thus:

Introduction   500

Section 1: How does WW2 poetry differ from WW1?   1,500
- Attitudes more 'realist' from the start – no early period of jingoistic optimism or romanticism about combat
- The war less confined to specific war-zones – aerial bombardment meant all were 'combatants'
- Battle more 'impersonal' – fighting mainly at a distance (e.g. bombs, torpedoes, long-range artillery)
- General mood less heroic, and long periods of waiting, inactivity, boredom, stalemate, etc.

Section 2: Who wrote and published poetry in WW2, in what styles, and on what topics?   1,500
- Officers, ordinary soldiers/sailors/airmen, nurses and auxiliaries, civilians

Section 3: Three 'case-study' poets
- Sidney Keyes   2,000
- Alun Lewis   2,000
- Keith Douglas   2,000

Conclusion   500

The structure in this case shows a gradual movement from broad considerations to a series of close-up case studies on individual poets. The introduction, as always, would explain the scope and emphasis of the dissertation as a whole. The first two sections have titles in the form of a specific research question, which is a useful aid in maintaining theme and focus as the writing progresses. Since the poetry of the 1914–18 war is so much better known, it is worth asking at the start why that of 1939–45 is so different and so much less popular. The second section asks (among other things) if 1939–45 poetry was more democratic in feel, representing the views and attitudes of a wider social spectrum, and voicing a pervasive sense of uncertainty, doubt and self-mistrust rather than heroic conviction or sudden disillusionment. In the case-study section, four or five representative poems by each figure would be considered, aiming to shed light on the various facets and stages of the poet's technique, experiences and concerns.

Preliminary reading

It might seem strange at first that a section on preliminary reading should come second rather than first in the present chapter. Surely, the reading and research comes first in the process, and the writing follows. Of course, you cannot write about novels and poems you haven't read, but think for a moment what will happen if you undertake a large amount of secondary reading first (that is, the reading of critical and contextual books and articles): as you read, you will probably make print-outs of downloaded articles, and then read them with a high-lighter pen in hand, possibly using several colours, each coded for a particular aspect of the topic (let's say, green for points about historical background, yellow for points on narrative technique, pink for useful comments on characters' motives and desires). After a morning's work, you may have read four articles or chapters, and, because you are a conscientious student and are keen to do well, you will have done a great deal of highlighting, so that every page is a dazzle of green, yellow and pink. You may have refined your coding, adding, for instance, a star system in the margin, putting one, two, or three stars against the highlighted points, according to the importance you attach to them. If you work hard along these lines for a week, you may have read about forty items and accumulated two or three hundred highlighted points. I think the problem with this method is obvious – you now have such a mass of data that the problem of organising, sequencing and synthesising it all into a running argument will seem bewildering and insurmountable. After your week's work, you will feel that you are now further away from writing your dissertation than you were when you started.

To non-writers, it seems logical to assume that firstly you do the thinking and the research, and secondly you write it all out. But writers know that writing is thinking, and as we *write* it out we are *thinking* it out, rather than simply writing down what we thought out on some earlier occasion, such as when we were highlighting, or making notes in a notebook. It boils down to this: you have to write as you go, not write retrospectively. Let's think again about the topic of illness in Victorian novels and try to demonstrate what this means. If we go back to the stage when we have read the novels we intend to use, what should we next be doing? Firstly, your text will no longer be 'clean', for you will have underlined plenty of passages (the briefer the better) that struck you in some way as you read, and you may have turned down the corners of pages which seemed especially relevant to the theme. I would take an obviously significant scene (one where the situation is realized, or the illness diagnosed, or a relapse, or a temporary rally, or a death scene). If I am unsure exactly what I want to focus on in the scene I feel will repay close reading, then I sometimes just begin open-endedly, merely 'writing back' to the scene, so that I am at the same time both re-reading it (the book open at my elbow) and responding to it in writing, *following* a train of thought that may begin to develop, rather than trying to *push* it in any particular direction at this stage. The aim here is to write fairly passively, commentating, making connections which occur, pondering the connotations of particular phrases, or the nuances of emphasis and setting.

As I do this, I begin to get a sense of the kind of secondary reading that might be useful: I think, for example, that I would like to read an article with a title like 'Deathbed scenes in Victorian fiction', and there it is, in *English Studies*, vol. 67, no. 1, 1986, pp. 14–34, by Margarete Holubetz. I also realize that the atmosphere of most death scenes in Victorian novels is determined by the strong religious beliefs of the period, so I look at books like Michael Wheeler's *Heaven, Hell, and the Victorians* (Cambridge University Press, 1994). Its four main sections are Death, Judgment, Hell and Heaven, so I read the forty-page section on Death, which has a great deal that is relevant. It is typical of research reading that I am usually reading just chapters or sections rather than complete books, and also that when I do this secondary reading, I have already drafted my main line of argument, because I don't want to be just 'slip-streaming' behind the argument of others, no matter how eminent they may be, summarising what they say and simply making minor adjustments or precision calibrations of their views. There is a lot of academic writing of that kind available, but it ought not to be the model for an undergraduate dissertation. Rather, we should try to use the authorities to add strategic depth to a point of our own, or extend its ramifications, or draw attention to comparable situations in the work of other novelists of the period who have not been the focus of our work. Rather than reading the secondary material open-endedly (and thereby building up pages and pages of notes), I am reading in a more utilitarian way, looking for things which relate to points that I have already floated in some form in my drafts. In other words, I am in the driving seat of my own writing, conducting my own argument, assembling my own evidence, and with my own goals in mind.

As well as this 'thematic' reading (concerning death and illness as aspects of Victorian literature and culture), we would be doing critical reading on the specific literary texts we are studying. We will have read our chosen novels in good-quality editions (such as Penguin, or Oxford World's Classics), which have a substantial scholarly introduction, annotation and a secondary bibliography. After reading the text, we will read the introduction, and a couple of the articles listed in the bibliography. Reading the introduction first will reveal in advance all the details of the plot and will steer you in the direction of particular lines of response and interpretation. Of course, an introduction of this scholarly kind usually makes a very good prelude to a second reading, but is likely to pre-empt the pleasure and satisfaction of a first reading. The fact that it is called an introduction does not mean it is best read first, just as your 'preliminary' reading should not be the first stage of your dissertation.

13

The Text as Text

On avoiding textual embarrassment

It's not unusual to pick up a book and read it, taking it for granted that what you are reading is (uniquely) the text named on the cover. You might, for instance, be asked to read Henry James's famous 'novella' (short novel) *Daisy Miller* for a seminar. This is currently available in paperback from Penguin, Wordsworth Classics, Dover Thrift Editions and Oxford Paperbacks. There are also several expensive scholarly editions, plus electronic texts in various formats. However, you may notice during the seminar that when your tutor or other students quote from the text, the wording in your own edition is not always the same, and that sometimes the differences even seem quite significant. Why is this? Ultimately, it is because (unlike the birth of a baby or the launching of a ship) the writing of a book is not a once-and-for-all event. On the contrary, it may take years, and in the author's eyes the book may never be a finished and closed account at all, so that each reprint or new edition may be seen as an opportunity for further revisions. Perhaps it is sometimes literally the case (as Ecclesiastes says) that 'of the making of many books there is no end'.

Daisy Miller is a good example of a book whose writing never really had an end, for James first published it in the *Cornhill Magazine* of June–July 1878, when he was 35. It was revised for its first appearance in book form in England in the following year, and it was given its final substantial revision for the collected New York Edition of James's work, which appeared in 1909, when the writer was an

eminent man of letters of 66. So the writing of *Daisy Miller* is an
'event' which lasts for 30 years. This story was James's only popular
'hit' – the American book edition which appeared later in 1878 (a
few months after the story's first publication in the *Cornhill*) sold
20,000 copies in a couple of weeks. It is probably because of its very
success that it is 'one of the most extensively revised of all James's
works for the New York Edition. (It has been estimated that 90 per
cent of the sentences were altered in some way and some 15 per
cent more material added.)' [1]

Yet will it matter, really, which text of *Daisy Miller* you have
taken into the seminar with you? Perhaps a discussion develops
about the characterization of Daisy: one group sees her as a kind
of proto-feminist who disdainfully rejects the codes of behaviour
considered appropriate at the time for 'nice girls'; in evidence they
quote Giovanelli's remark at the end (referring to the fatal visit to
the Coliseum) that 'she did what she liked'. But this group have a
text based on the New York Edition (probably Jean Gooder's Oxford
paperback); yours (probably the Penguin) is based on the 1879 text,
which doesn't contain that line: in your text Giovanelli just says 'she
wanted to go', which is quite different in tone and implication.[2] If the
seminar registers the difference and begins to spend a little time
on the textual question, you may look down Gooder's list of variant
readings. An obvious task for a tutor to set would be to ask you to try
to describe any patterns or tendencies you can detect in the changes
– what is it that James was seeking to achieve by making them?

One answer would be that he often seems to be aiming for a
'retrospective thematization'; that is, he is belatedly heightening
what was widely perceived to be the central conflict in the story:
that between American 'nature' and European 'culture'. Daisy is

---

[1] Quoted from the 'Note on the Texts' (p. xxix) in *Daisy Miller and Other Stories*, ed.
Jean Gooder, Oxford Paperbacks, reissue edition, 2009. This excellent edition contains
a list of variant readings, so that some of the main differences between the 1879 and
1909 texts can be seen at a glance.
[2] I am drawing quite closely here on Phillip Horne's chapter 'Henry James at Work:
The Question of Our Texts', pp. 63–78 in *The Cambridge Companion to Henry James*,
Cambridge University Press, 1998. Horne's chapter is about 'Daisy Miller', and he is
also the author of *Henry James and Revision: The New York Edition*, Oxford University
Press, 1990. In thesis form, this was one of the sources used in Gooder's Oxford
paperback.

the 'natural' American whose free and open behaviour is untainted by over-conventionalized European norms; hence, several of the changes made for the New York Edition introduce words like 'native' or 'natural' into descriptions of Daisy. In 1879 Giovanelli (with whom the scandalized high-class, American expatriate society in Rome had assumed she could be having an affair) says of Daisy (in the same passage at the end of the story) that of all the women he has met 'she was the most innocent'. In 1909 this becomes 'Also – naturally! – the most innocent.' In 1879, earlier in the story, 'Daisy turned to Winterbourne, beginning to smile again', whereas in 1909 this becomes 'Daisy at last turned on Winterbourne a more natural and calculable light'. The older James must have thought this an improvement, or he wouldn't have made the change, but I don't want to evoke the contrast (which Horne gently parodies) between a youthful 'freshness' of style and the more orotund phraseology of James's maturity. Frequently, the later Jamesian style works well for the often older characters of the later fiction, but seems less appropriate for describing a character as young as Daisy. In any case, it is notoriously easy, in the case of a writer who was a heavy reviser, to get our prose stereotypes mixed up, as a critic as eminent as F. R. Leavis did when he inadvertently quoted the revised 1909 text of an 1875 Henry James novel to illustrate the superior 'freshness' of James's *early* style. Leavis (it should be said in mitigation) made his mistake only in a review, and later admitted his error, though in a form which evidences a very high level of might now be called spin-doctoring: Leavis admits that the bits of James that strike us as 'characteristic felicities' are often late revisions, but the point is that the late revisions aren't needed to 'make the writing wonderfully intelligent, brilliant and sensitive'.[3]

The general point being made here, then, is that the text often has a double, and that it *does* matter which one we read. At the very least, in order to save ourselves possible textual embarrassment, we should make a point of knowing the source of the text we are

---

[3]Quoted by Horne, 'Henry James at Work', p. 72. Leavis's error was discussed by John Butt in *Art and Error: Modern Textual Editing*, eds Ronald Gottesman and Scott Bennett, Methuen, 1970, and is mentioned from time to time in discussions of Leavis (for instance, in George Watson's *Never Ones for Theory: England and the War of Ideas*, Lutterworth Press, 2000, p. 76).

reading (which will nearly always be indicated in a 'Note on the text' printed after the introduction) and we should also be aware of the existence of any alternative versions. Thus, there are 'Quarto' and 'Folio' versions of *Lear* and *Hamlet*; there are different endings for well-known Romantic and Victorian poems like Coleridge's 'Frost at Midnight' and Tennyson's 'The Lady of Shalott'; there are significant differences between the magazine and the book versions of controversial novels like Hardy's *Tess of the d'Urbervilles*, and T. S. Eliot's *The Waste Land*, a key modernist work, exists in two very different versions.[4] As English specialists, these are matters which must concern us, even though it is very far from my purpose to provoke a debilitating 'textual anxiety' of the kind which is sometimes evident at conferences and graduate seminars. Rather, my emphasis is on how much can be learned from some consideration of 'textual variants' and the issues they raise. This is the focus of the next section.

'In two minds' – Blake and Keats

Some kinds of reading feel like trespassing. Sometimes this can be a pleasurable thrill, as when we read the published letters or diaries of well-known writers. Even when these have been written with half an eye on publication, they still offer a special sense of intimacy with the author which other kinds of writing do not provide. But when we read the unpublished manuscript drafts of well-known poems, then

---

[4] Most general books on Shakespeare have a chapter on the question of the text: for an excellent example see Russ McDonald, chapter six, 'What is your text?', in *The Bedford Companion to Shakespeare: An Introduction with Documents*, 2nd edition, Bedford St Martin's, 2001. The different versions of Coleridge's 'Frost at Midnight' are discussed in the chapter 'The politics of "Frost at Midnight"' in Paul Magnuson's *Reading Public Romanticism*, Princeton University Press, 1998, though this more extreme style of discussion represents the kind of 'textual anxiety' which I am *not* recommending here. For 'The Lady of Shalott' see chapter four of the present book, and for *Tess of the d'Urbervilles* see J. T. Laird's compact and fascinating book *The Shaping of "Tess of the d'Urbervilles"*, Oxford University Press, 1975. To compare the original *Waste Land* with the published text see *The Waste Land*, Valerie Eliot ed. a facsimile and transcript of the original drafts, including the annotations of Ezra Pound (Faber, 1971). To read about the re-discovery of the original manuscripts of this poem as the story first broke, see Donald Gallop's 'The "Lost" Manuscripts of T. S. Eliot' in *The Times Literary Supplement*, 7 November 1968, pp. 1238–40.

the sense that we shouldn't really be there at all is stronger still, for we are looking at what the author explicitly rejected as wrong, or inadequate, or clumsy. We know that authors didn't want us to see these lines because they were not the lines they published. Of course, this fact gives these authorial rejections an irresistible fascination. In them we see the great author groping in the dark towards the light switch of inspiration, and often just missing. It is sometimes rather like that famous lager advert seen on TV in the 1980s, which showed William Wordsworth beginning to compose a poem and starting with the rather flat line: 'I used to walk about a lot on my own.' It clearly wasn't quite right, so he screwed up the paper and tried again, this time producing the line 'I used to wonder around the countryside by myself.' Still no good, so he takes a long draught (or draft?) of lager (the one which reaches the poets other beers can't reach), and then, with immense confidence, rolls out the lines 'I wondered lonely as a cloud / That floats on high o'er vale and hill'.

In poets' drafts we often find lines that, in their self-evident inadequacy, can be surprisingly like 'I used to walk about a lot on my own.' But sometimes the difference between the published lines and the lines in draft is only a matter of a single word. Yet it can be the crucial word, the one which seems most characteristic of the whole poem. This, for instance, is the start of William Blake's famous poem 'London', as published:

I wander through each chartered street,
Near where the chartered Thames does flow,
And mark in every face I meet
Marks of weakness, marks of woe.

These lines seem to have a kind of majestic inevitability, as if they had always existed, and the voice has an unmistakable air of poetic confidence and authority. Perhaps we could all imagine ourselves being William Blake, but surely we *couldn't* quite imagine ourselves writing those lines. There is something about that strange word 'chartered' that (I take it) you just couldn't ever imagine yourself choosing. But what does 'chartered' mean, precisely? Critics have never really agreed. The streets are owned by the corporations of the City of London; they are the mortgaged territory of proto-capitalism which generates both great wealth and great poverty, and the word 'chartered' seems to hint at this trumping of the human by the legalistic – but there is surely more to it than that. And anyway, even if we *could* imagine ourselves using the word 'chartered' once, we could never imagine repeating it immediately in the next line. This word 'chartered', in fact, seems to encapsulate the sombre individuality of Blake's poetic vision, and it's impossible to imagine the poem without it. But it isn't what Blake first wrote. Behind these mesmeric lines there is a first draft equivalent to 'I used to walk about a lot on my own':

> I wander through each dirty street,
> Near where the dirty Thames does flow,
> And mark in every face I meet
> Marks of weakness, marks of woe.

It's quite a shock, isn't it? If we could imagine ourselves being Blake – an impoverished, passionately left-wing poet – aren't these exactly the lines we *can* imagine ourselves writing? They seem the kind of poetic language which the Victorian poet Gerard Manley Hopkins called 'Parnassian', by which he meant the competent and elevated poetic diction that can be rolled out all too readily by poets who have learned their craft too well. Parnassian is not ridiculous or despicable; on the contrary, it is often dignified and competent. It has the characteristic tone and timbre of a particular poet, but it lacks that additional twist of strangeness, or unpredictability, or some such extra quality which the poetry reader craves. Hopkins realized, with a sudden loss of faith, that his great contemporary Tennyson wrote in Parnassian nearly all the time. He defines it in a letter to his friend Baillie (of 10 September 1864):

> Now it is a mark of Parnassian that one could conceive oneself writing it if one were the poet. Do not say that *if* you were Shakespeare you can imagine yourself writing *Hamlet*, because that is just what I think you *cannot* conceive.[5]

---

[5] Hopkins' letter to Baillie is discussed by Christopher Ricks in his essay 'Literary Principles as Against Theory' in his book *Essays in Appreciation* (Oxford University Press, 1998). Ricks sees it as an example of a literary *principle*, rather than a literary *theory*.

It is very curious, too, that eminent people can be taken in by Parnassian. The major critic F. W. Bateson (whom I greatly admire, in spite of his occasional critical aberrations) actually believed that the original version of Blake's poem was better than the final one. He writes in his book *The Scholar Critic* (1972) that 'the explicit "dirty" seems better to me than the more pretentious and obscure "chartered"'. Be that as it may, what we sometimes see in poets' manuscripts is how very thin the line can be that divides the production of routine Parnassian from that something more which poets can produce at the height of their powers.

Let's look now at another manuscript example of textual variation from another Romantic poet – John Keats and his narrative poem 'The Eve of St Agnes'. This poem, as you will probably remember, is a re-telling of a medieval tale. The young man Porphyro has hidden himself in Isabella's bedroom because he wants to be there when she wakes up. There is a legend which says that young women dream of their future husbands (or husband) on the Eve of St Agnes. He hopes that his hidden presence on this night in the room of his beloved Isabella will influence her into dreaming about *him*. At least, that's his excuse. Verse 26 is the one in which Keats describes the unsuspecting Isabella undressing for bed, watched by the hidden Porphyro. As you might be able to imagine (whether or not you can imagine yourself being Keats), this verse presents the writer with a number of problems. For many readers, this is the verse for which they have been waiting impatiently for all the way through the previous twenty-five stanzas. But clearly, it has to be done tastefully, otherwise it might seem like a deliberately titillating soft-porn scenario. Not surprisingly, therefore, Keats's manuscript shows him experiencing some difficulty with this stanza, and there are crossings out and fresh starts in abundance. Below is a printed representation of these hand-written sheets (as they are reproduced in the section called 'Poems in Process' at the back of the fifth edition of the *Norton Anthology of English Literature: The Major Authors*). Words which were different in the first draft are italicized, and the original word or phrase is given in square brackets at the end of the line.

John Keats, 'The Eve of St Agnes', Stanza 26

1 *Anon* his heart revives: her *vespers* done, [But soon] [prayers]

2 Of all its wreathed pearls her hair she *frees*;   [strips]

3 Unclasps her *warmed* jewels one by one;   [bosom]

4 Loosens her *fragrant* bodice; by degrees   [bursting]

5 Her *rich* attire *creeps rustling* to her knees: [sweet] [falls light]

6 Half-hidden, like *a mermaid in sea-weed*, [a Syren of the Sea]

7 *Pensive awhile she dreams awake*, and sees,
           [She stands awhile in dreaming thought]

8 In fancy, fair St Agnes in her bed,

9 But dares not look behind, or all the charm is *fled*.   [dead]

The questions I would I ask about this stanza are these:

- Can we detect any patterns in these changes?

- If so, do they give us any clues about the kind of effect Keats is aiming for?

- Are all these changes for the best?

- If not, in which cases were first thoughts best?

I will incorporate tentative answers to these questions in my own comments on Keats's manuscript changes. One evident pattern is that the second thoughts tend to prefer a word or form which is antique or 'medieval' in tone, so that, in the first line, 'Anon' is preferred to 'But soon', and 'vespers' to 'prayers'. This seems to fit the evoked atmosphere, which is mystical and mysterious, and hence suited to the re-telling of a romantic legend. In the second line the word 'frees' seems more in keeping with this dreamy atmosphere than 'strips', which would suggest a much more brisk and purposeful undressing. 'Frees' also implies both the thickness of the hair and the elaborateness of the coiffure, which has richly intertwined it with adornments. The word 'frees' is similar in implied pace and mood to 'unclasps' in line three, which again suggests an unhurried, musing atmosphere. 'Warmed' in the same line (pronounced as two syllables) replaces 'bosom': the former is vividly sensuous without being explicit, whereas the latter is crudely explicit, but without any particular force. Exactly the same could be said about the rejected 'bursting' bodice in line four – it is almost comically explicit, evoking at best a snigger, like the comic sexuality of the British *Carry On* films of the 1960s. By contrast, 'fragrant' is strongly sensuous, and it is interesting how both these words ('warmed' and 'fragrant') evoke by implication the intense arousal of the hidden observer rather than the sensibility of Isabella, since neither of these qualities would be particularly apparent or remarkable to the wearer herself.

The rejected 'sweet' in line five would have done the same, but Keats prefers 'rich' (an objective rather than a subjective description) to enhance the sound effect which is the main quality of line five. The sound depicted is the rustle of the heavy, layered material of the dress as it is gradually removed: the effect is to emphasize, again, the antique, medieval setting and perhaps the restrictions and conventionalities from which the couple wish to escape. The escape from the garments is gradual, not an instant floating free, as would be implied by 'falls light', and this allows the 'freeze-frame' effect in line six, as the moment when the garment is half on and half off suggests the image of a mermaid half-hidden in seaweed. This is preferred to the 'Syren of the sea', which would suggest a malign female force (the Syrens, in classical mythology, enticed sailors by their haunting song, bringing them in too close to the shore, and hence resulting in shipwreck). The implication of using the word 'Syren' would be almost that Isabella is deliberately enticing Porphyro to his ruin, hence Keats switches the image to the mermaid, sometimes reputed to be the rescuers of shipwrecked mariners.

The freeze-frame effect continues in line seven, as Isabella pauses, half in the dress and half out of it, momentarily lost in thought, but this line is more completely recast than any other in the stanza, though the resulting shift in meaning is very slight. 'Pensive' has a slight 'soft-focus' effect in comparison with 'thought', but Keats seems mainly to be slowing the stanza before its climactic moment of the mental vision of St Agnes in the bed. The slowing of the pace is achieved by varying the metrical regularity of the stress pattern. In the draft, the iambic beat has its regular alternation, which can be represented by showing the stressed syllables in bold and breaking the line into its iambic feet:

She **stands** / a **while** / in **dream** / ing **thought** / and **sees**

This is a completely regular iambic pentameter line, which is to say that it has five feet, each foot having two stresses, the heavy stress coming after the light one. This is the metre of vast amounts of English verse, and the iambic drum beats with complete regularity through the first five lines of the stanza, so that you can take any of them and mark the stress pattern in exactly the same way ('Of **all** / its **wreath** / ed **pearls** / her **hair** / she **frees**', and so on). But the pattern shifts in line six, so that we could not stress it in this way without making it sound ridiculous. Without getting over-technical about it, we can say that the effect of breaking (and braking) the iambic pattern in lines seven and eight is to focus on and increase the impact of the vision of St Agnes, and this seems to be the reason why Keats makes a major re-shaping of line seven without otherwise altering the sense or feel of the line to any great extent.

The final change in line nine, by contrast (of 'dead' to 'fled'), has no bearing on the form of the verse at all, since one monosyllabic word is substituted for another that has the same rhyme. But 'fled', again, has a softer and more evocative tone, helping to maintain the romantic, suspended atmosphere which culminates with Keats's famous line representing the sexual consummation in words which are erotic without, again, being sexually explicit, for as she lies in bed dreaming of her future husband, 'into her dream he melted'. Looking at a poet's drafts, then, can give us a remarkable insight into the workings of the poetic process, so that we seem to be colluding and participating in the dilemmas and verbal choices which are the essence of the art and craft of poetry itself.

Searching for the one true text

But which one, we might ask ourselves, the first draft or the revised version, is the 'true' text of Keats's stanza? How much should the editor of a text tell us about the composition process we have just been examining? Let's start our consideration of this question with a discussion exercise, one which takes up issues already raised implicitly during this chapter. The case is hypothetical, but the issues are fundamental. Imagine that you are editing a definitive critical edition of the stories of Ima Jeenius (1880–1956). The first story in the collection was written when Jeenius was twenty-three. The question is, which of the available versions of this story will you use as your copy text (that is, the one which will provide the basis of your printed edition)? In other words, which, in your view, is the 'true' text? Here are your choices:

Text 1: This is a hand-written manuscript (a 'holograph'), signed and dated '1903' by Jeenius. It is the earliest known version of the story. It contains deletions and substitutions, and it is possible in these cases to read both what Jeenius first wrote and what Jeenius later decided was better.

Text 2: This is also a holograph. It is the manuscript Jeenius sent to the magazine which first published it. Essentially, it is a fair copy of Text 1, mostly with the substitutions from that text preferred, but occasionally with the original deleted wording restored. There are also some changes entered in a different handwriting, known from external evidence to be that of the magazine's editor.

Text 3: This is an office-made typescript on the magazine's headed paper. It is essentially the same as Text 2, but there are some corrections and changes made in the handwriting of the author. The alterations in another's hand from that text have been incorporated, and none of these have been altered back.

Text 4: This is a set of corrected printer's proofs for the version printed in the magazine. The proof corrections are in the author's hand, and contain further deletions and substitutions, mostly very minor, except for an added paragraph.

Text 5: This is the version actually printed in the magazine. There are a few minor changes which were not indicated in Text 4; it is not known whether or not these were instigated by the author. (They *may* have been – the author would have received one proof copy to retain and one to return, and might have re-read the retained copy after returning the corrections and subsequently sent a telegram, let's say, with further changes).

Text 6: In 1923, twenty years after its first magazine publication, the story appeared in book form in a collection of Jeenius's stories. This version makes some further changes from the magazine version, all presumed to have been instigated by the author. Generally, they tend towards greater detail and explicitness on sexual matters, enabled partly by the greater broad-mindedness of the 1920s. In this book the story has a certain title and contains a certain line which was widely quoted, and indeed became virtually synonymous with Jeenius in the public mind. No other new version of the text published in Jeenius's lifetime used this title or this line, but this edition was *reprinted* many times over the next quarter century and became the main source of Jeenius's considerable income and status. In the 1953 lecture (see below, Text 8) Jeenius expressed dislike for both the well-known title and the famous line. All the same, critics have always referred to the story by this title, and most critical discussions of Jeenius have something to say about this line.

Text 7: In 1950, to mark the seventieth birthday of the now-famous Jeenius, a Collected Edition of the works was published. Jeenius revised many of the stories for this edition, and this one contains an unusually high number of changes. Jeenius reversed some of the changes made in the 1920s published version, partly in response to critics' tendency to prefer the earlier (less sexually explicit) version (on the grounds that it was more subtle). This is the last version of the text actually seen through the press by Jeenius.

Text 8: In 1953, in a British Academy lecture, Jeenius reminisced about the publication of this first story and indicated some dissatis-faction with *all* the published versions of the tale. The author's ideal version, it was indicated, would probably contain elements from all seven of these versions. The author was specific about some of these elements and vague about others. (So 'Text 8' is a notional text, not a physical text, but an editor might aim to construct it, following Jeenius's hints.)

Text 9: After Jeenius's death there was a demand for new editions of the works, which were now set texts on English courses. The story was republished in a collection called *The Portable Jeenius*, using Text 7 as the basic copy text, but incorporating the preferences which Jeenius had been explicit about in the lecture description of 'Text 8'.

As a first step in thinking about the problems of textual editing, as exemplified in this imaginary (but not untypical) case, you might try to decide upon your general editorial approach: here are some broad editorial options for you to consider.

Editorial primitivism

As 'primitivist' editors, we would try to reconstruct the story as it was in Jeenius's original conception of it, before it became 'contaminated' by the editorial process, by contact with the 'market', by the tastes of a readership that has specific culturally constructed preferences and prejudices, and by the later tinkerings of an older and well-established author keen to present a certain self-image, a certain 'narrative' for the career as a whole. So our over-riding aim as primitivists would be 'authenticity', and we would aim to restore the tale to its original state, in the form in which it first flowed from the pen of Jeenius. If Jeenius, being young and desperate for publication, was persuaded by editors to make changes or additions, for whatever reason (perhaps because the editor thought readers too prudish to accept certain incidents or phrases, or too dim to pick up anything not spelt out for them), then we will aim to remove these alterations and restore what Jeenius first wrote. We will even seek to save Jeenius from the later authorial self, whom we instinctively stereotype as a conservative compromiser, rather than an artist whose technique was constantly being refined as the career went on. The text which results from our editorial efforts may well please nobody at all except other editors, being, perhaps, clumsier and cruder than we had ever thought of Jeenius as being, and perhaps even lacking the parts readers came to see as most typical of Jeenius's genius. Lovers of Jeenius may even be rather scandalized at what we have done to the text, rather as the most recent 'restoration' of Michaelangelo's painting 'The Last Supper' produced a (to many) shockingly pale and patchy image, which, it is true, has been freed of all the work of past restorers, but now seems hardly to be a painting at all.[6]

The procedures of primitivist editing are highly technical and meticulous, but the approach seems to rest on very familiar attitudes to creativity which are rooted in ideas which go back to the Romantic period. The primitivist seems to believe that literary creativity is essentially about the lone, talented individual conceiving thoughts in isolation. It can never have a social dimension (in which friends, editors, readers etc. might play a part): it happens in an instant, not over an extended period of time, and it believes that only first thoughts are real thoughts, just as the Romantic novelists of the late eighteenth century (whom Jane Austen challenged in her novel *Persuasion*) believed that only first loves ('first attachments') are real, and that only young love is true love. Of course, the editorial primitivist would indignantly deny believing any such thing as this implies about creativity, but these are surely the attitudes the primitivist editorial endeavour embodies. Another name for it might be 'first intentionalism', since it strives to uncover the text which resulted from the first intentions of its author.

Last intentionalism

Hence, the opposite editorial approach might be called 'last intentionalism'. As editors of this persuasion, we would regard the creative process as something cumulative and sustained over many

[6]See Pinin Brambilla Barcilon and Pietro C. Marani, *Leonardo: The Last Supper*, tr. Harlow Tighe, University of Chicago Press, 2001, discussed in the *New York Review of Books*, 9 August 2001. The main aim of the year 2000 restoration of the painting was to remove the work of previous restorers so that all the paint which remained to be seen is paint applied by Leonardo. The result is to reduce a famous image to a ruin, because the original work began to deteriorate almost as soon as it was completed. Since previous restorers could see more of Leonardo's work than we can now, and presumably attempted to reproduce it, the process of removing what they did may seem arrogantly misguided. Likewise, the greater closeness of earlier editors to the author of the text should make us cautious about deleting their work. At any rate, it is helpful to think of textual editing as 'restoration' work which has many ethical problems in common with what happens in the art world.

years. We will seek to construct a text which incorporates the *culmination* of the author's work upon it; our ideal will be to offer the latest version of the text that had authorial approval and incorporates the author's mature thoughts upon it. Here the underlying assumption is that artists *grow* and that those whom the gods love don't always die young. Most writers reserve the right to revise works when they are being re-published, so that an individual poem (for instance) may have subtle differences between a first magazine appearance, its appearance in a first collection, a mid-career *Selected Poems* and a definitive *Collected Poems*. If the latter came out during the poet's lifetime and was seen through the press by the poet (meaning that the poet saw and corrected the proofs), then we can assume that this version represents final thoughts and completes the creative process as far as that poem is concerned. We may not feel ourselves that it is necessarily the best version, and it may well be that at some point in the process of re-visiting the poem over the years the poet lost touch with the original impulse that brought it into being. But all the same, if we think the poet a great poet (or even just a good one), then we may decide to allow the poet's judgement to over-ride our own. This strategy, though, does seem to be especially fraught in the case of poets who lived long lives and whose political views shifted during that time. Two well-known cases are William Wordsworth and W. H. Auden. In Wordsworth's case, the straight-down-the-line 'last intentionalist' editor would have to prefer the 1850 text of *The Prelude* to the original Wordsworth wrote as a young man, the version which readers have overwhelmingly preferred. In the case of Auden, we would have to accept the old Auden's repudiation of 'September 1st 1939', one of his best and best-known poems, and not print it at all, since Auden in his later years wanted to suppress it entirely, or at least amend the famous line 'We must love one another or die' to 'We must love one another *and* die', for as Auden said (in effect), not dying is not an option. It is perhaps becoming obvious, then, that neither first nor last intentionalism, pursued in exclusion of every other consideration, is likely to produce the best-possible all-round text. So what other editorial options are there?

Syncretism

Some editorial situations, by contrast, are fairly straightforward: Keats, for instance, was dead at the age of twenty-six, so did not live to re-visit 'The Eve of St Agnes' as an eminent middle-aged poet who might want to shift the emphasis of the material. It seems self-evident that his second thoughts (in the 'Eve of St Agnes' example just considered) usually refine the project and make the lines more effective, but the matter might become more difficult to decide as second thoughts become nineteenth and twentieth thoughts at an increasing distance from the original conception. Yet *sometimes*, much later thoughts are indeed improvements, and as an editor we might want to incorporate these into our text, even though we would not want to adopt either the full-scale 'last intentionalist' or 'first intentionalist' position. If we decide that our editorial aim will be to avoid privileging either the 'early' author or the 'late' author, while wanting to remain open to both 'early' and 'late' insights, then we might opt for 'syncretism'. As syncretist editors our aim would be to produce an 'ideal' text of this story. The version we print would incorporate early and late thoughts judiciously, using whatever external evidence is available and extrapolating from this where necessary. Once again, the possibility of pleasing everybody with a syncretist text is remote, and while the aims seem logical and laudable, the outcome may well provoke some unease. For one thing, the text we produce will never have appeared under the author's name during the author's lifetime, so that it may well seem to be under the ownership, not of its author, but of its editor, who may indeed then possess copyright of this new text (through the publishers) and expect to be asked for permission by scholars who wish to quote from it. This will seem an anomaly to most readers, and to many scholars, for how can an editor *own* a text? Yet something like this is the present situation with texts of James Joyce's *Ulysses*, a seminal modernist novel which in the 1990s generated competing and combative editorial teams, each dedicated to the goal of producing the definitive text. Editors of the competing texts point out that the original texts of the novel (which avoided prosecution for obscenity by being typeset in France by printers who did not read English) contained innumerable errors, but we might feel, all the same, that this error-ridden text is the one which made Joyce famous, and that this text, strictly speaking, is the 'true' *Ulysses* and therefore the one that should serve as the base text for modern reprints. But at this point the problem begins to seem deeply philosophical – is the 'real' *Ulysses* the text Joyce had in mind and had *meant* to give the public, or is it the text which the public actually received, with all its imperfections and accidents?

Populism

If you believe as an editor that the true text is the one actually received by the readership at the end of the publication process, then you might want to subscribe to the editorial principle of 'populism'. As populists, we will prioritise the text which has been 'canonized' by 'use and custom'. To publish means to give a piece of writing to the public. Neither author nor critic has the right to take back the gift, we would argue, even for the purpose of making a series of adjustments before returning it to its rightful owners. In the main, we would want to accept the book in the form in which it had its most definitive success, even if, for instance, its author had given it a different title or no title at all, or had placed the material it contains in a different order. This is the case with D. H. Lawrence's first collection of stories, which appeared in 1915 under the title *'The Prussian Officer' and Other Stories*. Lawrence did not call any of his stories 'The Prussian Officer' and he did not intend the one to which the publisher gave this name to be the 'flagship' story of the volume. His publisher, however, felt that, with the outbreak of the war, he could cash in on the widespread interest in German militarism by using this title, and he also changed Lawrence's proposed ordering of the tales so that this one became the culmination of the volume. Should a modern editor repudiate all this and aim to reproduce the manuscript as it was when Lawrence sent it to the publisher? Obviously, that manuscript is of great interest, and we want to know about it and about how Lawrence had intended the book to be. But we cannot reverse literary history and wish *'The Prussian Officer' and Other Stories* out of existence, for that book is what *actually* happened, and not the one which Lawrence had in mind. We cannot expect, surely, that readers can be corrected belatedly and begin to call it by a different name. To think otherwise would be to concede to editors not just the copyright and ownership of texts, but the overlordship of literary history itself. As with every other sphere of life, the events of literary history are sometimes the result of accident, and both writers and scholars, just like the rest of us, have to accept that.

I hope that the above discussion of some of the problems faced by textual editors will not result in the generation of too much 'textual anxiety' in readers. Its purpose is simply to show that what we refer to without a second thought as (say) *The Great Gatsby* or 'Frost at Midnight' may in fact exist in several different versions, all of which have their claims, and between which editors have to adjudicate. I have tried to indicate in a generalized way the grounds and principles on which editors base their choices. It is possible, in the case of major writers, to consult 'variorum' editions, which record all the different extant versions of every line or sentence. Naturally, these editions are massive, cumbersome and expensive (they often occupy teams of textual scholars for their entire careers). They are designed for 'consultation' rather than for reading, and they don't solve the problem of which text to supply for modern readers in general (rather than for scholars and critics). The important thing is that as students of literature we should be aware of the layers of editorial mediation that often lie between ourselves and the text we read.

14

English at MA Level

The term 'M Level' in this chapter means a postgraduate degree at master's level in English Studies. At a British university, this will usually be taken as a full-time, one-year course, or part time over two years. This degree is usually called an MA, but sometimes it has a different title, partly to distinguish it from the MAs at Oxford and Cambridge (and Trinity College Dublin), which do not require postgraduate study and are awarded after an interval of five to seven years to holders of the corresponding undergraduate degrees. At Scottish universities the MA is the undergraduate award given after four years of full-time study. Hence, master's degrees awarded at these universities are usually called MLitt degrees (Master of Letters, in which 'Letters' means 'Literature'). Sometimes an MRes (Master of Research) is also available, designating a course which provides specific research training for PhD work, or one in which the main requirement is a large-scale dissertation.

Varieties of MA in English in the UK

The notion of 'English', as we have seen, encompasses the fields of literature, creative writing and language studies or linguistics, and the broadest kind of English MA will enable you to continue your studies across a fairly wide spectrum in one of these three fields. Programmes of this 'panoramic' kind have correspondingly broad names, such as MA English Studies, MA Creative Writing or MA Linguistics, and they are usually structured much like undergraduate degrees. Thus, they offer a combination of core and option modules, and the programme is rounded off with the writing of a dissertation, or (in the case of creative writing) with a final project of similar length. UK examples of courses like these are the MA in English Literature at Edge Hill University, the MA in Linguistics at Birmingham City University, the MA in Creative Writing at King's College London and the combined MA in English and Creative Writing at Cardiff Metropolitan University. These are typical of what I will call the Type A model of the master's degree, being courses which have a title that designates the subject area in the broadest terms (English, Linguistics, Creative Writing, etc.). In practice, the breadth of study in most cases will be less extensive than the course title implies, as students will probably be encouraged to choose modules which 'cluster' or cohere in some evident way, and then connect meaning-fully with the topic chosen for the dissertation or portfolio.

The Type B model of the master's, by contrast, offers a greater amount of specialization. For example, there is an MA in Literature and Landscape at Bath Spa University, where the specialization is thematic rather than generic or period-based; at Durham University there is an MA in Romantic and Victorian Literature – an example of specialization by period – and the same university has an MA called Studies in Poetry, where the specialization is by a specific genre (poetry) which is studied across various periods. In creative writing, similarly, the Type B model offers a focus on a single aspect of the field, in varying ways: thus, at Bath Spa University, there is an MA in Script Writing, which includes tuition in the writing of dramatic scripts for radio, television and film, as well as for all forms of broadcasting in which scripts are used, such as news, current affairs, documentaries, discussion programmes and the like. The same institution has an MA in Writing for Young People – in this case, the writing of fiction comes first to mind, but young people also read poetry, factual books and materials, 'how-to' books and dramatic material, so this too is a specialization based on audience or readership rather than genre. At Bournemouth University, finally, there is an MA in Adaptation, where the specialization is in *re*-writing, that is, in the transformation of material from one genre to another, as when a full-length novel is adapted to be read on the radio across a series of episodes, or a short story is re-worked as a half-hour play for radio or television.

In linguistics, the Type B model can be exemplified by the MA in Sociocultural Linguistics at Goldsmiths, University of London, the focus of which is the study of language in society; topics covered include such things as global English, the nature of talk at work, the question of language and gender, including gendered differences in ways of talking, writing, and reflecting on experience, and issues concerning the relationship between language and social class. This MA is not a 'vocational' course (that is, one which might be expected to lead directly to entry into a particular profession), but many MAs in language or linguistics are vocational in this sense. An example is the MA in Applied Linguistics offered at Birkbeck, University of London, which is for people interested in working professionally with some aspect of language. Hence, this course covers major areas of profes- sional linguistic expertise, such as the field of TESOL (the teaching of English as a second language) or the 'international English' in which a great deal of international business and commerce is conducted. This is the medium in which (for instance) a meeting between Japanese and Nigerian business people is most likely to occur, and it will not correspond exactly to any major national form of English (British, North American, Australian or Caribbean English, for instance), being, rather, a hybrid form which has grown up in response to interna- tional conditions of communication with a modified tense system and grammatical structures. Other possible areas of focus on this kind of applied linguistics MA would be issues concerning trans- lation, aspects of psycholinguistics (which explores the relationship between mind and language) and the matter of language acquisition, including 'mother tongue' acquisition in childhood, and second- language learning in adulthood.

A third type of M Level course in English is the so-called 'MRes' (or Master of Research) degree, which emerged in the UK in the first decade of the present century, mainly in response to pressures from the UK research councils for the provision of specific and identifiable training in 'research skills' as a prelude to embarking upon PhD study. In the early days of the MRes, there was much emphasis on teaching the use of electronic sources (about which students usually know more than the people teaching them), and giving information about referencing, footnoting and bibliographies, with follow-up exercises. Thankfully, that early phase seems to have passed, and the prescriptive hold of the research councils has loosened in this area at least since they no longer fund master's-level work. Today, the foundation or 'core' modules on the MRes will draw not just on a check-list of 'skills', but on a set of key 'issues' (for example, theoretical, ethical, intellectual and editorial matters).

The major distinguishing feature of the MRes is that the dissertation is worked on for the whole year, or nearly the whole year, whereas on other M Level programmes it is usually a feature of the latter stages of the degree and is written mainly during the summer (the notional 'third semester' of the one-year, full-time MA), when all the taught modules have been completed. For both MA/MLitt and the MRes, the dissertation is usually handed in during September, a year after initial enrolment on the programme. So the backbone of the MRes is the dissertation, supervised individually on the same model as PhD work, and taking much longer than the 'summer dissertation' of other MAs. Whereas the MA/MLitt dissertation is usually around 15,000 words, the specified length for the MRes will be 20,000, 25,000, or 30,000 words, making it roughly a third of the length of the average PhD thesis. This seems logical, given that the MRes takes one year of full-time study and the PhD three: of course, MRes students also take taught modules, both core and options, but these days, so do PhD students.

It should be added that it is possible to discern Type A and Type B models for the MRes degree, just as for the MA/MLitt. Thus, in the broader-scale (Type A) category, there is an MRes in Literary Studies at Southampton University; at Keele University there is a Humanities MRes; at Ulster there is an MRes in Arts. The Keele and Ulster MRes programmes follow the trend of combining the MRes across several subject boundaries into an integrated administrative structure. The format in these two cases is to link up the programme's administration and some of its core elements across what would, until recently, have been called a Faculty (and may now be termed a College or an Institute), though probably the only part of the course taught in an integrated way will be the earlier parts of the foundational 'Skills' module. The more specialized Type B MRes course can be exemplified by the History of the Book MRes at the Institute of English Studies (part of London University's School of Advanced Study), which presents itself as 'one third coursework, two thirds research', which is pretty well a reversal of the usual proportions of a taught MA/MLitt course. This programme is divided into three terms, with the second and third entirely devoted to the dissertation. In the first, three modules are taken (Research Methodology and two options), and all the teaching takes place on the same day of the week, which perhaps somewhat restricts option choice, but benefits those studying part-time or on a day-relief or secondment basis from paid employment. Another example of the more specialized kind of MRes is the one in Medieval Studies at Birmingham University. In this case, the balance between taught modules and research looks to be in the ratio of about 2:3, since there are four taught modules, which are on Resources and Methods for Medieval Literary Studies, Bibliographical Methods, Approaches to Medieval Studies, and a topic from Medieval Texts, Cultures and Societies. The dissertation, at 20,000 words, is at the lower end of the MRes length-range, but the distinctive feature of this course is that it is based not just in an English Department, but in a cross-disciplinary Centre for the Study of the Middle Ages, which combines the expertise of archaeologists, historians and linguists as well as that of literary scholars. It is noteworthy that many recent significant advances of our knowledge of this period have been made by this kind of cross-disciplinary work.

Mention should also be made here of the MFA (Master of Fine Arts) degree in creative writing, which originated and is long established in the USA, and has more recently become available at a number of UK universities. The MFA is a two-year full-time course which teaches both creative writing and the teaching of creative writing and it has long been the primary qualification for those who wish to teach creative writing at an American university. At Glasgow University, the MFA is in two distinct parts: the first year is the MLitt course in creative writing, in three sections, centring, respectively, on creative, critical and practical issues. The second year consists of the structured course in the teaching of creative writing, which is also followed by students undertaking a PhD in creative writing. Elsewhere, the two years of the MFA may integrate the creative and the pedagogical elements across the two years, but Glasgow's sequential rather than combined format seems attractive, giving the added advantage that an MLitt qualification is available to those who might decide (for instance) to bypass the second year of the

MFA and instead proceed straight to the creative writing PhD. Since there is some evidence that there may be an on-going shift towards regarding the PhD as the universal entry-level qualification for all university teaching, including the teaching of creative writing, this would seem a sensible option to have available.

Variations of teaching format

M Level courses now come in a variety of formats, though a given course is not usually available in all the modes I will mention here. However, all MA/MLitt/MRes courses I am aware of can be taken in both full-time and part-time mode, the former meaning from start to completion in twelve months, and the latter in twenty-four months. A newer format, originating in the United States and at present almost exclusively applicable to courses in creative writing, is the so-called 'low residency' structure. Typically, this means that the course is taught primarily by distance learning, but with (usually) two residential weeks of intensive tuition, one around early September and the other in the early summer (most often June), these weeks being chosen to fall just outside the undergraduate teaching terms so that plentiful campus accommodation is available. An example is the MA in Creative Writing (low residency) at Kingston University, which follows this pattern. Of the core modules on this course, one is the dissertation, one is the introductory module taken in the first residency, another is a 'Structure and Style' module taken in the second and the other two are small-group workshops, taught by distance learning, one in each semester. At Oxford University there is a low-residency Creative Writing course using a slightly different model, which is a two-year, part-time MSt (Master of Studies in Creative Writing) offering 'a unique combination of high contact hours, genre specialization, and critical and creative breadth'. This course includes a series of brief 'residencies' (of four days each) and writers' 'retreats' (slightly shorter), and a 'placement' period with a publisher or literary agent, or similar.

A small number of MAs in English are currently available at British universities, taught entirely, or almost entirely, by distance learning. According to postgraduatesearch.com, on which I am drawing freely here, there are currently (in 2013) nine of these, offering a wide variety of courses, some of them quite innovative or even experimental in character, and others tailored to a very specific market. For instance, Birmingham University offers an MA in Shakespeare and Education, run by the University's Shakespeare Institute in Stratford-upon-Avon, but entirely distance-taught and aimed at practising teachers. It consists of two core modules (Shakespeare's Theatre, including research and study skills, and Shakespeare and Education) and two options (taken from Shakespeare's Craftsmanship, Shakespeare's Legacy, The Text of Shakespeare, Acting and Directing Shakespeare and Shakespeare's Women). The course is completed with a dissertation. There is an MA in World Literature at Sunderland University, a Colonial and Postcolonial Literature MA at Newman University College (Birmingham) and an MA in Children's Literature at Roehampton University. All the distance-learning MA programmes so far mentioned are on the more specialized Type B model mentioned earlier.

By contrast, the MA in English at the Open University – a part-time degree (extending over thirty-two months) taken by distance learning – might be called a Type A/B hybrid. It has two sections, the first being in two segments: the opening segment explores five clusters of literary texts from the ancient past to the present, considering, for example, rewrites and adaptations of literary texts in different genres, languages and media; in the second segment the main focus is on issues of literary history and book history with reference to Byron's satirical poem *Don Juan* and Kipling's *Kim*. The second part of the MA is the dissertation of up to 15,000 words. Here the emphasis on the reception, transmission and cultural roles and functions of literary texts is distinctive and quite specialized, whereas the period spread is very broad, which is why I am calling it an A/B hybrid. At Sheffield University, too, the MA by distance learning seems to have something of this hybrid character and can be taken in one year full time or two years part time, both by distance learning. There is a core module on research methods in English studies followed by optional modules, which include Shakespeare and early women dramatists, the language of eighteenth-century literature, the poetry of contemporary Ireland and psychoanalysis and the arts, and the whole is rounded off with the dissertation.

Finally, mention should be made in this context of the English Language Testing System (IELTS), set up under the auspices of the British Council and Cambridge University, which administers standard language tests for students whose first language is not English applying for university-level academic courses taught in English. The tests are administered at approved local centres worldwide, and they give separate scores for listening, speaking, reading and writing as well as an overall score. Overseas applicants from 'MESCs' (Majority English Speaking Countries, such as the USA, Australia, the Caribbean and so on) are exempt from these tests, but applicants from other parts of the world will have to obtain the required scores on the IELTS tests in order to qualify for acceptance on to an M level course. Until recently, the requested average score for UK postgraduate enrolment was generally 6.5, but there is widespread evidence that applicants accepted with this score sometimes have difficulty in participating fully on postgraduate courses and achieving the pass standard, especially for dissertation and thesis work. Hence, higher scores are now frequently asked for, such as an average of 7.0 across the three components of the test with a minimum of 7.5 in the written part. Many universities will also interview applicants by Skype and some ask for a specific piece of writing to be completed and returned by e-mail to the admissions tutor before the interview. At some institutions it is also the practice to arrange for part of the interview to entail discussion of a specific text (such as a short story or a small selection of poems), which has been agreed in advance with the applicant.

Of course, the portfolio of MA courses offered by individual institutions tends to shift and change quite frequently as conditions and demand alter, but the above outline will represent the range and scope of what is on offer for the foreseeable future. In the next section, I will assume that you have selected your postgraduate course and been accepted on to it, and will offer some advice on how to tackle its written assignments.

Scholarliness vs readability

Students beginning their first postgraduate course are often (under-standably) anxious about whether their work will be perceived as sufficiently academic or scholarly to merit an award at this higher level. In some cases this can result in a writing style too densely packed with footnotes, references, citations, quotations and sub-clauses, making the piece difficult to follow. I will exemplify the kind of thing I have in mind from a published example and perhaps the fact that there is so much writing of this kind in print partly explains why students often believe it is the model they should imitate. The (genuine but anonymous) example chosen is not especially shocking or culpable, but it does illustrate clearly the characteristics I have in mind. In rare cases, the subject matter in question is so complex that no other way of writing is possible, but in most academic situa-tions a rather more humane style is possible, and desirable. The example below is perhaps, or even probably, a case in which a very dense style is the only possible medium for the material. It is taken from a fascinating book about French influences on Shakespeare, centred on three plays and making intricate co-ordinations between events and documents, most of which are manuscripts in archives rather than printed and published secondary sources. What follows is the second sentence in one of the sub-sections of the chapter on *Hamlet*:

> As early as 24 May 1561, Cardinal Grandvelle (a marginal note by the translator, in La Place, *The fyrst parte of commentaries*, adds that the latter 'might rather be called Grandvillan, or greate villane' [1573, p.166])[60] was writing from Brussels to his master Philip II that he feared a protestant move to take the throne from the Hapsburgs, and that the Duke of Saxony, perhaps even the King of Denmark, had his eye on it (Grandvelle, 1841–52, 6: 320 [No 51]).

This is a very brief sample of a style of writing immediately recog-nisable as academic, most obviously in the elaborateness of the referencing, for every statement is supported with a reference giving sources and page numbers, or linking to footnotes and to entries in the bibliography. Another characteristically academic feature is the use of 'embedded' or 'interrupting' clauses, which are inserted into the main sentence and delay its completion. Thus, the 'core' statement made is that 'In May 1561 Cardinal Granvelle wrote to Phillip II that he feared a protestant move to take the throne from the Hapsburgs.' A long, bracketed interruption about a marginal note made by the translator of a source document is inserted into this statement between its subject ('Cardinal Granvelle') and its main verb phrase ('was writing from Brussels'). Indeed, that bracketed interruption itself contains an interruption of its own main statement. Thus, the core statement of the bracketed insertion is that 'a marginal note by the translator adds that 'the latter' [that is, presumably, Granvelle] 'might better be called 'Grandvillan'. But this statement is itself interrupted by the insertion of a source reference ('in La Place, *The fyrst parte of commentaries*'), and then there are square brackets within the cursive brackets to contain the page data, followed by a footnote number. Towards the end of the lengthy sentence there is another interrupting clause ('perhaps even the King of Denmark'), this time closed off with commas rather than brackets, before we get to the main verbal phrase 'had his eye on it'. Of course, it is taxing to read prose of this kind at length, and if spoken aloud, as in a lecture, it would be impossible for an audience to understand it if they did not also have sight of the text. In its favour, on the other hand, we note that a large quantity of complex information has been arranged with maximum economy and that each snippet of the historical information it contains is contributing to a gradually unfolding thesis which requires this intricate chain of data to be placed before the reader. There is no way of quick-reading material of this nature, and there is a recognition in the very manner of the writing that its audience will necessarily be small and highly specialized. I do sometimes wonder if the 'embedding' or 'interrupting' structure, of which academics seem inordinately fond (as you will have noticed, I am doing it now), is really always helpful or necessary, but it has the *look* of learnedness and intellectual efficiency and can sometimes save words when words are tight. Also, when an argument is based upon multifarious archival sources, it is inevitable that the referencing will be dense and complicated. Yes, it *is* sometimes possible to relegate all the referencing to footnotes, so that the sentences of the main text will have a less cluttered appearance, but that can make reading the material more difficult if the footnotes are not printed on the same page. Anyway, my point is simply that this kind of prose is not a suitable model for academic writing in general and that most critical arguments in the discipline should not require such impacted density of annotation, expression and referencing. We should aim to be fluent, specific and detailed in argument, but this can be done without the premature acquisition of a fussy, over-annotated, old-fashioned academic style. In other words, the ideal of scholarliness is not the only requirement, for the ideal of readability is just as important.

Your voice and 'their' voices

A related problem is finding an appropriate balance between the space devoted to discussing the views of established scholars on the topic set for an essay or assignment and presenting and defending our own views on the matter. At undergraduate level a student's primary engagement should be with the 'text' itself, whether the text be a work of literature, a piece of writing in some other form, a film, a performance, an image or a concept. The text should be discussed in what I would call a 'fully instanced', close-up way, rather than being surveyed from a generalising distance or viewed exclusively through a single theoretical, historical or conceptual perspective. At M Level, this requirement is not entirely superseded, but it must be supplemented, for we must also engage with the interpretive body of material which has grown up in response to the text, re-situating our own response to the text within the context of that body of work. Thus, the balance required is quite a delicate one, for we might well feel somewhat in awe of the household-name critics and theorists who have been there ahead of us and have made their pronounce-ments on the texts we are now reading (belatedly, we may feel). When we are influenced by the views and voices of these eminent (or, at least, published) personages we must acknowledge the fact with appropriate referencing and citation, and much emphasis will be placed on the business of 'acknowledging sources'. But citing 'authorities' for almost every point we put forward can make it very difficult for an essay to develop its own voice and momentum. In extreme cases, the writing can become merely a form of 'critical braiding', in which the views of a series of critics are woven together to make what I am tempted to call a facsimile of a scholarly essay, leaving little room for the voice and opinions of the person who is writing the essay. In such cases, the student's primary engagement can seem to be with published academics, so that the text itself is only encountered by critical proxy. So how can a balance be struck between your voice and their voices?

We can begin a brief consideration of this matter by considering the following question: Which (if any) of the following statements require a supporting reference?

(1) Queen Victoria reigned from 1837 to 1901.
(2) Dickens was one of the most famous and successful novelists of the nineteenth century.
(3) Hemingway's prose style is terse and laconic.
(4) The poet Tennyson was very short-sighted.
(5) Coleridge was in love with Wordsworth's sister-in-law, Sara Hutchinson.
(6) In Conrad's fiction there is often a decisive 'watershed' moment of self-loss or self-discovery.

With the first of these, you may well have checked these dates in a printed or online source, just to make sure that your memory is accurate, but does that mean that you need to cite that source in a footnote? Of course, it doesn't mean that, but why not, exactly? The reason is that this data is a matter of public record, locatable in thousands of printed and other sources. Anyone who felt he or she ought to record the source in which these dates were checked would also have to do so every time he or she checked the spelling of a writer's name or the name of the capital city of a given country. The second is simply a matter of opinion of the most generalized kind – disproving this statement would be almost as difficult as proving it, and it really says nothing very specific in any case, since being 'one of' the most popular novelists of a given period could mean that you are the third most popular (by sales figures, etc.), or the two hundredth and third. The third of these statements is something of a critical commonplace, so far as the sentiment goes, and it would only need to be referenced if the precise phrase 'terse and laconic', as applied to Hemingway's prose style, is a comment you found in a critical article or chapter about this author's work. If that is the case, then you are obliged to enclose the phrase in inverted commas and provide a reference for it. Otherwise, it is so typical of the consensus on the nature of this author's style that no specific reference or citation would be needed. In the case of the fourth, the statement is true, and I believe that it accounts for the ultra-close-up feel of some of Tennyson's poetic descriptions of objects. I found out about it by reading a biography of Tennyson and looking at a reproduced sketch, in the same book, of Tennyson reading, in which he is holding the book a couple of inches from his eyes. So in this case, I would want to reference the biography and give a specific page reference. This fact isn't common knowledge, but it seems to me of great interest, so I would certainly want to cite a source and would feel that I ought to do so if I were to mention the fact in the course of an argument about Tennyson's writing. In the case of Coleridge, the fifth example, the fact is more widely known and is usually mentioned in even a very cursory account of Coleridge's life and career, but I would want to cite a major biography (such as Richard Holmes's) and indicate the chapter in which detailed information on this topic can be found. The final example is a very specific critical opinion, and if the insight and/ or the formulation is not your own, you are obliged to cite a critical source for it. In extreme cases, failure to do so could mean that you would be suspected of unfair critical practice by seeking to pass off as your own an insight or opinion which is the intellectual property of somebody else. Overall, then, of these six statements, only three would definitely require a reference or citation to an external 'authority' or source of expertise.

Book chapter vs journal articles

An MA assignment essay should address clear-cut questions and issues, focusing on a specific and well-defined aspect of a text, author, genre or issue rather than aim to provide an overarching, open-ended survey of the topic. There should be a fully articulated and explicit running argument flowing through the essay, leading to specific conclusions. This means, in effect, that an M Level essay should be more like a (recently published) article in an academic journal than a chapter in an academic book. The editors of journals usually impose strict limits on the overall word count, discourage the proliferation of footnotes and require a briskness of pace, a transparency of purpose and a clear style that makes a real effort to engage and sustain the reader's attention. Articles, too, are usually pinpoint interventions into a field, written first and then sent on spec to a journal, whereas books are usually commissioned and contracted first, and then written. Books are larger items and they have to cover a substantial stretch of ground, so they usually have broader and more open titles, which are as general as possible. Of course, a book entitled *The Novel in Mid-Victorian Britain* will probably cover only a small number of major authors and a limited number of themes, so the implied promise of overview is often in practice confined to the opening chapter. The core chapters might then look at major thematic areas, so there could be one with the title 'The Provincial City in the novel, 1850–1870'. Again, this title suggests a breadth of scope and treatment rather than a piece that homes in on a specific question or issue. A book of this kind will want to remain in print for ten or twenty years and will need to have wide appeal across the whole subject body, so it will probably avoid the extremes of up-to-the-minute, 'cutting-edge' methodologies on the one hand and head-on challenges of the prevailing consensus on the other. In other words, the book chapter is not the best model for you to follow when you are writing an MA essay.

Consider, by contrast, an article on the same area. Instead of the implicit, open-ended promise to provide an overview of a broadly designated topic, a journal article will have more of a precision 'micro-brief', as we might call it. Whereas a book chapter can move at a leisurely pace, typically extending to 10,000–12,000 words – and does not need to focus very tightly on a specific issue – a journal article has to move at a brisker pace (with a typical length of 6,000–8,000 words) and will address a tightly defined issue or problem, with a more purposeful brief and a specific micro-focus. So an article in this area might have a title such as the following 'Representations of elsewhere: the image of London in novels set in provincial cities, 1850–1870'. An article of this this kind will need a much shorter list of relevant secondary material, for articles have to break new ground and conceptualize and analyze a topic which has not previously been formulated. In years to come, the author of the article and the editor of the journal hope, a whole new sub-field will grow up, with all subsequent critics citing their debt to this pioneering piece. All the weight of effort and thinking is directed to the new conceptualization and the engagement with secondary materials will be, well, secondary, because as yet there may hardly be much directly relevant secondary material to cite. From the point of view of an ambitious postgraduate student, there is the possibility, in a piece of this narrower kind, of saying something new and getting noticed. By contrast, in attempting to write an overview piece on the mid-Victorian novel, the chances of achieving this are more remote, for that means competing with scholars who may already have behind them half a lifetime of immersion in the material. The other advantage of adopting the article rather than the book chapter as a model is that articles need to state their methodology explicitly, and foreground and signpost the stages of their argument as they proceed, which is an excellent discipline for an emerging writer and scholar to follow.

Even when writing assignments for modules explicitly devoted to theory, students should include 'text work' in some form, otherwise originality is almost impossible. No student can say something original about (for example) gender roles; he or she may be able to say something original about gender roles in *Hard Times*, but only if he or she goes to text-level and engages with language and nuance in a particular scene. There is little point in discussing film theory or literary theory without – at some point in the essay – considering in detail stills or sequences from an actual film, or lines, stanzas etc. from an actual poem, or scenes from an actual novel. This is the primary material that needs to be 're-seen' or 're-read' in the light of the theory, and the result will probably be to highlight strengths and weaknesses in both the theory and the text. But that juxtaposing of theory and text – that *specificity* of enquiry – is surely the heart of it. In cases where the essay opens with the explication of some aspect of 'theory', that part also needs to make a succinct case for using specified elements of the theory in relation to the text in question, rather than attempting to provide a general overview of what (say) deconstruction is or how new historicists approach literary texts. Generally, I would add, it is inadvisable for a student to write an overview account of a theorist with whom he or she is in almost complete agreement: the result will be a bland 'parallel paraphrase' of what the theorist says. Where such total agreement exists, a detailed application of a specific aspect of his or her work to a text he or she never discussed is likely to be more fruitful, and the process should aim to raise some fundamental issues about the outlook and practice of the theorist in question.

The excesses I am hoping to discourage in what has been said in this chapter about writing at M Level arise from the fact that so many of us are anxious to make study at this level look and feel distinctly different from undergraduate work. But we have to do that by making the syllabus different and distinctive, as well as the methods of study, rather than by insisting on an over-conformist style and an often tedious, manner of writing. Indeed, I would want to emphasize instead that everything said about writing at undergraduate level (as represented here by the contents of chapters eleven and twelve) remains true and valid at postgraduate level. We want students to bring those virtues with them as they cross the border into postgrad land rather than seeking to disguise themselves instantly as middle-aged, jobbing academics with several little-read books behind them.

Postscript

In 1998, the American Council on Education and the University of California conducted a survey on the habits and aspirations of 275,811 new college students entering 469 institutions. The survey found, among other things, that 80.4% of these students had occasionally played a video game in the past year, while only 18.7% had frequently taken out a book or journal from a school library. Among their reasons for going to college, the ability to make more money ranked highest among 74.6% of these new college students.[1]

The statistics have a dubious air of precision (18.7 per cent!), but as the survey was made quite a long time ago we can only assume that the figure would be lower still today. Playing online games is undoubtedly a more popular leisure activity than reading literature. It's easier, and it may well give most people a more immediate sense of pleasurable relaxation. Gaming is fine, but it isn't everything. Reading literature, rather than just spending the evening in front of the TV or the games console, requires conscious effort, even for professors, but it can give a longer-term sense of satisfaction, which may well in the end add up to a greater measure of human contentment. In the same way, getting off the sofa and going for a run or a swim isn't always the most attractive option, but mostly (surely?) we find it more pleasurable in the end. Pleasure isn't everything, either, but if we don't read, then we become trapped in our own individual minds, never allowing somebody else's thoughts to alter our mental climate in subtle ways by thinking themselves inside us (that slightly spooky yet somehow thrilling way of thinking about what reading is). Without reading, we can end up living in a mental weather system which is always the same, so that rain and

---

[1] Information from D. W. Fenza's article 'Creative Writing and its Discontents' in *The Writer's Chronicle*, March/April, 2000.

sunshine become the same thing and a sameness which isn't really total living begins to take hold of us. Of course, we can be moved and challenged by films and TV and other electronic entertainment too, but the City of Words has a unique intimacy and power, and that is where we live when we study English.

As Ezra Pound said, education is what remains when we have forgotten everything we set out to learn. Perhaps when we revisit our own City of Words in later life, we will find much of it vanished, with only isolated sections of apparently unimportant suburbs remaining, or puzzling bits of broken monuments, which presumably once stood in an impressive urban centre of some kind, but are now stranded in territory which has reverted to desert. This, I realized as I wrote it, is the scenario of Shelley's short poem 'Ozymandias', so it's a literary recall still reverberating in the mind many years after the original literary encounter. But it's also an echo of the ending of the film *Planet of the Apes*, in which a puzzling fragment of stone is recognized as a piece of the Statue of Liberty, half-buried in land which has now become desert. Film image and literary image, then, can express the same thing, can work together, each with its own vividness, each with the characteristic tang of its own textuality. All true cities are several cities, and in studying English we are not looking for an embattled citadel opposed to everything else in our own time and place. It would be very rash to try to predict what comes next. Perhaps one day only fragments of the City of Words will remain. But let us hope that at this very moment that strange and frightening beast *The Next Big Thing* is slouching towards the City of Words, to be born.

What Next? Annotated Bibliography

Chapter 1 Introduction

The following books all give an overview of literature or literary studies. Bradford and Pope are big textbooks covering both criticism and theory and designed for systematic use as part of an English course (Pope's being a 'recast' of his earlier *The English Studies Book*). Eaglestone's is a short book which aims to bridge some of the gaps between A level and degree-level English. Gribble's is an older book which defends more traditional methods in the face of the onslaught of theory. Widdowson's is a succinct and thought-provoking reflection on a vast topic.

Bradford, Richard ed., *Introducing Literary Studies*, London, 1996

Eaglestone, Robert, *Doing English*, 3rd edn, London, 2009

Gribble, James, *Literary Education: A Revaluation*, Cambridge, 1983

Pope, Rob, *Studying English Literature and Language: An Introduction and Companion*, London, 2012

Widdowson, Peter, *Literature*, London, 1999

Chapter 2 Reading Poetry

Close reading remains potentially a radical and transforming pedagogical practice, but many of those who have explicitly defended it in recent years have tended to become identified (sometimes unfairly) with mainly conservative allegiances. Abrams', Alter's, Ricks' and Steiner's are books of this kind with great character and originality. Hopkins' is a textbook working usefully to a systematic brief.

Abrams, M. H., *Doing Things with Texts*, New York, 1989

Alter, Robert, *The Pleasures of Reading in an Ideological Age*, rpt, New York, 1997

Hopkins, Chris, *Thinking About Texts*, 2nd edn, London, 2009

Ricks, Christopher, *Essays in Appreciation*, Oxford, 1998

Steiner, George, *Real Presences*, London, 1989

Chapter 3 Reading Fiction

All these books are about prose fiction. Forster's was first published in 1927 and is relaxed but systematic. Hawthorn's is an excellent study book, detailed, practical and comprehensive, and drawing upon the more 'high-tech', 'narratological' approach of Bal and Genette (both of which are written with pithy concision). Lodge's is a compendium of his very short pieces (originally published in a Sunday newspaper) on different aspects of fiction (beginnings, endings, the use of symbolism and so on).

Bal, Mieke, *Narratology: Introduction to the Theory of Narrative*, 2nd edn, Toronto, 1998

Genette, Gerard, *Narrative Discourse*, Cornell, 1993

Forster, E. M., *Aspects of the Novel*, Harmondsworth, 1962

Hawthorn, Jeremy, *Studying the Novel*, 6th edn, London, 2010

Lodge, David, *The Art of Fiction*, Harmondsworth, 1992

Chapter 4 Reading and Interpretation

Allen gives an orderly account of the many different versions of intertextuality within literary studies, whereas Chandler, in his chapter six, 'Textual Interactions', covers the same terrain from a perspective which takes in non-literary media as well. Clayton and Rothstein unravel notions of literary intertextuality from the related idea of literary influence. Newton takes a broader all-round view of matters of literary interpretation. Rylance and Simons offer a series of contextualized readings of major literary texts, illustrating the officially approved way of doing English in the UK.

Allen, Graham, *Intertextuality*, New Critical Idiom, 2nd edn, London, 2011

Chandler, Daniel, *Semiotics: The Basics*, 2nd edn, London, 2007

Clayton, Jay and Eric Rothstein, (eds), *Influence and Intertextuality in Literary History,*Wisconsin, 1991

Newton, K. M., *Interpreting the Text: A Critical Introduction to the Theory and Practice of Literary Interpretation*, London, 1990

Rylance, Rick and Judy Simons, *Literature in Context*, London, 2001

Chapter 5 English and Creative Writing

This is currently a rapidly expanding field, with many excellent books competing for sales and influence. Bell has contributions from around forty writers and covers a wide range of topics – viewpoint, setting, characters, endings – and the book is associated with the creative writing course at the University of East Anglia. Brande is an older and very popular book now re-issued (it's actually about fiction-writing, in spite of its broad title). Newman's is a lively and practical book from the creative writing course team at Liverpool John Moores University. Singleton is also a practical workbook, closely associated with a degree course, and Marshall is a book which has very quickly established wide popularity.

Bell, Julia, Paul Magrs and Andrew Motion, *The Creative Writing Coursebook*, London, 2001

Brande, Dorothea, *Becoming a Writer*, new edn, London, 2004

Morley, David, *The Cambridge Introduction to Creative Writing*, Cambridge, 2007

Newman, Jenny, Edmund Cusick and Aileen La Tourette, *The Writer's Workbook*, 2nd edn, London, 2004

Marshall, Evan, *Novel Writing*, London, 2004

Singleton, John and Mary Luckhurst, *The Creative Writing Handbook*, 2nd edn, Basingstoke, 2000

Chapter 6 English Now and Then

All these are about the history or the future of English Studies. Court and Graff have a North American perspective, and Potter and Palmer centre on England. The appropriately named English takes a fascinating and detailed look at the present state and future prospects of literary English Studies worldwide. These, then, are various 'then' and 'now' overviews of literary studies in English.

Court, Franklin, E., *Institutionalizing English Literature*, Stanford, 1992

English, James, F., *The Global Future of English Studies*, Oxford, 2012

Graff, Gerald, *Professing Literature: An Institutional History – Twentieth Anniversary Edition*, Chicago, 2007

Palmer, D. J., *The Rise of English Studies*, Oxford, 1965

Potter, Stephen, *The Muse in Chains*, London, 1937

Chapter 7 Online and Digital English

The Department of Digital Humanities at King's College London gives a useful overview of what is available online. Burdick (also available in electronic formats) is modestly described as 'a compact report on the state of contemporary knowledge production'. Clark is a free online public information resource giving basic data on literature in English worldwide. Section two of Goring is a very useful updated guide to electronic media in literary studies, and Siemens is an immensely helpful and wide-ranging collection of essays.

The Department of Digital Humanities at Kings College London (the DDH), formerly the Centre for Computing in the Humanities, http://www.kcl.ac.uk/artshums/depts/ddh/about/index.aspx

Burdick, Peter et al. (eds), *Digital Humanities*, Cambridge, MA, 2012

Clark, Robert, Emory Elliott, and Janet Todd, *The Literary Encyclopedia and Literary Dictionary*, http://www.litencyc.com/editors.php

Goring, Paul, Jeremy Hawthorn and Domhnall Mitchell, *Studying Literature: The Essential Companion*, 2nd edn, London, 2010

Siemens, Ray and Susan Schreibman, *A Companion to Digital Literary Studies*, new edn, Oxford, 2013

Chapter 8 Literary Criticism and Literary Theory

All these books are introductions to literary theory for students. Eagleton's was the pioneer, the first book to try to make literary theory make sense for undergraduates and the first to present its development as a single integrated narrative. The others are all 'second-generation' texts which build on that approach but have much more material on practical applications of literary theory.

Barry, Peter, *Beginning Theory: An Introduction to Literary and Cultural Theory*, 3rd edn, Manchester, 2009

Bennett, Andrew and Nicholas Royle, *An Introduction to Literature, Criticism, and Theory*, 4th edn, London, 2009

Eagleton, Terry, *Literary Theory: An Introduction*, 25th anniversary edn, Oxford, 2008

Lyn, Steven, *Texts and Contexts: Writing about Literature with Critical Theory*, 3rd edn, 4th edn, London, 2004

Tyson, Lois, *Critical Theory Today: A User-Friendly Guide*, 2nd edn, New York, 2006

Chapter 9 English as Language

This chapter touches on four areas within a vast field of study: Bradford is a general introduction to the first of these, stylistics, and Toolan covers the area of the *narrative* stylistics, balancing the fact that my own comments under this heading are mainly on poetry. Holmes is one of the best student introductions to sociolinguistics, and Burchfield is an able and engaging writer on matters of historical linguistics. Matthews is a fine introductory overview of the field of linguistics.

Bradford, Richard, *Stylistics*, *New Critical Idiom* series, London, 1997

Burchfield, Robert, *The English Language*, Oxford, 1985

Holmes, Janet, *An Introduction to Sociolinguistics*, 3rd edn, London, 2008

Matthews, P. H., *Linguistics: A Very Short Introduction*, Oxford, 2003

Toolan, Michael, *Narrative: A Critical Linguistic Introduction*, 2nd edn, London, 2001

Chapter 10 English and History

This chapter deals with history and contextuality, and while there are plenty of books and series which place individual writers in context, there are very few which raise the question of contextuality as a general issue. Brannigan gives an overview of the strengths and weaknesses of new historicism. Chandler exemplifies the full-scale new historicist approach applied to Romanticism. Cunningham's lively and provocative book argues against the view of the literary text as self-contained and self-reflexive, seeking to reinstate the importance of reference and context, while Gallagher and Greenblatt show historicist approaches in practice. Parvini's discussion is probing and well informed and Veeser offers a very useful collection of material, not restricted to a single historical period.

Branningan, John, *New Historicism and Cultural Materialism*, London, 1998

Chandler, James, *England in 1819: The Politics of Literary Culture and the Case of Romantic Historicism*, Chicago, 1999

Cunningham, Valentine, *In the Reading Gaol: Postmodernity, Texts, and History*, Oxford, 1994

Gallagher, Catherine and Stephen Greenblatt, *Practising the New Historicism*, Chicago, 2000

Parvini, Neema, *Shakespeare and Contemporary Theory: New Historicism and Cultural Materialism*, London, 2012

Veeser, Aram, H., *The New Historicism Reader*, London, 1994

Chapter 11 The Essay: Crossing the Four Frontiers

Marggraf-Turley is an extremely popular and user-friendly practical guide to essay writing, written by an English lecturer rather than a general educationalist. Gaskell too is an English lecturer and the book has both general guidance on correct usage and a series of quoted examples from critics with commentaries. Evans is a lively and sensible book by a former newspaper editor writing for journalists about clear style, and valuable for English students too. Elbow's book is compulsive reading – I have found it an enormous help as a writer over many years. Hennessy's is a 'cure for essay-phobia', its users say.

Elbow, Peter, *Writing with Power*, 2nd edn, New York, 1998

Evans, Harold, *Essential English*, new edn, London, 2000

Gaskell, Philip, *Standard Written English*, Edinburgh, 1998

Hennessy, Brendan, *Writing an Essay*, 5th edn, London, 2007

Marggraf-Turley, Richard, *Writing Essays: A Guide for Students in English and the Humanities*, London, 2000

Chapter 12 The Undergraduate Dissertation

Surprisingly little is available which addresses the specific issues of the undergraduate dissertation. Greetham is a well known and invariably helpful writer on all aspects of student writing; Grobman is an interesting collection of essays from the USA's National Council for Teachers of English; Swetnam is a useful and successful book which has stood the test of time.

Greetham, Bryan, *How to Write Your Undergraduate Dissertation*, London, 2009

Grobman, Laurie and Joyce Kinkead, *Undergraduate Research in English Studies*, Illinois, 2010

Swetnam, Gareth and Ruth Swetman, *Writing Your Dissertation*, London, 2000

Chapter 13 The Text as Text

All these are about literary editing. Pettit is the best one to start with as it introduces the issues for non-specialists, with essays on the texts of major novels. Kastan and McKenzie are brief books by excellent writers, using telling examples to focus the issues involved. Murphy's collection links literary editing and literary theory in provocative ways and McGann/Greetham is a major work which had a profound effect on literary theory, literary editing and literary criticism.

Kastan, David Scott, *Shakespeare and the Book*, Cambridge, 2001

McGann, Jerome and David C. Greetham, *A Critique of Modern Textual Criticism*, Virginia, 1993

McKenzie, D. F., *Bibliography and the Sociology of Texts*, Cambridge, 1999

Murphy, Andrew ed., *The Renaissance Text: Theory, Editing, Textuality*, Manchester, 2000

Pettit, Alexander, *Textual Studies and the Common Reader*, Georgia, 2000

Chapter 14 English at MA Level

Belsey's is a very interesting chapter in Griffin. The contributors to Da Sousa are mostly staff at the UK's Open University, so it is quite closely geared to their courses and distinctive cultural point of view, but it has general interest too. Griffin is one of the very few available overview books on what is distinctive about postgraduate study in English. Sword's is a challenging and deliberately provocative book about academic style with which I have a great deal of sympathy.

Belsey, Catherine, 'Textual Analysis as a Research Method', is Chapter 9 in the next-but-one item

Da Sousa Correa, Delia and W. R. Owen (eds), *The Handbook to Literary Research*, 2nd edn, London, 2009

Griffin, Gabriele, ed., *Research Methods for English Studies*, Edinburgh, 2005

Sword, Helen, *Stylish Academic Writing*, Harvard, 2012

Index

acronyms 158
aesthetic quality 35
'Affective Fallacy, The' 129
All for Love 129
American literature 80
American New Critics 98
Amis, Kingsley 103
Amoretti 32–6
analysis 24, 25–30, 195–7
Angel in the House, The 89
annotation 237
Antony and Cleopatra 129, 131
'Apology for Poetry' 127
'Aposiopesis' 28–30
applied linguistics
    master's degrees 229
Aristotle 127
Armstrong, Isobel 74, 75–6, 78
Arnold, Matthew 150–1, 152
art galleries 188
Associated Writing Programs
    (AWP) 79
Auden, W. H. 83, 223
Austen, George 178
Austen, Jane 10–11, 12, 20, 39,
    113, 117, 172–80, 222
    novels 12, 30
authenticity 221
authorship 57–8
AWP *see* Associated Writing
    Programs

back-formations 158–9
Bailie, Joanna 62
'Ballad of Religion and Marriage,
    A' 120–1
Barbauld, Anna 62
Barthes, Roland 73, 128, 134

Bateson, F. W. 130, 215
'Beggars' 54–6
Beloved 39
Belsey, Catherine 133–4
Bengal Asiatic Society 160
Bennett, Andrew 183–5
Beowulf 95
Beyond Formalism 133
Biographia Literaria 128
biography, literary 181
Blake, William 212–15
Bloom, Harold 132, 133
books, chapters in 239–42
borrowed words 167–70
'Boyhood of Raleigh' 37–9
Bradbury, Malcolm 82
Braine, John 103
'Break, break, break' 97
'Break of Day in the Trenches'
    123
British Council 234
British *Intute* Consortium 105
broadcasting 228
Brontë, Charlotte 11, 191
Brontë, Emily 129, 130
Brooks, Cleanth 99, 129
Browning, Robert
    dramatic monologues 58
Bunyan, John 93
Butler, Marilyn 186
Byron, Lord 61, 233

'Cambridge revolution' 98
Cambridge University 94
Camelot 68
Cameron, Julia Margaret 88–9
Carry On films 217
Carter, Angela 82, 103

case studies 205
cataphoric words 152
catchphrases 157
Caxton, William 168
celebrity culture 159
Cento Novelle Antiche 74–5
'Church Going' 24
citation 237
Clark Lectures 128
*Classic American Slave Narratives,
    The* 7
classification systems 197
close reading 101, 131, 133,
    153
  closed 130
  critical 134
  open 130–1
  seen 130
  unseen 130
closed close reading 130
cognates 163
cohesive chains 152
Coleridge, Samuel Taylor 23, 40,
    60–1, 128, 212
collocational clashes 152
*Colonial American Travel
    Narratives* 7
commentary 24, 192–3, 194
Commonwealth 91
computers 159
concordances 107, 117
Conrad, Joseph 41, 44, 46, 47
  grammar 46
contextual reading 130
contextualism 171–80, 184, 188
  resonant 189
contextuality 49–50, 51, 62, 77
Cornell University 80, 92
Cornhill Magazine 209–10
Crawford, Robert 91
creative writing 8, 79–89, 227
  Canada 79
  courses 85, 89, 234
  degree courses 79, 80

doctoral degrees 231
English departments 84–9
higher education 81–3
master's degrees 228
UK 81–3
USA 79–81
creativity 222
Creeley, Robert 17–18
critical close reading 134
Critical Difference, The 140
Critical Practice 133
critics 31, 70
Cuddon, J. A. 140
Culler, Jonathan 133
cultural
  practices 102
  stereotypes 138
  studies 101
  tradition 68
Culture and Imperialism 172
Cummings, e. e. 12
curriculum, higher education 95

'Daffodils' 52
  parody 59
Daisy Miller 209–12
  editions 209–12
Dale, Thomas 94
databases 106–7
  full-text 107, 117
David Copperfield 39
'Death of the Author, The' 73
deconstruction 132, 138, 140–3, 145
  definition 140
  process 141
Deconstruction and Criticism 132
'Defence of Poetry' 127
degree courses 101, 199
  preliminary reading 206–8
  secondary reading 207–8
  writing 206
degrees 7
  classification 200
  grades 200

marking process 200
  part-time 233
deixis 149–50
delineation 42
Derrida, Jacques 128, 132, 133, 134, 140
description 191–2
Dewey, John 80
diaries 212
Dickens, Charles 39
  novels 50
dictionaries 158, 159
Dictionary of Literary Terms, A 140
disbelief, suspension of 40
discussion 193–5, 196
dissertations 199–208, 228, 230, 233
  assessment 199
  preliminary reading 206–8
  secondary reading 207–8
  structure 200–5
  writing 206
distance learning 232–3
doctoral degrees 231
docu-poetry 87–8
domain 41–3
Don Juan 233
Donna di Scalotta 74–5
Donne, John 130
Doolittle, Hilda *see* HD
dramatic monologues 58
Dryden, John 129
Duchess of Malfi, The 15
Duhig, Ian 23
Duke of Edinburgh 137–8
'Dulce et Decorum Est' 123

Eagleton, Terry 140
early English 91
  degrees 96
  UK 94–6
  USA 92–4
East Anglia, University of 82

ecocriticism 132
editorial process 221–2
editors 221
Education Act of 1870 95
Egley, William Maw 69
ekphrastic poetry 85–6
ekphrastic writing 87
Electronic Literature Foundation (ELF) 114
electronic resources 105
Electronic Text Center 105
Elephants Teach, The 81
ELF *see* Electronic Literature Foundation
Eliot, George 19, 73
Eliot, T. S. 29, 58, 103, 127, 128, 131, 212
elitism 94
Elizabethan World Picture, The 100
ELTS *see* English Language Testing System
Empson, William 98, 99, 128
English as a Foreign Language 101
English Language Testing System (ELTS) 234
English Reformation 136
epic poetry 32
essay writing 8, 191–7
essays 202
etymology 97
euphemisms 156–7
evaluation 31, 128, 129
'Eve of St Agnes, The' 215–18, 224
  manuscript 215

Feaver, Vicki 12, 15–16
Felluga, Dino Franco 113
feminism 132
fiction 37–47
fictionalization 57, 58
film studies *see* theatre, film and television studies

financial crisis of 2008 105
First World War Poetry Digital
    Archive 123
    Tutorials 123
Foerster, Norman 80
Folger Shakespeare Project 121
footnotes, footnoting 235–7, 238
Ford, Ford Madox 43
foregrounding 17, 44
formalism 49, 171, 172, 188
Foucault, Michel 128
Freeman, Edward 95
Freud, Sigmund 73
'Frost at Midnight' 212, 226
Frost, Robert 27

galleries *see* art galleries
Gaskell, Elizabeth
gateway sites 112
gaze 123
gender 57, 59–62, 70, 71, 138–9,
    154–6
gender politics 59–60
Germany, universities 92
Google 110
Graff, Gerald 92, 93
grammar 25, 34
Great Gatsby, The 226
Greek 94, 160
Greenblatt, Stephen 186–8
Greene, Graham 103
Grimm, Jakob 164
Grimm's Law 164
Grimshaw, John Atkinson 69

Hallam, Arthur 75, 97
Hamlet 73, 212
    film versions 121–2
Hamlet on the Ramparts 121
Hardy, Thomas 129, 130, 212
Hartman, Geoffrey 132, 133
Harvard Composition Course 93
Harvard University 92
HD 140–3

head nouns 152
Heart of Darkness 13, 16, 44
Hemans, Felicia 62
Henry V 20
Henry VIII 136
higher education, curriculum 95
historicism 49, 171
history (as academic subject) 8, 135
Holman Hunt, William 69
Hopkins, Gerard Manley 49–50,
    214
Hughes, Arthur 69
Humbul 106
hypertext 109

'I Know a Man' 17–18
Idylls of the King, The 68, 75
Indiana University 119
intention 222, 224
'Intentional Fallacy, The' 129
internet 8, 107, 118, 159
Internet Shakespeare Editions 117
interpretation 31, 42, 49–78
intertextuality 47, 49–50, 51, 57–8,
    59–62
Introductory Guide to Critical
    Theory 113
Intute 106
Iowa Writers' Workshop 80
Iowa, University of, School of
    Letters 80
'Ironing' 16
Ishiguro, Kazuo 82

Jackson, Julia 88
Jakobson, Roman 149
James, Henry 47, 145, 209–12
*Jane Austen and the French
    Revolution* 181
Jane Eyre 11, 191
jargon 156–7, 159
Johnson, Barbara 140
Johnson, Samuel 128
'Jolly Corner, The' 145

Jones, William 160
journals, articles 239–42
Joyce, James 41, 103, 131, 224–5
judgements 31

Keats 181–2
Keats, John 61, 130, 181–6,
    212–18, 219, 224
  biography 181–2
Keats, Narrative and Audience 183
Keele University 230
Kim 233
King Lear 13, 29, 212
King's College, London 94
Kipling, Rudyard 233
Kirkpatrick, Johnston 27–30, 31–2
Knights of the Round Table, The 68
Kureishi, Hanif 103

'Lady of Shalott, The' 8, 63–78,
    119, 212
  interpretation 69–78
  representation in art 69
  versions 68, 69
Lancaster University 82
language 135, 140, 147–70
  acquisition 229
  groups 162
  master's degrees 229
  relationships 162–4
  studies 227
languages, Indo-European 164
Larkin, Philip 24
Latin 94, 160
Lawrence, D. H. 77, 225–6
'Leach Gatherer, The' 52
Leavis, F. R. 98, 128, 129, 130,
    131, 211
letters 212
Levinson, Marjorie 186
Levy, Amy 119–21
lexico-semantic deviations 152
lexis 154
liberal humanism 134

linguistics 227
  applied 229
  definition 147–8
  historical 148, 160–2, 170
  literary 132
  master's degrees 229
  terminology 152
linguists 147
literariness 133
literary
  biography 181
  criticism 20, 31, 85, 127–45
    differences between British
      and American 128–30
    extrinsic 130–1
    intrinsic 130–1
  critics 147
  historians 147
  linguistics 132
  scholars 51
  studies 61, 80
  theorists 147
  theory 8, 85, 100, 113, 127–45
Literary Theory 140
literature 5–6, 227
  Australia 5
  Canada 5
  Caribbean 5
  Indian sub-continent
  Ireland 5
  South Africa 5
  teaching 96
  USA 5, 80
  Wales 5
Liu, Alan 112
Lives of the Poets 128
Living Principle, The 129
loan words 167
'London' 213
London University 94
Longfellow, Henry Wadsworth 93
Longinus 127
Lowell, James Russell 93
Lynch, Jack 113

Majority English Speaking
    Countries (MESCs) 234
Malcontent, The 15
Malory, Thomas 68, 74, 75
de Man, Paul 132, 133
Manchester Metropolitan
    University 82
Mansfield Park 113–16, 172–80,
    185–6
    Electronic Literature Foundation
        version
        114–16
Marston, John 15
Marxism 132
master's degrees 227–42
    assignments 239–42
    distance learning 232–3
    specialized 228
    structure 227
    teaching 232–4
McEwan, Ian 82
McGann, Jerome 183, 186
meaning 13, 25
media and communications
    studies 101
media studies 84
MESCs *see* Majority English
    Speaking Countries
metaphor 16, 57
Meteyard, Sidney 69
MHRA *see* Modern Humanities
    Research Association
Middle English 95
Middlemarch 19, 73
Millais, John Everett 37–9, 46
Miller, J. Hillis 132
Milton, John 34
MIT Shakespeare Project 121
MLA *see* Modern Language
    Association
*MLA Handbook for Writers
    of Research Papers* 105,
    109–10, 112
mobile devices 106

Modern Humanities Research
    Association (MHRA) 110
    referencing 111
    Style Guide 111
Modern Language Association
    (MLA) 93, 109
modernism 47, 103
Monty Python and the Holy Grail
    68
Morrison, Toni 39, 103
Morte Darthur 68, 74
Motion, Andrew 82, 181–2
multi-media 107
multitextuality 62, 68
Mulvey, Laura 122
museums 188
'My Last Duchess' 58
Myers, D. G. 81
Mystery of Hamlet, The 122
myths 74

Nabokov, Vladimir 81
narratee 39–40, 44–7
narrative 43
    closure 46
    process *see also* story telling
        38, 39, 40
narrator 40–1, 43, 44–7
    unreliable 44
National Association of Writers in
    Higher Education 83
Navvies, The 119
NAWE *see* National Association
    of Writers in Higher Education
neologisms 155
never-ending story 46
New Bearings in English Poetry
    128
New Criticism 101, 128, 129, 132,
    133
New Criticism, The 99, 129
New Historicism 132, 186–9
new words 157–9
newspapers 154, 158

headlines 154
Nielsen, Asta 122, 123
Norton Anthology of English Literature 215
Norton, Charles Eliot 93
novelists 6
novels 11, 19, 131

Oedipus Rex 29
Old English 95
Old Norse 95
On the Sublime 127
Once and Future King, The 68
online resources 105–24
open close reading 130–1
'Oread' 141–2
originality 241
Othello 15
Owen, Wilfred 123–4
Oxford University 94, 95, 106, 123
'Ozymandias' 244

Paradise Lost 34
part-time degrees 233
Patmore, Coventry 89
patterns 26
personal experience 58
Persuasion 10–11, 222
Peterloo 181–6
philology 93
phonetics 148
phonology 148
Pindar 50
Pindaric ode 50
plagiarism 109
Planet of the Apes 244
plot 11
Poetics 127
Poetry 123
poetry/poems 15, 23–36, 57, 58, 131, 149, 151, 185
  analysis 24, 25–30
  commentary 24
  criticism 149

difficulties of 26
docu-poetry 87
drafts 213, 218, 219
ekphrastic 85–6, 88
epic 32
metre 26
rhyme 26
Romantic 150
short 23–30
structure 25
Victorian 150
Welsh 50
polytechnics 82
Pope, Jessie 123–4
populism 225–6
portfolios 199
postcolonialism 132
postgraduate degrees 227–42
  specialized 228
  structure 227
postmodernism 103, 132
postmodification 152
poststructuralism 132, 134
Pound, Ezra 131, 244
Practical Criticism 99, 128, 129
practical criticism 132, 134
Prefaces to Shakespeare 128
prejudice 155, 156
Prelude, The 223
premodification 152
Pride and Prejudice 11, 20, 39
Principles of Literary Criticism 99
'*Prussian Officer, The' and Other Stories* 225–6
Prynne, J. H. 25
Psomiades, Kathy 69–70
psychoanalysis 135, 139–40
psycholinguistics 148
  master's degrees 229
public speaking 93
puns 159

Queer Theory 132

rabbinic tradition 133
Ransom, John Crowe 80, 99, 129
readability 235–7
reader response 43
reading 9, 10, 49–78
Reaganism 134
'Reality and Sincerity' 129, 130
redundancy, verbal 35
referencing 235–7
Reform Bill of 1832 75
regional accents 156
register 154, 159
representation 46
Re-Reading Literature 72
research councils 230
research degrees 229–31
'Resolution and Independence' 52
resonance 187, 188
'Resonance and Wonder' 186–7
Revaluation 130
revisions 219
rhetoric 93
Rich, Adrienne 142–5
Richard III 14–15
Richards, I. A. 98, 99, 128, 129
Roberts, Warren 181
Romanticism 61
   British 61
Rosenberg, Isaac 123
Rossetti, Dante Gabriel 69

Said, Edward 172–4, 176–9,
   185–6
Sanskrit 160
Scholar Critic, The 215
scholarliness 235–7
Scotland, universities 102
Scottish Invention of English
   Literature, The 91
seen close reading 130
semantic change 167
semantic shift 168
semantics 32, 34, 148, 164–7
Sense and Sensibility 10

'September 1st 1939' 223
set-pieces 50
Seven Types of Ambiguity 99, 128
Seventeenth Century Background
   100
sexism 69–70
Shakespeare, William 13–15, 29,
   117, 129
   editions 93
   sonnets 19–20, 135–40
'She Being Brand' 12
Sheffield Hallam University 82
Shelley, Mary 62
Shelley, Percy Bysshe 61, 127,
   244
shifters 149–50, 153
Sidney, Philip 127
Siegel, Kristi 113
significance 13
simile 57
Sinclair, Clive 82
Sir Gawain and the Green Knight
   68
site 41–3
Skype 234
slang 155, 159
smartphones 106
Smith, Charlotte 62
social justice 94
social networking 159
social self 72
sociolinguistics 148, 153, 154,
   156, 159, 160
sociology 101
soliloquy 14
Sonnet 73 (Shakespeare) 135–40
   gender 138–9
   history 135–6
   language 137–8
   psychoanalysis 139–40
sonnets, Elizabethan 19–20
Sophocles 29
Southampton University 230
spelling 34

Spenser, Edmund 31–6
  editions 93
stative verbs 152
Steggle, Matthew 106
'Stopping by Woods on a Snowy
  Evening' 27
story telling *see also* narrative
  process 39, 45, 46, 192
structuralism 132, 134
Structuralist Poetics 133
stylistics 148–9, 152, 153
Sullivan, Dick 119
suspension of disbelief 40
Sutherland, John 175, 176–8,
  181
syllabus 102, 134, 242
Sylvia's Lovers 20
syncretism 224–5
synopsis 74–8
syntax 148, 154

tablets 106
taxonomies 197
teaching of English as a second
  language (TESOL) 229
technical terms 157
television studies *see* theatre,
  film and television studies
Tennyson, Alfred Lord 8, 68, 71,
  73, 75, 97, 119, 212, 214
  dramatic monologues 58
  Memoir 74
Tennyson d'Eyncourt, Charles 72
TESOL *see* teaching of English as
  a second language
Tess of the d'Urbervilles 212
text-based study 98
textual variants 209–26
textuality 63–9, 77
Thatcherism 134
theatre, film and television
  studies 84
thematization 194, 196
theorized reading 133

Thompson, Ann 122
'Thyrsis' 150–1, 152
Tillyard, E. M. W. 100
Times, The 49
Times Literary Supplement, The 28
'To Autumn' 181–6
  political meanings 183
To the Lighthouse 89
Tolstoy, Leo 14
topic sites 106–7
'Tradition and the Individual Talent'
  58, 127
'Transit' 142–3
  absences 145
  aporia 143–4
  contradictions 143
  linguistic quirks 143–4
  omissions 145
  shifts 144
Tremain, Rose 82
TutorPro 106
tweeting 34
  grammar 34
  spelling 34

University of Ulster 230
Ulysses 224–5
'Ulysses' 58
undergraduate dissertations
  199–208
  assessment 199
  structure 200–5
Understanding Poetry 99
University College, London 94
unreliable narrator 44
unseen close reading 130
URLs 110, 111
USA 102
  New Critical revolution 99
utility 33–4

*Varieties of Metaphysical Poetry,
  The* 128
Verbal Icon, The 129

verbal redundancy 35
Victorian Poetry: Poetry, Poetics and Politics 74
Victorian Web 118, 119
Victorian Women Writers Project 119
Vining, Edward P. 122
Virago Book of Wicked Verse, The 59
Virginia, University of Electronic Text Center 105
VIRGO 105
vocabulary 26, 154
voice 43, 237–9
Voice of the Shuttle 112

Wales 102
Warren, Robert Penn 99
Waste Land, The 29, 212
Waterhouse, John William 69
websites 158
Webster, John 15
Well Wrought Urn 129
Wendell, Barrett 80
White, T. H. 68

Wilberforce, William 175
Willey, Basil 100
willing suspension of disbelief 40
Wilson, Angus 82
Wimsatt, W. K. 129
Winters, Yvor 80
Women in Love 77
Women's Indian Captivity Narratives 6
wonder 188
Woolf, Virginia 41, 47, 89, 103, 131
   novels 19
word-splices 159
Wordsworth, Dorothy 51–7, 60–1, 62
   diary 51–4, 56–7, 58, 59, 60–1
Wordsworth, William 51–7, 58, 60–1, 128, 213, 223
workshops 84–5
'Wreck of the *Deutschland*, The' 49
writers 6
writing
   process 87
   style 235
   techniques 102